PAUL

ELMER

MORE

PAUL

ELMER

MORE

LITERARY CRITICISM AS THE HISTORY OF IDEAS

Stephen L. Tanner

Brigham Young University

For Bill and Norma Gillespie

Library of Congress Cataloging-in-Publication Data

Tanner, Stephen L.
  Paul Elmer More : literary criticism as the history
of ideas.

  Includes index.
  1. More, Paul Elmer, 1864–1937—Knowledge—Literature.
2. Criticism.   3. Continuity.   I. Title.
PS2432.T36   1985   801'.95'0924   86-6847
ISBN 0-88706-560-0

Brigham Young University, Provo, Utah 84602
Copyright 1987 by Brigham Young University.
All rights reserved
Printed in the United States of America

Distributed by State University of New York Press,
State University Plaza, Albany, New York
12246-0001

Contents

Preface

Some words must be said at the outset regarding the scope of this book. First of all, it was not intended as a study of the New Humanism in general. My focus is entirely on Paul Elmer More; his relationship to the New Humanist school or movement is treated only incidentally. I have made no attempt to describe his interaction with Irving Babbitt or other humanist critics. Also, I have made no attempt to describe and analyze the "battle of the books" in the late 1920s and early 1930s in which More and Babbitt and their allies squared off against the liberal critics in a melee of journalistic skirmishes. These subjects are interesting and important to an understanding of American literary criticism, but they do not fall within the scope of my particular goals and interests in this study.

My concern is with one particular aspect of More's literary criticism—continuity. I have drawn upon his writings on philosophy and theology only as they throw light on the philosophical and historical continuity within his literary criticism, which I have attempted to define and synthesize. Unfortunately, in order to make that synthesis, I have had to slight some noteworthy aspects of his critical essays—such things as the details of his biographical and aesthetic concerns, the finer discriminations of his appreciative responses, and the balance of his critical praise and blame. I hope that the value of my presentation of philosophical and historical continuity adequately compensates for such omissions.

More's own statements are used generously throughout this book for two main reasons. First, they are used for the sake of clarity and authority. I feel it is important for the reader to see just how More expressed his concepts, particularly since some of those concepts are easily distorted in tone and subtly altered in meaning when paraphrased. In a significant way, what he said was determined by how he said it. Second, to display his graceful and lucid style, which has been praised by friends and detractors alike. It seems desirable to allow the flavor of that style to manifest itself as much as possible, commensurate with my attempt to interpret and synthesize the philosophical and historical aspects of his criticism.

CHAPTER ONE

Introduction

The Argument

From one point of view, it is surprising that Paul Elmer More is not better known. He wrote thirteen volumes of literary and social criticism and seven volumes treating philosophy and religion. In addition to these volumes of the *Shelburne Essays, New Shelburne Essays,* and *The Greek Tradition,* he did a biography of Benjamin Franklin; translations of Plato, Aeschylus, and Sanskrit epigrams; an edition of Byron; and, in collaboration with others, a text on English literature and an anthology of seventeenth-century religious literature. He was also the author of two novels, a collection of poems, and a considerable amount of uncollected literary journalism. Much of this is distinguished work. Robert Spiller has described the criticism as "the most ambitious and often the most penetrating body of judicial literary criticism in our literature."[1] Austin Warren has praised "his range, his comprehensiveness, his staying power, his not too heavily insisted upon sobriety."[2] Russell Kirk considers him "the greatest of American critics."[3] T. S. Eliot considered him one of the two "wisest" men he had known.[4] Even H. L. Mencken, who had no sympathy for More's way of thinking, conceded that he was the "nearest approach to a genuine scholar" America had.[5] In 1930 he came very near to being the first American to earn the Nobel Prize for literature, when it went to Sinclair Lewis instead; and again in 1933 reports spread that he might receive it.

From another point of view, however, it is not surprising that More is little known. Literary reputation in America, particularly that of a critic, is notoriously short lived. Moreover, he had the misfortune of just preceding the dominant critical movement in America during our century—the New Criticism. Besides this, the sociopolitical surge to the left in literature and criticism during the 1930s thrust him, and the New Humanism in general, over to the sidelines away from the main action. Most damaging to his literary reputation was the myth or caricature of the New Humanists created by their enemies. According to the myth the New Humanist was a horrid old conservative curmudgeon, a hard-hearted old man, devoid of humanitarian feeling, determined to maintain his authority against aspiring youth; he was fixed in ancient ways and petulantly annoyed with novelty; arrogantly he tried to elevate his own narrow preoccupations into universal edicts. Pairs such as the following were set up: critical-creative, repressive-liberating, old-new, narrow-broad, reaction-progress, authority-individualism, tradition-experiment, etcetera. In this system of simplistic labeling, the New Humanist was consistently awarded what was considered the negative side. Though a ridiculous caricature, the myth still diverts people from reading More.

It is unlikely, therefore, that he will ever be widely known or read; but he certainly will not be forgotten. The *Shelburne Essays* alone, with their breadth of subject matter, informed perceptions, enduring insights, and moral seriousness will insure a continuing sympathetic readership among those who find literature and moral values inextricably blended. And although this group of readers has not been conspicuous in the formalistic and antimimetic criticism of recent years, it is nevertheless large and enduring. Austin Warren once said that the New Humanism did not become extinct with the deaths of More and Babbitt; it simply "went underground."[6]

2

It is the nature and achievement of the literary criticism within the *Shelburne Essays* that is the concern of this book.

The organization of the *Shelburne Essays* has generally been considered loose and arbitrary. This looseness of arrangement is explained by the fact that most of the essays comprising these volumes were published separately in a number of places between 1898 and 1921.[7] Some were originally lectures, but most are the products of literary journalism. The apparent arbitrary arrangement of these essays cannot be denied, and they probably would constitute a more coherent work if they were rearranged and properly indexed. But looseness in arrangement should not prevent recognizing and appreciating a fundamental unity underlying all of these essays. The fact is that too frequently evaluations of More's criticism have been crippled by a failure to take this unity into account. Francis X. Duggan hints at it as "a consistent philosophical or moral purpose."[8] I see it as a continuity operating on two primary levels, and the central purpose of this book is to define and describe that continuity.

The first major thread of continuity is the concept of dualism. This philosophical concept, with its moral, social, religious, and aesthetic corollaries, constitutes a body of first principles that determines More's taste, method, and judgment as a critic. In its essential form this dualism appears as the contention that man has a dual nature comprised of two opposite tendencies. The key for understanding human behavior and for evaluating artistic representations of it lies in recognizing the nature of the struggle between these opposing tendencies. Louis J. A. Mercier, in summarizing how dualism functions in More's criticism, accurately describes it this way:

There must be a solution of a conflict between the two contrary principles, and the greater the conflict the greater the interest. This applies to the form of art as well as to the content. That form is the most beautiful which most adequately orders the most complex material. As to the content, a work of literature will move us in proportion as it enables us to see struggling within man the vital urge, made up of his inner desires and outer impressions, and the power of ordering in man, which is categorically distinct from the flux of appetites and sensations to be ordered, and which is felt to be superior to the natural intellect, will, and feelings.[9]

Throughout his criticism More treats writers primarily in terms of their simultaneous perception of what is changing and what is unchanging in man, awarding praise or blame on the basis of how cognizant they are of the contrast between man's passion of the moment and the eternal law above and within him.

The second major thread is a consistent history of thought since the Renaissance implicit in the *Shelburne Essays*. As a student of intellectual history, More felt that man and his society can profitably be studied by considering the major ideas which influence human action and in large measure shape the course of history. From his earliest days his life was dominated by an unremitting intellectual and spiritual quest, and therefore literary criticism for him was rarely an end in itself. Almost always the work of literature in question served to precipitate a discussion of some philosophical, moral, or religious issue. Walter Lippmann described him as "a man who, in the guise of a critic, is authentically concerned with the first and last things of human experience."[10] Scattered through the *Shelburne Essays* is More's interpretation of what he once referred to as "the long battle of the spirit." Natural and moral law, faith and reason, and the opposing tendencies of liberalism and conservatism in the individual and society are some of the large issues that interested him. He was also much concerned with romanticism, science, humanitarianism, and evolution. From his treatment of these issues emerges a historiography which, though piecemeal and repetitious, is consistent with itself and comprehensive when taken as a whole. In the chapters that follow I put the pieces of this history together in an attempt to clarify its consistency and comprehensiveness. This needs to be done before an accurate estimate of More's achievement in the totality of his criticism can be made.

More's Objectives

The proposition I wish to establish, therefore, is that dispersed throughout the *Shelburne Essays* are the pieces of a consistent spiritual-intellectual history conceived on the basis of a dualistic interpretation of human nature and experience that provides a unity for the essays as a whole and makes it necessary for individual essays to be seen in relation to the whole in order to be adequately understood and appreciated.

The first question raised by this proposition is to what extent was More conscious of this history and how deliberately did he construct it? There are several facts which indicate directly or indirectly that More intended his criticism to express not only the character of individual writers in relation to "the first and last things of human experience" but also the character of the age in which they lived and the connection of that age with the ones preceding and following it.

The fact that the history is there is, of course, evidence of its deliberate creation, but aside from this we have More's statement to a friend that his purpose in the *Shelburne Essays* was to compose "a kind of history of human thought and ideals of life," chiefly in England but with excursions into other countries.[11] Another indication of his concern with the historical tracing of great formative tendencies is that in his major work following the *Shelburne Essays*, his six-volume work on *The Greek Tradition*, he explicitly states his purpose of tracing a consistent continuity of thought from the death of Socrates to the Council of Chalcedon in A.D. 451.[12] It appears to me that More was doing explicitly and systematically in *The Greek Tradition* for an early period in history what he did implicitly and unsystematically in the *Shelburne Essays* for the period since the Renaissance. It may be that the historical thread of formative thought and ideals in the *Shelburne Essays* was a natural outgrowth of his propensity for seeing literature always in the perspective of the currents of thought of the age in which it was written. What began as an unconscious tendency became increasingly deliberate, and the *Shelburne Essays* became a kind of trial run in a method displayed in its perfected form in *The Greek Tradition*.

A good deal can be learned about More's objectives in his own criticism by considering the statements he made concerning the purposes and ideals of criticism. Several of these statements go a long way in explaining why he was so consistently preoccupied with the history of ideas. In one place he says there is a kind of criticism that limits itself to looking at the thing in itself, or at the parts of a thing as they successively strike the mind. This is the way of sympathy, he says, and the concern here is not for what is ugly, false, or incomplete in a work of art. "But there is a place also for another kind of criticism, which is not so much directed to the individual thing as to its relation with other things, and to its place as cause or effect in a whole group of tendencies." Actually most criticism is a combination of both these kinds and the highest criticism would balance these methods "in such a manner that neither the occasional merits of a work nor its general influence would be unduly subordinated." More acknowledges that his essays do not always succeed in striking such a balance but justifies himself by saying that

there are times, are there not? when the general drift of ideas is so dominant that a critic may at least be pardoned if, with his eye on these larger relations, he does not bring out quite so clearly as he might the distinguishing marks of the writer or book with which he is immediately dealing. And if to his mind this general trend [he had in mind here specifically romanticism] appears to be carrying the world toward the desolation of what he holds very dear, you will at least understand how he may come to slight the sounder aspects of any work which as a whole belongs to the dangerous influences of the age.[13]

More not only thought that the critic was obliged to see the individual work of literature in relation to other things and "to its place as cause or effect in a whole group of tendencies," but he saw this as a high and creative calling.

Yet, certainly, the best and most durable acts of mankind are the ideals and emotions that go to make up its books, and to describe and judge the literature of a country, to pass under review a thousand systems and reveries, to point out the meaning of each, and so write the annals of the human spirit, to pluck out the heart of each man's mystery and set it before the mind's eye quivering with life,—if this be not a labour of immense creative energy the word has no sense to my ears. (SE, III, 76-77)

An important part of the critic's task in writing "the annals of the human spirit" is to separate the mutable from the immutable in man's nature and experience. In order to do this he must exercise what More calls "the historic sense."

That sense has a double function; it points out the differences that creep in from age to age, the changes of manners and forms that come with time and make the generations of men like foreigners to one another. And here the training of the day will keep any scholar from error. But we are also justified in demanding that clearer faculty of vision which pierces beneath those transient modes and discovers what each age has attained of essential and permanent truth. (SE, IV, 68)

The critical history of literature is, according to More, the finest exercise of the historic sense.

By literature we do not mean books that record facts merely or those that amuse merely, but books that carry from age to age the high endeavor of the race to build for itself a world of faith, a world in which beauty is made real, human responsibility certain, and human aspirations assured. The Bibles of the world are a part of this literature, and the poems that invest faith with beauty, and every true work that interprets the dignity of man's spiritual life are a part of it. Now historical criticism is no less than an attempt to coordinate the scattered phrases of this long document, and to bring out the progressive harmony of their meaning; it is, in a word, an attempt to trace the history of the human spirit.[14]

Clearly, More's own objective in his criticism was to cultivate within himself the historic sense and thus trace the history of the human spirit. I use the term spiritual-intellectual to describe the type of history reflected in the *Shelburne Essays* to distinguish it from the usual kind of intellectual history. More's historiography has a distinctive religious and moral bias. He touches on political thought, but rather incidentally. He deals with scientific thought, but not really for its own sake. Likewise, economic issues come in for consideration but are never the center of attention. His main concern is always the concept of human nature held by a particular writer or by his age, and this concern is often shaded with religious questioning. He always deals with the fundamental questions of what is the nature of man and how should he believe and act.

More believed that if his criticism was to endure, it would have to present itself as a total unit. He no doubt realized that the very nature of his method and objectives demanded that individual essays be seen in the light of other essays. Perhaps with Sainte-Beuve (whom he admired greatly) in mind, he wanted his reputation as a critic to rest on a large body of work; therefore, he used one general title for all his volumes of collected essays, even though these essays deal with a wide variety of topics. Both William Roscoe Thayer and Irving Babbitt urged him to publish some of his work under separate titles, reasoning that it would have a better chance for proper recognition and acclaim. More acknowledged the validity of these arguments for "the short haul," but he was more concerned about "the long haul" and concluded, "In the long run will not such work be most effective and make a better fight for remembrance by its very bulk and massiveness?"[15] It remains to be seen how More's criticism will succeed in its fight for remembrance. In the forty-eight years since More's death it has slipped into the shadows of American literary history. This is not surprising considering how much his moral approach has been out of joint with the general critical tenor of the last four or five decades. But a writer's reputation is seldom set permanently after forty-eight years, and More's criticism along with his philosophy and theology may yet prove to be of enduring quality. At any rate, the continuity which I am trying to demonstrate in the *Shelburne Essays* suggests strongly that they are best understood as a whole, for only then can the basic interpretation of human experience which underlies them all be adequately distinguished and evaluated.

Another question raised by my thesis is why More chose the Renaissance as the starting point for his history. It certainly was not because his tastes and interests were confined to the period since the Renaissance; his writing as a whole displays an extraordinary breadth of interest in literature and philosophy of many cultures and many ages. A more adequate explanation is that he saw the Renaissance as the seedbed for the important formative tendencies which were to collide and interact in the centuries to follow. Specifically, he saw two basic forces emerging in the sixteenth and seventeenth centuries, the products of the developing new science. He uses the terms "humanism" and "naturalism" to describe these forces, whose central difference lies in their respective acceptance and rejection of the dualistic nature of man. "The recognition of this dualism of the natural and the supernatural in man (or of a higher and lower nature, for the word 'nature' is as unstable as the sea) is precisely the philosophy of humanism, as contrasted with the philosophy of naturalism which denies that the distinctive mark of man is a consciously directive will. And the history of European culture since the Renaissance turns on the varying fortunes of these two hostile views" (*NSE,* I, x). In More's tracing of thought since the sixteenth century there are many apparently conflicting theories of life, many isms—deism, romanticism, scientism, humanitarianism—but they all have roots in the naturalism which began in the Renaissance, particularly with Bacon, that single philosophy "which bears in itself the inevitable seeds of contradiction" (*NSE,* I, ix).

As a final comment on More's objectives, it should be noted that many aspects of his history are not original. He would have been the first to admit this and would have considered such an observation in his favor. He was not attempting to be novel or original, but rather to give comprehensiveness and consistency to generally recognized truths regarding the development of thought in Western Europe and America. The concept at the core of his interpretation, dualism, he did not consider new or of his own invention. He viewed it as a fundamental truth available in common to men in all ages and societies. The originality of his contribution lies in his uncovering subtle or obscure cause-effect relationships and in tracing ideas and attitudes through transformations wrought by time, circumstance, and individual minds.

The Development of More's Thought

More's thought, of course, underwent a process of development during the course of his career. This is only to be expected for the thought of any man over a period of so many years. Harry H. Clark put it this way: "Mr. More has not been a static thinker, and when one claims agreement with his position, it is essential to indicate *which* position is meant."[16] This fact, on the surface, seems to militate against my thesis regarding a consistent historiography operating in his criticism, but this is only an apparent difficulty, for his thought evolved within the framework of a pattern of first principles that did not change significantly.

Near the end of his life when he had reached a distinctly theistic position, More outlined at one point in his short autobiographical work, *Pages from an Oxford Diary,* the development of his intellectual and spiritual life, saying, "In a way I have come about a great circle, and my end is close to where I began; for I was born, so to speak, a theologian, and my first literary work was a sermon, printed, without my knowledge, at the tender age of eight" (*POD,* V). In the same section he describes the steps in this circle. In his youth he fell under the sway of German romanticism and "sucked folly even out of Goethe. The thoughts of God were supplanted by a morbid introspection and the practice of worship gave way to indulgence in a self-commiserating egotism." Then came a reaction into hard rationalism and materialism. "A thick note-book was filled with the project of a New Philosophy which should prove once for all that the world and men are the product of a fatalistic Law of Chance and Probability." But this project went the way of fire, probably because of his "deep-seated interest in humanity." He could not bring himself to believe that men are only machines, and he could not smother in logic "the sense of mystery that broods upon the world, nor find any place in the network of blind chance and fate for human will." And so, disillusioned with metaphysics, he gave himself for years to the study of literature. These years of criticism gave the stamp to his reputation, which he reflects upon in this way: "Unfortunately I was too much addicted to literature to be accepted by the philosophers, and too fond of interpreting art by an ethical criterion to find favour among the literary." Following his years as literary critic, he began "a passionate search to discover the eternal verities behind the veil—the realm of Ideas which Plato taught." In his final years he seemed to attain his goal in the form of a Platonized Christianity and said "I shall end my days a conscious, as I was born, an unconscious, Platonist."

Through these changes More's fundamental beliefs regarding human nature did not change in any essential way. As Barrows Dunham rather playfully points out, More's dualism was full and complete when he was ten years of age. At that time he wrote on certain scraps of paper that composed a kind of sermon, "Ther are 2 ways to do anything, they are the right way and the rong." "In the years to come," says Dunham, "More improved his orthography, but he could not improve the insight, for it was perfect as it stood."[17]

More serious evidence that the changes in More's thought were not of a nature that would weaken my thesis is the fact that most of these changes came in his youth and were over by the time he began the *Shelburne Essays*. Just preceding his years as literary critic, and following the romantic and rationalistic phases of his youth, he retired to a cabin in Shelburne, New Hampshire, for two years of study and meditation. He confessed that he did not discover the secret of the meaning of life during this "contemplative sojourn in the wilderness," but he learned that the attempt to criticize and not create literature was to be his labor in this world. And although he returned from the woods without solving the riddle of existence, the direction of his thinking was fixed by those years of solitary reflection, and the essays that followed, at least the more serious of them, were successive attempts to discover the meaning of life.

The attempt to discover the meaning of life is reflected in two ways in the *Shelburne Essays*. One is the continuity of history already mentioned; the other is what Walter Lippmann described as the "record of continuous religious discovery" expressed in the essays. The latter is what most interested T. S. Eliot, a good friend of More. "What is significant to me," says Eliot, "—and it is of objective significance as well—is not simply the conclusions at which he has arrived, but the fact that he arrived there from somewhere else; and not simply that he came from somewhere else, but that he took a particular route." Eliot remarks on the maturity of both the late and the early *Shelburne Essays* but points out that "between the first and the last a very long journey has been taken." He then adds, "Not that there are not everywhere evident, as in the work of every good mind, principles that remain unchanged."[18]

The evolution of More's thought is interesting, but it will not be emphasized in this study; it has already been treated adequately elsewhere.[19] My primary concern is with his "principles that remain unchanged," primarily dualism. I agree with Folke Leander's comment on More that "No one ever insisted more on the ultimately alogical character of religious dualism. His earliest word can be placed beside his last, on this point at least, without the charge of inconsistency."[20] There is also the same constant insistence upon the vitally sensed moral and religious realities as against the laborious constructions of rationalizing metaphysics or theology. More himself recognized a stable element underlying the fluctuations of his thinking and philosophy. After mentioning the various phases in the development of his thought, he says the kindest explanation of them "would be to say that I lived through successive distractions, under which, however, ran one strong steady current, often out of sight, but at the last coming broadly to the surface, and, by gathering all other movements into itself, giving in appearance at least, a unity of direction to them all" (*POD*, XXIX). The "strong steady current" More speaks of here is dualism, the preoccupation with which came early in his career. An illustration of this is the fact that in the introduction to one of his earliest works, *A Century of Indian Epigrams,* published in 1898, he calls attention to dualism. In providing background for his translation of the Sanskrit epigrams, he makes the unorthodox statement that although "we read constantly of the monism of the Hindus, of their attempts to reduce all things to one substance . . . in fact their intellectual attitude is the result of a keen perception of the dual nature of man and the world at large; and this holds true even in the Vedanta, commonly cited as the most radical of monistic systems" (*CIE,* 13). Just as the aspect of dualism was at the center of his interest in Indian literature in 1898, so was it the center of interest in his criticism of Western literature over the next thirty-odd years.

A final example to show that although More's thought underwent changes during his process of continuous religious discovery, these changes were, in scholastic terminology accidental rather than substantial is a passage from *Christ the Word,* one of the volumes of *The Greek Tradition* written in 1927 when the focus of his work was theistic. This passage illustrates two points which are important to my argument. First of all, it points up once again what I have indicated More's main objective to be—to trace the continuity of the permanent elements in human experience. Secondly, by comparing it with the statements in the preceding section on "the historic sense," we can see that although More's thinking became increasingly oriented toward religion, the basic patterns underwent no essential change—they simply took on religious shadings.

> Literature and art, so long as they remain true to their high function and do not sink into mere flattery of man's baser instincts, are an effort to interpret life and the phenomena of nature in the light of the logos, and to build here and now a home for the soul in the world of Ideas. And for the scholar the finest and most comprehensive name ever yet devised is the old Greek term *logios,* signifying one who is skilled to trace the operation of the logos, to distinguish its genuine expression in literature from shams, to know the truth, and so dwell in the calm yet active leisure . . . of contemplation. The scholar, the *logios* in that noble sense of the word, is he who by study and reflection has recovered the birthright of humanity and holds it in fee for the generations to come. (*CW,* 300-304)

Here More has given the scholar a new name and has emphasized the religious nature of his task, but his duties are essentially the same as More outlined them twenty-one years earlier in discussing "the historic sense." The noble scholar or critic, seeing beneath the surface modes of thought and behavior, will discover what each age has attained of essential and permanent truth.

Characteristics of More's Method

All of More's criticism is founded on the syllogistic notion that art cannot be separated from life, and life in turn cannot be separated from moral values; therefore, moral considerations should be a part of any criticism of art. He once said that the critical temperament consists primarily in the "linking together of literature and life, and in the levelling appli-

14

cation of common sense" (*SE*, III, 81). What he said of Sainte-Beuve could also be said of him: "What attracted him chiefly was the middle ground where life and literature meet, where life becomes self-conscious through expression, and literature retains the reality of association with facts" (*SE*, III, 78). Indeed, the major criticism leveled against More has been that he allowed the historico-moral view to override the poetical or aesthetic view; that his work as a whole seems to deny that poetry is an entirely distinct although not totally independent way of looking at life. More acknowledged that his essays would appear old-fashioned "to those caught by the present trend of ideas. For the one thing characteristic of modern criticism, as exemplified eminently by so influential a writer as I. A. Richards, is the complete absence of any search for the meaning of life, and in place of that an absorbing interest in what might be called the problem of aesthetic psychology." He offered no apology for this old-fashioned note in his criticism because he was "utterly convinced that literature divorced from life is an empty pursuit."[21]

More, himself, described most accurately the tradition of criticism to which he aspired. He said of Matthew Arnold what could likewise be said of him, that Arnold belonged

to one of the great families of human intelligence, which begins with Cicero . . . and passes through Erasmus and Boileau and Shaftesbury and Sainte-Beuve. These are the exemplars—not complete individually, I need not say—of what may be called the critical spirit: discriminators between the false and the true, the deformed and the normal; preachers of harmony and proportion and order, prophets of religion and taste. If they deal much with the criticism of literature, this is because in literature more manifestly than anywhere else life displays its infinitely varied motives and results; and their practice is always to render literature itself more consciously a criticism of life. (*SE*, VIII, 218)

It is obvious from the earliest *Shelburne Essays* that More's own purpose, taking Sainte-Beuve and Arnold as his mentors, was to render literature more consciously a criticism of life.

One of the most important characteristics of More's

method in relation to my thesis regarding continuity is that he was never content to confront an idea, attitude, institution, or philosophy without looking before to see where it came from and after to see its consequences. This tendency is the source of the historiography I hereafter trace in his criticism. Lynn H. Hough describes him as a detective of ideas. He commends his erudition, his knowledge of Greek culture, of Latin, of the whole of English literature and says, "He sees everything in the terms of everything else. He knows the ancestors of ideas which call themselves modern. He traces out the true paternity of institutions. He is a marvelous detective who follows an idea through all the changes with which, like Proteus, it moves through civilization after civilization and age after age."[22] The following chapters are, in one sense, a correlating and editing of the results of More's "detective" work regarding the period since the Renaissance.

In a typical essay the method functions in this way: In response to a recent edition or biography of an author, More will launch into his own essay on the writer in question. He will first discuss the man's life and then relate his life to his works. Then at some point he will connect those works to the main intellectual or spiritual currents of the age. An additional step is frequently included, which is an explanation of the sources and implications of those currents of thought based on a dualistic conception of human nature and experience. Somewhere along the way value judgments are made. These usually come at strategic places. Horace Gregory observes that "More practiced the art of suspending his esthetic and moral judgments, and one waits, quite as one waits for the fall of an ax, for the place and the moment at which the sharpened edges of his discrimination are going to fall."[23] Such judgments are made in accordance with what H. J. Harding has called "master ideas."

The broad underlying basis of all his evaluations is the presence of a dualistic attitude to life; but in individual essays, the touch-stone is not dualism in general, but one concrete aspect of it, the

One and the Many, Altruism *versus* Egotism, False *versus* True Illusion. This use of *master ideas,* as opposed to the more superficial use of master phrases adopted by his famous mentor, Arnold, at once lends coherence to individual essays and cohesion to the whole series.[24]

Theorists of criticism generally agree that there are three aspects of criticism which in practice are actually combined in a single organic process. These aspects are re-creative criticism, historical criticism, and judicial criticism. More implies in his practice and suggests in certain theoretical remarks that he recognized this threefold function of criticism; for him it was a matter of appreciation, an ascertainment of the historical context, and a judgment of value. There is not an equal blending of these aspects in his criticism, however. In fact, the second most frequently takes precedence over the other two. Because of his philosophical bent, he was most keenly interested in the historical context, which he viewed as primarily a context of ideas.

This partly accounts for his frequent treatment of what are generally considered minor writers. In searching for the continuity of the *Shelburne Essays,* one must realize that an essay on a particular writer might appear, not because of his stature as a literary figure, but because he dealt with issues which interested More. At first it is puzzling to consider why the essay is there and how it fits into the More canon, but further thought often reveals that it is there because the writer in question reflects some element in the continuity of human thought as More interprets it. More once called attention to this passage from Sainte-Beuve: "The illustrious writers, the great poets, scarcely exist without having about them other men, themselves essential rather than secondary, great in their incompleteness, the equals in the inner life of thought with those whom they love, whom they serve, and who are kings by right of art" (*SE,* XI, 97). Since More was so concerned with "the inner life of thought," it is not surprising that he took an interest in such minor figures. As a matter of fact, minor writers are often the clearest and most distinct reflections of their age and provided the best examples for More in his historiography. His treatment of minor figures, therefore, is of interest only partly for what it reveals about those writers themselves; it is more important in what it reveals about More himself and his interpretation of the history of ideas.

I do not wish, however, to give the impression that his interest in minor writers was limited to their position in an intellectual history; he also was sensitive to the pleasure they provide in and of themselves. "The commonplace or the small may in its own sphere be commendable and may afford a true relish to the finest palate; and, indeed, one of the functions of criticism is to set forth and so far as possible rescue from oblivion the inexhaustible entertainment of the lesser writers" (*SE*, VII, 26).

In a rather early essay, More makes a distinction between "the essential and the contingent" in literature which has significant implications in an understanding of his method. He says

we must recognise that there are two kinds of poetical genius, the essential and the contingent, and that their claims on our memory are as diverse as their faculties. Nor is this division quite coterminous with that into major and minor poets. Keats and Wordsworth both belong to the major group, yet one is essentially, whereas the other is in large measure contingently, poetic. We judge the work of Keats in itself, and its value rises or sinks purely in proportion to its own intrinsic interest; it would be almost the same to us if we had never heard the writer's name. On the contrary, no small portion of Wordsworth's verse, and that not always the least cherished, derives its weight and significance from what we know of the poet's own character and of his philosophy. It is the High Priest of Nature to which we are listening, and behind his words is the authority of a grave teacher. Take away the memory of that systematic life with its associations, forget the hallowed beauty of the Lake Country, and how much of Wordsworth's celebrity would be annulled! (*SE*, IV, 21-22)

18

More wrote essays on both "essential" and "contingent" writers, but it is interesting to note that he gives both groups what might be called a "contingent" treatment. Even when he writes about Keats, whose work he says in the above passage "rises or sinks purely in proportion to its own intrinsic interest," the major part of the essay is devoted to showing Keats's relationship to the Elizabethans. The fact is that although More was not insensitive to aesthetic considerations or the beauty of a work of literature in and of itself, he was most interested in how the work and its author fit into the continuity of human thought and experience.

Limitations and Procedures

The justification for this study of continuity is not that it provides a new evaluation of Paul Elmer More's criticism, but that it is a necessary step which must be taken, and which heretofore has not been taken, before such an evaluation can adequately be made. More's achievement cannot be accurately calculated without taking this continuity into consideration. Harry H. Clark suggests that "Mr. More's actual distinctive superiority lies not so much in any weighty contribution to the understanding or criticism of individual authors as in, first, the impressive spectacle he presents of a cultivated mind approaching a vast gallery of authors of many ages from the unifying standpoint of one pattern of critical criteria; and second, in his native ability to transmute criticism into literature of rare value in its own right through the virtues of a style of singular charm and felicity."[25] This study is intended to define and explain that "one pattern of critical criteria" and describe and correlate its application. As for More's style, it does not receive the study and analysis it deserves, but I hope that the generous amount of quotation in this volume makes its merits self-evident.

One service this study should render is to make more intelligible the philosophical sections of individual essays which sometimes give readers difficulty. Stuart Sherman complains of the difficulty of some of the *Shelburne Essays,* saying that occasionally one "stumbles" on a statement dealing with a philosophical concept and goes "tumbling head over heels into the abyss of recondite philosophy."[26] This should not happen once the first principles of More's philosophy have been mastered. He is never obscure, but frequently the central ideas of one essay must be complemented by those of other essays to be thoroughly understood. This is true despite the frequent repetition of basic themes and principles.

Austin Warren, in a sympathetic but penetrating evaluation of More, applies to him the term "generalist," which he defines as those "who, starting from the particular studies of their training and profession, widen their scope of interest— either by instinct or conscious intent, their hypothetical goal being the whole range of basic and liberal knowledge, being perspective and wisdom."[27] Such persons are subject to adverse criticism from the professionals in particular fields because to be a generalist in an age of specialization is unavoidably to be an amateur, of however high a level. More knew this and faced it after considering the cost. How one judges his work rests finally on the weight one assigns to balance and centrality.

More was perhaps the last American scholar-critic to handle the large moral, religious, and philosophical issues as they have unfolded in history. Critics now are more intimidated by the complexity of knowledge and information, and perhaps rightly so. More dealt with fundamental and universal questions with a remarkable boldness. He made mistakes and oversimplifications but still accomplished a significant thing. Schools now produce brilliant men, but specialists, often lacking in a wise and comprehensive historical perspective. More felt the need for a larger view.

Much of the flightiness of modern minds, much of the waste of our powers, is due to the fact that we look on too small a segment of the great circle of history; we misjudge human nature thereby and we lose sight of forces lying too deep for our hasty ken. To have the beginnings firmly fixed in memory, to have followed these forces through the long unfolding of human history, gives a gravity to judgment, an ability to discriminate between ephemeral change and organic growth, a steadiness of purpose against the shifting winds of opinion, a total wisdom, that are not likely to come to a man from any other source.[28]

The fact that More was a generalist, a detective of ideas, a kind of cultural critic with a definite moral stance, must be appreciated if we are to evaluate his achievement accurately. The following statement by Louis Kronenberger fits the case of More precisely:

The exclusively literary critic performs a very narrow function, yet must have the broadest possible sympathies—must in theory be as eclectic as an auctioneer. He cannot let personal quirks, or philosophical or political theories, blur the precision of his responses. The cultural critic, on the other hand, can perform a far broader function with far narrower—or at least far more personal—views, his subject matter being in fact so large that if it isn't harnessed to a point of view it becomes unwieldy. And though even for him literature can never be merely a tract, it can be a test, it can help determine the master currents of his age.[29]

My method is necessarily more descriptive than critical. I say necessarily because More was an extraordinarily expansive intellect: his erudition and wide range of study make it highly unlikely that another single person would be competent enough in the same areas to authoritatively and justly criticize him. The task I have undertaken here is to describe the unifying threads of principles and historiography in his criticism. I have made some evaluative comments, but for the most part the accuracy and validity of his judgments regarding individual works, writers, periods, and tendencies of the human spirit must be judged by those trained and qualified in respective areas. I have also chosen not to compile and repeat the criticism of others because much of that criticism is polarized and the biases at each pole destroy objectivity.

21

Furthermore, much of that criticism does not meet More on his own terms. What Gorham B. Munson said in 1928 has unfortunately remained generally true until today. He suggested "that More is a force that has not been encountered on its own plane and surely our present mileau suffers insofar as such forces are not permitted open-minded hearing and direct opposition. For a direct clear-seeing opposition to More I would have to discuss such questions as the whole view versus the contemporary view, the validity of More's philosophic and religious sources, dualism versus monism, and the nature and role of skepticism."[30]

I fully realize that by focusing on continuity I have been prevented from doing justice to the breadth of More's criticism; the re-creative or appreciative aspects and the aesthetic judgments have been particularly slighted. This is unfortunate and the only justification I can offer is that my emphasis on the history of ideas is commensurate with a similar emphasis in More's criticism as a whole.

The intention governing my organization was first to define the unifying pattern of More's critical criteria and then discuss its application to specific literary periods. Therefore, the next chapter is a discussion of first principles, and it is followed by chapters on the consecutive centuries since the Renaissance. American literature is treated in a separate chapter because More viewed it in an intellectual tradition of its own. The essays in the eleven volumes of the *Shelburne Essays* along with those in the two volumes of the *New Shelburne Essays* which are comprised of literary criticism (volume II of that series is exclusively on religion) constitute the subject matter of this study, but references to More's other works are made when they serve to clarify the continuity I wish to demonstrate.

CHAPTER TWO

First Principles

Art and Life

The logical starting point in a presentation of the first principles of Paul Elmer More's critical philosophy is a consideration of the vital connection he saw between art and life, aesthetics and ethics. He is a representative of a long tradition of writers and critics, dating back at least as far as Plato, who have attempted to describe and justify the connection between the beautiful and the good in literature. Matthew Arnold expressed the keynote of this tradition: "It is important, therefore, to hold fast to this: that poetry is at bottom a criticism of life; that the greatness of a poet lies in his powerful and beautiful application of ideas to life—to the question: How to live."[1] More shared this view; indeed, he believed that art in general, so long as it is human, must concern itself with the portrayal of human character in search of values by which to live. And literature in particular, though related to the other spatial or temporal arts, seems by its very universality to be more essentially a function of life. In fact, what distinguishes literature from the other arts, according to More, is its moral quality. Moral standards might not be relevant to an art like music, but they seem to be as relevant to literature as they are to life itself. Living necessarily involves values. One can scarcely act without implying that it is right to do so. And of all the arts literature is the one that most persuades us of the qualities of actual experience, with its dramatic and symbolic representations of ideas, action, and emotion. Literature is important to us precisely because of the values we find there. In short, literature by its very nature reflects life and it should reflect it truly.

More felt that the problems of literature and society are essentially the same, and if the great critics of human actions and values deal much with the criticism of literature, "this is because in literature more manifestly than anywhere else life displays its infinitely varied motives and results" (SE, VII, 218). He accounted for confusion in literature as the result of confusion in ideals for living, for "as we live, so shall we paint and write." If there is formlessness and lack of higher emotion in literature, then we can find the same thing in society. "There can be no great and simple and sincere art without ideals of greatness and simplicity and sincerity prevailing in society" (NSE, III, 3). Homer and his successors are preeminent artists, he says, "not by reason of form alone, but because they present a fairer criticism of life—than is readily to be found elsewhere." Therefore, it is a "contradiction" that Homer and Sophocles "should be reckoned unsurpassed as poets, and their views of life be regarded as immature" (SE, II, 189).

As noted in the preceding chapter, More's central interest was in that middle ground where life and literature meet, and for him the critical temperament consists mainly in the linking together of literature and life. But the artist, of course, prior to the critic, must recognize the link between art and life, and for More, the real task of the artist is to present in his writing the streams of life in such a way as to be consistent with the pattern of life apart from art. Much of his effectiveness, indeed, will depend on the ingenuity he displays as he personalizes and adorns the workings of ethics and morality, but he will not be a true artist if he thinks his characters can escape the moral laws inextricably bound up with human life.

Of the intimate relation between ethics and any form of art that deals directly with human nature I do not see how there can be a reasonable doubt. Such a relation, in fact, means no more than that he who would depict life must be familiar with the springs and consequences of action, and that in the large matters of experience the tradition of the ages is probably richer in content than his own limited observation. The problem for the artist, more especially for the novelist, is not how far he shall accept the obligations of this law—his art will gain in depth in proportion to the measure of his acceptance—but how he shall manifest its operation. (*NSE,* I, 102)

An important implication of this statement is that literature cannot avoid involving moral judgments. "If there be any conclusion to be drawn from the history of literature, it is that the writer of stories 'must teach whether he wish to teach or no' [Trollope's words]: his very denial of the pertinence of the moral law to art becomes in practice inevitably a form of teaching"(*NSE,* I, 105). "The simple truth is that all literature, except perhaps the humblest and least pretentious kind of fiction, is interpretive"(*NSE,* III, 87). As might be expected from these statements, More was not much interested in literature merely as escape (though he did like detective stories). For him relatively little could be an escape; literature that is simply and completely "escape" literature probably does not exist, for even the most trivial item may contain the seeds of far-reaching consequences.

More goes even beyond the contention that there exists an intimate relation between ethics and art: "The fact is that ethics and aesthetics are inseparable in art. Or, more precisely, just in proportion as the practice or criticism strikes deeper, ethics and aesthetics are more and more implicated one in the other until they lose their distinction in a common root" (*NSE,* I, 108-9). (That common root, according to More, lies in the awareness of dualism in the human consciousness and is considered in the next section.) But to say that ethics and aesthetics have a common root is not to say that they are the

25

same thing. "I know that a man may be sturdily, even intelligently, moral, yet withal a dull writer, that the temptation to preach may invade the region of art disastrously. Morality is not art" (*NSE,* I, 99-100). "The 'greatness' of literature cannot be determined solely by literary standards; though we must remember that whether it is literature or not can be determined only by literary standards." More thought this famous statement by T. S. Eliot to be "a complete truth perfectly expressed" (*NSE,* III, 195) because it precisely embodies his own philosophy. His most complete statement of this philosophy is found in a letter to a friend:

Can or cannot art be divorced from ethics? . . . Well I say flatly that art, any art, worth considering very seriously cannot be so divorced. Of course you will understand that by ethics I mean no narrow or specific code of morals, but the laws of man's ἦθος. And another point: I do not mean that ethics and aesthetics are the same thing. They are not. And it is perfectly possible, and may be valuable, to study a work of art, or a movement of art, from the purely aesthetic point of view. Only, in my opinion, it should be remembered that such a study is abstracting for a special purpose what in practice cannot exist separately. . . . I would not for a moment deny that technique and aesthetic enter into the criterion of art and are factors of tradition. Indeed I have said as much. But I think you will find that of the two, aesthetic is far more changeable than ethic, and that the continuity of taste depends more on the latter than on the former—though I would not press this point too far. But, after all, the great enduring things are the primary emotions, and about all I would say is that the higher emotions feed the better and more enduring art.[2]

Because More viewed ethics and aesthetics as inseparably connected in an organic bond, he was highly critical of any attempts to achieve "pure" art or pursue art for art's sake. "The point is," he says, "that the pursuit of art as an abstraction divorced from the responsibilities of life leads to nothing, and idealistic beauty loosed from belief in the higher reality of spiritual ideas is no more than a mist fluttering in the infinite inane" (*NSE,* III, 80). Art cannot be left to work "under the canons of beauty alone independently of outside control, but is to be judged by a standard embracing interests of a far wider order; art must be subservient to ethics" (*P*, 180). "Life is more than art: if to be true to art it were necessary to be false to life, then only a shallow dilettante would choose art; and if to seek beauty it were necessary to forget righteousness, then a whole-hearted man of experience would say, Perish the name of beauty" (*NSE*, I, 101). More was not only critical of artists who attempted to escape the relevance or consequences of ethical truth in their writing, but he also at one point took another critic to task for slurring over the "impudicity" of a certain author saying of that critic, "To belittle in this way the importance of ethical truth in literature is to surrender the most decisive instrument in the hands of the critic" (*SE*, X, 75).

To conclude this exposition of More's views on the connection of art and life, here is a statement which summarizes the points that have already been made and fits them into a scheme which More sees as the "tradition of agelong practice . . . what we mean, or ought to mean, by classical."

Always the great creators have taken the substance of life, and, not by denying it or attempting to evade its laws, but by looking more intently below its surface, have found meanings and values that transmute it into something at once the same and different. The passions that distract the individual man with the despair of isolated impotence they have invested with a universal significance fraught with the destinies of humanity; the scenery of the material world they have infused with suggestions of an indwelling overworld. And so by a species of symbolism, or whatever you choose to call it, they have lifted mortal life and its theatre to a higher reality which only to the contented or dust-choked dwellers in things as they are may appear as unreal. (*NSE*, I, 36-37)

Dualism

Mention has already been made of the critical tradition More outlines in his essay titled "Criticism," a tradition running from Cicero through Erasmus, Boileau, Shaftesbury, and Sainte-Beuve to Matthew Arnold, whose practice is always to render literature more consciously a criticism of life. This is the tradition to which More himself aspired; but in doing so he wished to perfect this tradition by eliminating the faults of these critics. They had the critical efficiency and moral earnestness that he valued, but they were lacking in another direction: "They missed a philosophy which could bind together their moral and aesthetic sense, a positive principle besides the negative force of ridicule and irony; and, missing this, they left criticism more easily subject to one-sided and dangerous development" (SE, VII, 233-34). More, therefore, was interested in achieving two principal aims in formulating a theory of criticism. First, because of "an invincible feeling that true art is in some way based on truth" (SE, X, 145), he sought some philosophy of life and human nature that could provide an adequate test for the truth of a literary work. Second, he sought a way to relate the beautiful and the good, the aesthetic and the moral. He found what he thought was a solution to both of these problems in his philosophy of dualism.

Dualism is the first principle of More's philosophy, theology, and literary criticism. In a rather autobiographical article published just a year before his death, he acknowledged that obviously "the dualistic thesis stood out as the binding thread running through all my work." But he was quick to clarify what he meant by the term: "Emphatically I have not meant by it to set up an ironclad rival to the various metaphysics of the One." His intention, he says, was less ambitious and implies no more than this, "that in every field of experience, if I push my analysis to the end of my resources, I find myself brought up against a pair of irreconcilable, yet interrelated and interacting, contraries, such as 'good' and 'bad,' 'mind' and 'body,' the 'One' and the 'Many,' 'rest' and 'motion.' "[3] He observes that from his childhood he was conscious, at first only vaguely and inarticulately, of "the two worlds between which my soul was compelled to choose its allegiance"—the world of sense and a higher, intangible world of impressions. Within his consciousness there was a "kaleidoscopic oscillation" of attraction between these two alternating worlds. He found that the world of sense was at first solid-seeming, but the more one concentrated on it the more it gradually betrayed itself—it being inconsistent and illusory. With the other world it was just the opposite. "It was evasive at first, but with the effort of attention took on a firmer and firmer body, and to the stability of your interest it responded by assuming ever more stable hues and outline."

It is scarcely too much to say that the development of my noetic life, the history of the altering attitude toward certain fundamental articles of belief from book to book as these were written, has been governed by the intermittent endeavor, from varying angles of approach, to discover some instrument, some formula of thought, which would give a fixed solidity to the tenuity of a vision always present, always inviting, yet always threatening to vanish away—this rather than any transaction with a logical rationalization of dualism.[4]

From childhood, then, More was preoccupied with the dualistic vision of human consciousness, and when he responded vigorously to any particular idea, philosophy, or work of literature, it was because it provided some insight into the nature of this duality. This was the case, as we shall see, with Eastern Philosophy and with Platonism and ultimately with Christianity. The first of such instances occurred in 1891 when he chanced upon Baur's *Das Manichäische Religionssystem:* "Such mental excitement as that book gave me I had never known before and have never felt since." What excited him so much was "the principle of dualism,—a crude mechanical sort of philosophy as taught by the Manicheans, but through the really magnificent allegory in which their mythology flowered hinting at a deeper and subtler truth."[5] More saw from the start "the extravagance and materialistic tendencies of the Manichean superstition," but it acted "as a powerful stimulus to the imagination" (*SE*, VI, 66).

In 1892 More entered Harvard to study Oriental languages and philosophy, and although Eastern philosophy and religion are generally considered thoroughly monistic, what interested More most was the remnant of dualism he saw in them. He saw dualism as the foundation of Buddhism (*CF*, 8); and the truth of the Upanishads, he thought, lies "in the vivid consciousness of a dualism felt in the daily habit of humanity" (*SE*, VI, 17). In "The Forest Philosophy of India" (*SE*, VI, 1-42), he argues his own dualistic interpretation of the sacred writings of the East against the non-dualistic interpretation of both ancient sage and modern scholar. More was never, in a strict sense, a believer, but he went to Vedanta "for strength and consolation" and enlightenment regarding the dualistic vision of human experience.

It was not long before he turned his focus of attention from Vedanta to Platonism, and he remained a Platonist during all of his adult life. Again, his response to the writings of Plato was a response to what he saw as a dualistic interpretation of life. In arriving at his Platonic position, he first had to disentangle the thought of Plato from that of Plotinus. Neo-Platonism he viewed as a monistic corruption of Platonism. The true key to Platonism, he thought, lies in its frank acceptance of a dualistic universe of the One and the Many, mind and matter, or perhaps, spirit and matter. But because man's mind is uncomfortable with the challenge of dualism, for it presents a puzzle at the heart of the universe, there has been a tendency among men to construct monistic theories through rationalism; these purport to provide unity and solve metaphysical puzzles. This is why Plato's dualism has not been widely accepted; usually the dualism has been covered over either by a frank materialism or some kind of Neo-Platonic idealism. The extent of the influence of Platonism upon More's thought is too vast to be considered here.[6] However, a statement by More regarding what he saw at the heart of Plato's philosophy is useful in indicating how Platonism blended into that dualistic consciousness which was, from his childhood, at the center of More's noetic life:

> At the root of Plato's philosophy lies the perception of a dividing cleft between our experience of that which comes to us as stable, eternal, immutable, unitary, possessible, joyous, peace-giving, somehow right, and our experience of that which comes to us as shifting, ephemeral, transient, various, elusive, mingled of pleasure and pain, distracting, somehow weighted with evil; on one side our knowledge of ideas, on the other side our opinions of phenomena. Yet this world of our experience is still one without confusion, two utterly disparate natures; and I who live in this double experience am still one person. (*CW*, 251)

According to Robert Davies, "Next to dualism itself the belief in the Platonic Ideas is the most constant ingredient in More's creed, and even the Ideas are actually a late specific crystallization of his dualism."[7] As a literary critic it is likely that the Platonic Idea was in More's mind associated with the criterion of universality as opposed to a writer's obsession with sensuous particulars (the Many).

In his later years when he gravitated to an increasingly theistic position, More found in his brand of Platonized Christianity or Christianized Platonism an ultimate symbolic representation of dualism. He came to view the Incarnation as the central dogma of Christianity: here was the Word or Logos made flesh, the divine paired with the human, the higher reality joined with the lower. In this dogma More found a dualistic concept of God to consummate his lifelong dualistic concept of man and the world.

The most explicit and extended formulation of his dualistic philosophy is found in "Definitions of Dualism" (*SE*, VIII, 247-302). This essay is not, and was not intended to be, a systematic treatise on the subject, but rather a series of definitions. It is rather sketchy in itself, hardly more than an extended outline, but when it is considered in the light of the *Shelburne Essays* in their totality, it becomes quite an illuminating document and a remarkable example of philosophical synthesis. Although this essay was written relatively early in his career (1913), his views altered in no significant way later. He never renounced the philosophical dualism he defines here or any of its major implications for philosophy, morality, society, or literature. The aphoristic quality of the essay makes it difficult to summarize, but a few excerpts will serve to indicate the basic principles.

There is an opposition within the human consciousness, says More, between two irreconcilable forces. First, there are the impulses which spring from the coming together of inner desires and outer impressions. The sum of these desires and impressions he calls "the great self-moving, incessant flux."

Beside the flux of life there is also that within man which displays itself intermittently as an inhibition upon this or that impulse, preventing its prolongation in activity, and making a pause or eddy, so to speak, in the stream. This negation of the flux we call the inner check. It is not the mere blocking of one impulse by another, which is a quality of the confusion of the flux itself, but a restraint upon the flux exercised by a force contrary to it. (247-48)

This dualism, which assumes the power of free-willed choice, within the human consciousness is a fundamental reality and we can know nothing more about it than the mere fact that it exists; it is "the last irrational fact, the report behind which we cannot go, the decision against which there is no appeal, the reality which only stands out the more clearly the more it is questioned" (248-49).

From this starting point, More goes on to define the various aspects of human nature and experience: reason, feeling, memory, imagination, happiness, etcetera. All of these terms are defined in the light of the scheme of dualism. For example, "character," which is an important and recurring term in his criticism, is defined in this way: "A man of character is one in whom a vigorous disposition is continuously controlled by the habit of attention, or the will to refrain [the inner check]. As character develops, the disposition takes on a more regular pattern; the impulses become harmonious as if arranged upon a centre, and display a kind of unity in multiplicity. The outcome in conduct is consistency, self-direction, balance of faculties, efficiency, moral health, happiness" (274-75).

Art is defined as the attempt to establish the experience of the individual in tradition.

Works of art are varied in so far as they are created by the imagination out of the material of the flux, and substantially they depend on the richness of the artists' experience. Formally they rise to a common standard of excellence in so far as the imagination of the artist is subject to the control of the unvaried inner check. So, too, taste, or the appreciation of art, passes from the impressionistic whim of the individual and from the larger convention of an age or a people to a universal canon just to the degree that it is regulated by the inner check. Criticism is thus not left to waver without a fixed criterion; and in the understanding of dualism it possesses further a key to the main divergences of thought and action, and a constant norm of classification. (264-65)

Talent is a man's ability to express his experience; genius is the degree to which the consciousness of dualism enters into that expression.

These are some sample definitions from the rather comprehensive series presented by More. They were selected because they have such a direct bearing on his standards as a judicial critic. Many of the other terms defined come up later and are discussed in connection with essays on particular subjects. One of the most interesting things about "Definitions of Dualism" is that in itself it comprises a close analogy to what More does in his criticism as a whole. Just as in this essay he defines familiar terms in the context of the concept of dualism, in his literary criticism he "defines" authors or discusses them in the same context. Thus, this essay is like a microcosm in relation to the macrocosm of his total criticism. The continuity of this individual essay corresponds to the continuity of his essays as a whole.

The central truth of experience for More, therefore, is what he sees as the truth of dualism, "a recognition of the absolute distinction between the two elements of our conscious being, and an admission of the impossibility of finding any rationally positive explanation of the mutual interaction of these two elements" (P, 187). Anyone who looks deeply into his own heart, More believes, must recognize there the two distinct principles governing his life—the will to act and the will to refrain—"and on the right understanding of these two faculties depends largely our insight into much that is best and much that is worst in literature" (SE, II, 116-17). The question which is finally raised in all of More's criticism is the question of dualism: "Is there, or is there not, some element of man's being superior to instinct and reason, some power that acts as a stay upon the flowing impulses of nature, without whose authoritative check reason herself must in the end be swept away in the dissolution of the everlasting flux?" (SE, VIII, xiii). In one way or another he applies this question to all the writers he studies. Looking at his method from this point of view, one might expect considerable sameness and repetition in his literary criticism; but as a matter of fact, although the repetition of principles is certainly there, the protean implications of his dualistic criteria and the original manner in which he applies them elicit something quite fresh with each author he approaches.

Just how central the concept of dualism is to the continuity of More's criticism can be seen in the following two statements. The way he delineates how the human race works out its spiritual history by confronting the final irrational fact of dualism is the chief concern of the subsequent chapters of this study.

But in one way or another, by the fervor of acceptance, by the very vehemence of denial, by the earnestness of the endeavor to escape it, this dualism lies at the bottom of our inner life, and the spiritual history of the human race might be defined as the long writhing and posturing of the soul (I mean something more than the mere intellect,—the whole essential man, indeed) to conceal, or deny, or ridicule, or overcome, this cleft in its nature. (*SE*, VI, 18)

It is possible, I believe, to view the ceaseless intellectual fluctuations of mankind backward and forward as the varying fortunes of the contest between these two hostile members of our being,—between the deep-lying principle that impels us to seek rest and the principle that drags us back into the region of change and motion and forever forbids us to acquiesce in what is found. And I believe further that the moral disposition of a nation or of an individual may be best characterized by the predominance of the one or the other of these two elements. (*SE*, III, 245)

Humanism

The term "humanism" has acquired a number of meanings, some closely related, but others radically different. It is a term whose meaning has become very fluid, much as the meanings of words like "romanticism," "conservatism," and "liberalism" have become fluid. Each of these words in practice is applied to a variety of attitudes, philosophies, and movements. Their usefulness decreases to some extent as their meanings become increasingly unstable, and we are forced continually to redefine them in order to preserve their usefulness. Since Paul Elmer More considered himself a humanist and literary history classifies him as a leader of the New Humanism movement, it is necessary to examine carefully his own definition of the term. A consideration of what humanism meant to him can take us a long way in understanding the fundamental principles of his philosophy of criticism.

> There are two laws discrete
> Not reconciled,—
> Law for man, and law for thing;
> The last builds town and fleet,
> But it runs wild,
> And doth the man unking.

These lines from Emerson (who wrote sympathetically on Plato's One and the Many) reflect what More thought to be the fundamental truth of humanism: there is a human law and a natural law—both are true and must be applied in their respective fields, but they are distinct and must remain separate. The natural law cannot be ignored or made of little consequence, but it should always come second in priority to the human law. "There is a truth of human nature as there is a science of material forces, and the better efficiency is that of a soul which has first come to terms with itself" (*SE*, XI, 255). The human law is of first importance to the humanist because he firmly maintains that it grows out of a "higher nature" in man "which is not of nature," an "ethical will" that is his "center," which does not merely react to stimulus, but in some measure controls and directs, which apprehends and seeks to realize values that are objectively real, not mere projections of his desires or rationalizations of his instincts.

The dualism in the preceding section is therefore at the center of More's humanism. Man is born with a divided nature. There is always a conflict within him between judgment and impulse, between his higher will and the flux of experience, between a better and a worse self, between that which we call god-like and that which seems to link him with the beast. The acceptance of this dualism (and its correlative emphasis on free-willed responsibility) is the distinctive attribute of the New Humanism and is that which makes it uncompromisingly antinaturalistic. For naturalism (and here is another term which must be defined in the context of More's thought) is precisely the denial or minimizing of the higher nature in man. Naturalism, for More, is the antonym of humanism; it is "the union of science and rationalism, that is to say the reassumption of nature and the soul under the same law" (*SE*, VIII, 270). Naturalism denies any revealed authority outside of nature and any higher nature or "supernature" within man. The point here can be summarized and fitted into the continuity we are concerned with by repeating this statement by More: "The recognition of this dualism of the natural and the supernatural in man (or of a higher and lower nature, for the word 'nature' is as unstable as the sea) is precisely the philosophy of humanism, as contrasted with the philosophy of naturalism which denies that the distinctive mark of man is a consciously directive will. And the history of European culture since the Renaissance turns on the varying fortune of these two hostile views" (*NSE*, I, x).

In addition to the distinction between law for man and law for thing, another important principle of More's humanism is what might be termed the law of measure. From the time of Socrates until today this, he believed, has been a fundamental precept of humanism. It is the law of the golden mean, nothing too much, a due balance. Humanism starts from the effort to understand man's true nature and thus determine his best way of life. It began and has lived as a critical activity— as a skeptical attempt to expose hollow pretensions which frequently have resulted from attempts to set up absolute systems, to set the law of measure aside in favor of one kind of extreme or another. (This tendency on the part of men to explain the world in terms of one absolute system or another More labeled "The Demon of the Absolute," and his criticism of it is presented in the following section.)

More's humanism was a kind of *via media* in which he attempted not simply to walk a line between two extremes, but to establish a middle ground which partakes of the extremes but remains stable. In writing to his friend Robert Shafer he said,

I think a true humanism should mediate between romantic revery which prescinds distinctions and floats away into a debilitating emotionalism in the manner of Schleiermacher and Rousseau who take this to be the essence of religion, and a cold harsh intellectualism which finds salvation in the bare distinguishing faculty of reason. And such a mediation is not a mechanical compromise or a flabby wavering between two moods, but an intimate marriage between passivity and activity, contemplation and self-direction, emotion and will, of which is born a certain *tertium quid*.[8]

More emphasized that such a middle view was not simply a compromise between the extremes but depended upon a positive choice of direction which is intrinsically different from compromise.

There are two basic ingredients which appear repeatedly in More's humanism. The first is an insistence on the dignity of the individual human life: "There is that in every human being which it behooves him to know and cherish, a potentiality which is worth his while to develop at any cost, a goal of perfection toward which all his energy should be directed—the high value of being a man" (*NSE,* III, 15-16). The second is a recognition of individual responsibility which comes with this individuality: "The cause of humanism is identical . . . with belief in free will and purpose as the traits that distinguish humanity from nature or, if you prefer, from the rest of nature" (*NSE,* III, 17). Free will and purpose necessarily entail responsibility, and "the beginning of humanism, as of religion, is the humility that goes with a sense of personal responsibility" (*NSE,* III, 5).

The first of these basic ingredients More shared in common with other humanists, not only his fellow New Humanists but humanists of any stripe. But the second ingredient involving the issues of free will, purpose, and responsibility became a point of divergence for More from humanism in general and the humanism of his good friend and fellow New Humanist Irving Babbitt in particular. The point of divergence lies in the answer to the question of where free will, purpose, and responsibility ultimately originate. This question, according to More, presents a dilemma for the kind of humanism that denies supernaturalism.

The intuition of free will; free will exercised for a purpose; purposes directed to clothe human life with value; value measured by happiness—the chain is perfect link by link, only at the end it

seems to be attached to nothing. And so I ask myself, reluc-
tantly, almost wishing my answer were mistaken, whether those
who advocate humanism, as an isolated movement, are not
doomed to disappointment. . . . Will not the humanist, unless
he adds to his creed the faith and the hope of religion, find
himself at the last, despite his protests, dragged back into the
camp of the naturalist? (*NSE,* III, 19-20)

More found the solution to this dilemma in what may be
termed theistic humanism.[9] He took the chain described
above and fastened it firmly to the spiritual order. The final
element of unity in human nature is not then, for More,
reason, but rather a sense of the eternal, an intuition of the
spiritual realm. He was critical of those who made humanism
a religion in and of itself, who viewed man as god and,
because of his powers of reason, inherently good. "Whatever
we do, whatever we believe, let us not shut our eyes to the
reality of evil" (*POD,* XXXI). This idea about evil is basic
with More, and many of the philosophies and literary movements he harshly criticizes are criticized primarily on the
grounds that they fail to acknowledge the reality of evil. His
theistic humanism, therefore, consists of a dualistic view of
human nature in which man's higher nature, the nature
which enables him to achieve the good through purposeful
free-willed responsibility, has its source in God. This higher
nature has real significance because it is balanced by a lower
nature which is subject to evil in a very real way.

Another important aspect of More's humanism is a distinction he makes between the true and the false illusion. This
doctrine appears as early as in the first volume of the *Shelburne
Essays* and is repeated with increasing fullness and widening
application throughout his criticism. In the beginning he
applies it to poetry, but later it becomes part of his criteria
for judging art in general and even government as well. He
explains it at one point in this way: "For there is a true
illusion, if the phrase will be accepted, whereby the lower
nature of man is charmed by the voice of his higher instincts;

and there is a false illusion, of the very contrary sort. The one is social and constructive, and is the work, properly speaking, of the imagination; the other is disintegrating and destructive, and is the product of the egotistical desires" (SE, IX, 174). More associates the true illusion with humanism and the false illusion with naturalism. The true illusion is to cast over the affairs of daily activity that illusory charm which will cause the reader to lift his thoughts and imagination to the eternal truths which lie beyond the realm of the physical senses. This is the artist's challenge, but if he fails in it, or ignores it, he will likely fall into the false illusion. In the false illusion the artist casts over the physical realities the illusory charm that leads the reader to believe the world of spirit is contained within the physical world itself. But because this is a false illusion, it fails to satisfy him and simply leads him deeper and deeper into the world of the physical senses in search of the spirit, which in reality is not there. Thus the true illusion leads men to a clearer perception of the lasting verities and the realm of spirit while the false illusion leads men away from such a perception into a morass of conflicting physical impulses. The true artist, according to More, is aware of the bestial in man, but he sees also something else, and in that something else looks for the meaning of life. This does not mean that the true artist is restricted to representing only the pure and innocent, nor should he be a preacher.

Rather he is one who, by the subtle, insinuating power of the imagination, by just appreciation of the higher emotions as well as the lower . . . gives us always to feel that the true universal in human nature, the faculty by which man resembles man as being different from the beast, is that part of him that is "noble in reason," the master and not the slave of passion. True art is thus humanistic rather than naturalistic; and its gift of high and permanent pleasure is the response of our own breast to the artist's delicately revealed sense of that divine control, moving like the spirit of God upon the face of the waters. (NSE, I, 24)

There is probably no better way to conclude this section on humanism than to present More's own summary of the subject, a summary which emphasizes free will, the reality of evil, and the antimechanistic or organic:

In a word, the humanist is simply one who takes his stand *on being human*. Against those who still hold that man is only a fragmentary cog in the vast machine which we call the universe, moved by the force of some relentless, unvarying, unconscious law, the humanist asserts that we are individual personalities, endowed with the potentiality of free will and answerable for our choice of good or evil. Against those who reduce man to a chaos of sensations and instincts and desires checking and counterchecking one another in endlessly shifting patterns, the humanist points to a separate faculty of inhibition, the inner check or the *frein vital,* whereby these expansive impulses may be kept within bounds and ordered to a design not of their making. Against those who proclaim that a man can only drift, like a rudderless ship, with the weltering currents of change, the humanist maintains that he is capable of self-direction, and that character, as different from native temperament, is a growth dependent on clarity of strength and purpose. Against those who, to appease the stings of conscience, assure us that we are what we are by no fault of our own, that, as we have no responsibility for our character, so the lesson of wisdom is to shuffle off any sense of regret or remorse or fear; and against those who go further in flattery and, through each and every appearance of delinquency, assert the instinctive total goodness of unredeemed nature—against these the humanist contends that as free agents we are accountable for defalcations and aberrations and that self-complacency is the deadliest foe to human excellence. (*NSE,* III, 7-8)

Rationalism

A corollary to the insistent dualism on which More's humanism is based is an opposition to monism that appears persistently in his work in the form of antirationalism. It is impossible to read any volume of his writing without coming across some negative reference to rationalism, or to metaphysics or monism, both of which he equated with rationalism.

What he really referred to by these terms was "reason un-checked by experience," an absolutism to which he was both temperamentally and philosophically opposed. He had a strong antipathy toward the systematization of life and belief because he felt that such rational systems generally ignore the facts of existence. Since those facts involve principles of good and evil and knowledge acquired both empirically and intu-itively, he saw no way of combining them into a unified rational system. Systems which purport to unify and explain all of human experience through some kind of rationalizing process he viewed as mere pretensions and the source of per-nicious thought and behavior.

Late in his career he coined the phrase "The Demon of the Absolute" to refer to man's propensity for rationalism. The Demon of the Absolute, he says, "is nothing else but rationalism . . . or, if you wish it in plainer English, reason run amuck" (*NSE,* I, 1). Reason, properly our guide and friend, has a perennial tendency to leap beyond "the actual data of experience" and "set up its own absolutes as truth." It craves to explain life in terms of a single formula and thus blurs that "double consciousness," that inexplicable sense of opposition in human nature between dust and deity, which is the source of great art and great conduct. There are no abso-lutes in nature; "they are phantoms created by the reason itself in its own likeness, delusions, which, when once evoked, usurp the field of reality and bring endless confusion in their train" (*NSE,* I, 2). He believed that this Demon can be seen in the fields of philosophy, politics, and religion in all periods of history; but nowhere, he says, "has it produced more stupid contrariety than among the critics of art and literature." In the area of criticism this "baleful influence" draws the critic to choose between "belief in absolute stan-dards or belief in an absolute irresponsibility of taste, whereas truth lies with the mediatorial view of common sense that we have standards vested with a certain amount of authority but never infallible" (*CF,* 169). This mediatorial acknowledgement of the attraction of both the One and the Many is of far-reaching importance in his work.

It should be obvious thus far that his use of the term "rationalism" would not be entirely acceptable to most philosophers. As Robert Davies has pointed out, what he has done is confuse method and content; "when he attacks 'rationalism' he is really attacking conclusions that have been reached by rationalistic methods."[10] More sees rationalism as a method or attitude of mind, but one which invariably leads to some sterile monism; hence rationalism, metaphysics, and monism become synonymous in his writings. However, he had too sharp a mind to overlook the distinction between rationalism as a method and the content of its conclusions. When he confuses the two we must conclude that he is deliberately slurring over a distinction he considered of minor importance in order to have a term which will serve his purposes. As already mentioned, he thought that his writing in order to stand must stand as a whole; therefore, he used such words as "rationalism," "metaphysics," and "naturalism" in his own way knowing that their meanings would be perfectly clear to anyone who read his individual essays in the context of his work in general and not as isolated and self-contained units. And besides this, in "Definitions of Dualism," which he must have intended as a kind of glossary for his published works, he defines all these terms in the context of his thought and philosophy.

More believed that when we push our analysis of the human consciousness to the end of our resources, we come up against a pair of irreconcilable contraries: good and evil, mind and body, One and Many. The dualist, he says, "is one who modestly submits to this bifurcation as the ultimate point where clarity of definition obtains. Beyond this he refuses to follow reason in its frantic endeavor to reconcile these opposites by any logical legerdemain in which one of the controlling factors of consciousness is brought out as an absolute while the other disappears in the conjuror's hat."[11]

The dualist acknowledges the reasoning faculty "as the governor of practical conduct, yet balks at its pretension to discover in its own mechanism the ultimate source and nature of Being. He remains half-brother to the sceptic, whereas the monist is a metaphysical dogmatist."[12] The danger of monistic rationalism, More insists, whether of the scientist or the metaphysical idealist, is that reason becomes regarded as mistress instead of servant of that within man "which lies deeper than any nameable faculty." The simplifying process demanded by reason tends to fly in the face of immediate concrete experience and common sense and denies one term or the other of the paradox which lies at the bottom of human consciousness. Hence, he defines metaphysics as an attempt on the part of reason to assume essential authority for the faculties, in which reason usurps the function of consciousness and undertakes to explain the ultimate reality of things by abstract conceptions (SE, VIII, 266). One of the "tyrannous obsessions" of metaphysics has been "the attempt to catch and hold the universe in a syllogism, denying thereby all our concrete experience, all our sense of multiplicity and change, all our knowledge of evil, denying life itself for an abstract unity of reason." In light of this, he says, "I confess that to me monism has always been merely another word for monomania" (SE, VII, 200).

For Socrates, says More, the beginning of philosophy as the wisdom of life was to know what we know and what we do not know, "and just this distinction is lost by the metaphysician who deals with words and logical formulae which have no positive content" (HP, 243). But let us not be deceived, he advises; "these questions that touch man's deepest moral experience are not capable of logical solution; indeed, they lose all reality as soon as they are subjected to dogmatic definition" (SE, II, 252-53). One of the hardest things for a student to learn, he says in another place, "is the simple fact that *brain power is no guarantee for rightness of thinking,* that on the contrary a restlessly outreaching mind, unchecked by the humility of common sense, is more likely to lead its owner into bogs of duplicity if not into the bottomless pit of fatuity" (*NSE,* I, 42). Why is this lesson hard for the student to learn? Why are the illusions of rationalism constantly springing up? He believed the answer is that men have refused to accept the terms under which they live, which according to him are basically these: "Man is intellectually impotent and morally responsible" (*NSE,* II, 89). Men reject this fact when, through the powers of reason, they try to set up some kind of unified, monistic system for explaining human nature and experience. He defines rationalism at one point as "the attempt to erect reason into an independent power within the soul taking the place of the inner check" (*SE,* VIII, 270). It is easy to see, therefore, why he was so adamantly opposed to rationalism as he interpreted it. In setting up reason in place of the inner check, rationalism claims to bridge the gap between the fundamental dual elements in human consciousness, in effect claims to resolve that dualism. This, in his view, is an illusion because that dualism is incapable of being resolved.

In fact, it should be emphasized here that the dualism More always had in mind was a genuine dualism, an absolute dualism in the sense that it is complete and unqualified. He made a distinction between what he called an "absolute" and an "absolved" dualism. An absolute dualism accepts the fact that there is a world of observation and a world of spirit—both real. The tendency of the human mind is to resolve this dualism into an absolved dualism whereby one of the factors, either the world of observation or the world of intuition, disappears into unreality, and we are back to monism. In other words, an absolved dualism might acknowledge a distinction between spirit and matter, but still hold that the spirit can attain to a condition of complete unity and changelessness in which it is absolutely free from involvement with materiality or the flux of change. Such a condition is the goal of all mystics. He explains the distinction between these dualisms as it applies to the area of religion in this way:

Any genuine dualism must be "absolute" in the sense that it postulates a radical distinction between spirit and matter and good and evil, with all that these distinctions imply. Admittedly such a conjunction of contraries involves an irrational paradox in the nature of things; but it is a paradox rooted in the nethermost stratum of human consciousness, and it may be the foundation of a perfectly reasonable superstructure of experience. . . . By an "absolved" dualism I mean that the absolute distinctions of dualism are maintained, but on the condition, so to speak, that the goal of religious endeavor shall be regarded as a final divorce of these opposites in such wise as to permit spirit to exist in perfect unity and immutability, absolved from any association with the feelings and thoughts and activities which pertain to the multiple and mutable element of normal consciousness. (*CF*, 66-67)

Of course an absolved dualism might also work in an opposite way, whereby the material world of flux becomes absolved completely from any association with the immutable world of spirit. An absolved dualism is rationalistic, he maintains, because it deals with incomprehensible abstractions while the absolute dualism deals with things we know and understand. Monism is the next step metaphysically after an absolved dualism.

More's particularized usage of the word "rationalism" naturally presented him with a problem when he wished to speak highly of the powers of reason and use them as a basis for rejecting certain propositions. When speaking of the process of sound reasoning, he could not very well use the term "rationalism," so he made use of another, similar term, "reasonableness." The difference between reasonableness and rationalism is the difference between "the act of reason dealing with the data presented to it whether in the sphere of the senses of the spirit, and the act of reason usurping the right to subvert the truths of experience to its own insatiable craving for finalities" (*HP*, 242). "However our pride of intellect may rebel," he insists, "there can be no intelligent attitude toward the greater problems of existence until we have learned that reason, though it may be the pragmatic guide of

46

conduct, is not the source of knowledge or even the final test of truth" (*CW*, 241). In clarifying the distinction between the two terms in his preface to *The Demon of the Absolute* he says, "The rationalism I denounce has no affinity to the reasonableness of common sense; it is rather just that defalcation of the reason to its own unreal abstractions which, obscuring the true function of the master faculty of our complete being, reduces the soul of man to a nonentity controlled by fatalistic law or to a puppet tossed in the winds of irresponsibility" (*NSE*, I, xii). In short, according to More, a view of life that bases its inferences on the intimately known facts of consciousness and which is docile enough to submit to control by the whole range of experience is more *reasonable* than *rational*.

Thus, in his thinking "reasonable" and "rational" are not convertible terms; in fact, rationalism is unreasonable. "It is odd, but true, that reasonableness and rationalism have never been able to dwell together peaceably; hence the need of humility" (*CNT*, 5). This distinction is of greater significance than first appears because from More's point of view reasonableness is the handmaiden of dualism while rationalism is the servant of monism. Any confrontation with the fundamental questions of life entails a choice between the two: "It should seem therefore that our only choice lies between a reasonable philosophy based on an irrational paradox [dualism] and an unreasonable metaphysic [monism] based on a rational presumption" (*CW*, 137). Therefore, when we see the way he thought rationalism functions in any approach to finding answers to the great questions of human nature and experience, we can better understand why he considered the most diverse appearing movements or philosophies as essentially the same if they attempt to rationalize human life on a monistic basis. This is what underlies the fact that he can place such apparently diverse philosophies as romanticism, scientism, humanitarianism, deism, and naturalism in the same camp. Just how he does this is considered in the following three sections.

Science

The New Humanists are generally characterized as being antiscientific, and it is true in More's case that his writings reveal an underlying distrust and even hostility toward "science." But this antagonism is not toward science *per se,* but rather toward science that is tainted by the rationalism just discussed. In arriving at an understanding of More's attitude toward science, we must keep in mind that he grew up in the late nineteenth century when science was almost an object of worship for many people, and its limitations were seldom clearly understood. Therefore when More attacks science, it is usually not science itself but the popular conception of science that is his target.

More's views on science are set forth at greatest length in his essay on T. H. Huxley (*SE,* VIII, 193-244). He begins by distinguishing between three types of science: positive, hypothetical, and philosophical. By positive science he means "the observation and classification of facts and the discovery of those constant sequences in phenomena which can be expressed in mathematical formulae or in the generalized language of law" (193). For this procedure we should have the highest respect. But it must be remembered that a law of science, no matter how broad its scope, does not go beyond a statement of observed facts and tells nothing of the ultimate cause of these facts. The mind of man is constituted in such a way that ignorance of causes acts as a constant source of irritation; we are almost irresistibly tempted to go beyond the mere statement of law to constructing a theory of reality that underlies the law. "Such a theory is an hypothesis, and such activity of the mind is hypothetical science as distinguished from positive science" (195). At this point, More distinguishes between two uses of the term hypothesis—for explanations of phenomena that "transcend the reach of our perceptive faculties," and for "scientific law which belongs to the realm of positive science, but which is still to be established." He rejects the former and prefers to call the latter "scientific conjecture" and includes it as part of positive science. As an example, he cites the case of Newton. Newton's formula began as scientific conjecture and when it was tested and proved to conform to facts it became scientific law. "But if Newton, not content with generalizing the phenomena of gravitation in the form of law, had undertaken to theorize on the absolute nature of the attraction which caused the phenomena of gravitation, he would have passed from the sphere of positive science to that of hypothetical science" (196). The chief danger of hypothetical science lies in the almost irresistible tendency of the human mind to glide from it into what More chooses to call philosophical science, "meaning thereby the endeavour to formulate a philosophy of life out of scientific law and hypothesis" (201). The trouble with philosophical science is that, with all its perspicacity, it can see no place within its scheme for "what is after all the heart of humanity and the source of true humanism—the consciousness of something within us that stands apart from material law and guides itself to ends of happiness and misery which do not belong to nature" (*SE,* IX, 85).

What More defines separately here as hypothetical and philosophical science is generally lumped together in his writing and given the term "rationalistic science." True science or positive science is a "reasonable" endeavor; it is primarily "the systematic accumulation of accurate knowledge" (*SE,* VIII, 258), "the habit of mind which searches for and clings to the actual individual fact independently of presupposition or theory and regardlessly of consequence" (*SE,* VIII, 67). Rationalistic science, on the contrary, "the science which really counts and which colours to-day our popular philosophy" (68), begins with presuppositions and begins to theorize too soon. The ultimate data of science are mass, motion, and energy; and the first fatal step toward rationalism is taken when the scientist, "not content to employ these immediate and inexplicable facts of sensation, tries, as it were, to go behind the returns, and seeks by some legerdemain of definition to comprehend what these phenomena are in themselves" (*HP,* 337). This process of rationalism inevitably leads to some form of desiccated monism: "Science, when it passes beyond the field of positive observation and metaphysical hypothesis into pure metaphysics, is an attempt to formulate a changeless law of change, to find some absolute cause of unity or development within the flux of nature without projecting into nature the equivalent of the inner check" (*SE,* VIII, 269). Thus, the real source of More's antipathy toward science is his fear that science is too vulnerable to the enticings and corrupting influence of a rationalism that denies his central premise of dualism.

A prime example of rationalistic science, in More's opinion, was the then current state of evolutionary biology. It is natural that the doctrine of evolution would loom large in More's consideration of science; he grew up in a time when America was experiencing the greatest impact of Darwinism. The impressiveness of Darwin's work and the simplicity of his theory had led to the imposition of the evolutionary hypothesis on education, morality, religion, and government—it seemed to explain everything. "Evolution is the living guide of our thought," More noted; "it has become as essentially a factor of our attitude toward the natural world as Newton's laws of gravitation" (*SE,* III, 253). He thought Darwin had confined himself to positive science until he tried to explain the cause of evolution by the theory of natural selection—here he passed into hypothetical science. And the natural step after that was for men to take Darwin's hypothetical science and convert it into philosophical science by formulating it into various philosophies of life.

In the preface to his ninth volume of the *Shelburne Essays,* More offers an explanation for his hostility toward evolution. He does not object to it as "a scientific law which states the facts of nature." What he is critical of is the philosophy which evolution "has wittingly, sometimes unwittingly" lent authority to (ix). "The point is," he says elsewhere, "that this rationalistic form of science depends on an invincible belief in some universal law of nature, and on a tendency to overlook if necessary the individual phenomenon in favour of this law" (*SE*, VIII, 68-69). It leads to a philosophy that amounts to "a faith in drifting; a belief that things of themselves, by a kind of natural gravity of goodness in them, move always on and on in the right direction; a confiding trust in human nature as needing no restraint or compression, but rather full liberty to follow its own impulsive desires to expand; an inclination to take sides with the emotions in their rebellion against the inhibitions of judgment" (*SE,* IX, viii-ix).

More's objections to science, therefore, are really objections to the "metaphysical extension of science." As soon as science overreaches itself and enters into the realm of metaphysics, he sees the Demon of the Absolute rearing its ugly head. The method of the rationalistic scientist, according to More, differs not one whit from that of the religious dogmatist; they are both the Demon's method. "The one, maintaining his faith in an unvarying cause, and untroubled by refractory details, formulates his experience with material phenomena into a scientific hypothesis; the other, holding fast to his faith in God's revelation of himself to the human soul, expands his inner experience into a mythology, unconcerned by individual facts that cannot be reconciled to his creed" (*SE,* VIII, 69). More's own posture in regard to both science and religion was to focus on immediate experience and intuition and maintain a skeptical attitude toward the ability of reason to answer the questions of ultimate cause and being.

Romanticism

As a young man More had been "immersed in the current of romanticism" (*SE,* VIII, 83), whose contributions to "the world's sum of beauty and sublimity" (36) he gratefully

51

acknowledged. But later, after having in his view "barely escaped" from the intellectual and moral dangers of the movement, he attacked with "violent revulsion" (83) its insidious elements: "the infinitely craving personality, the usurpation of emotion over reason, the idealization of love, the confusion of the sensuous and the spiritual, the perilous fascination that may go with the confusions. It is like a dream of fever, beautiful and malign by turns; and, looking at its wild sources, one can understand why Goethe curtly called romanticism disease and classicism health. He might have added that disease is infectious, whereas health must be acquired or preserved by the effort of the individual" (30).

More was not insensible to the beauty and magic that are commonly connected with the term romanticism in some of its manifestations. He acknowledges that in romantic literature "there is much that is simply true, much that is beautiful and magnificent, and there are moments that express the divine awe that belongs to the sudden inflooding of the veritable otherworld" (*SE,* VIII, 232); but he also observes in the preface to *The Drift of Romanticism* that the word romanticism is used in two quite different ways, and that the ignorance or neglect of this ambiguity has led to "endless confusion of standards" (*SE,* VIII, ix). On the one hand, the word is used to refer to certain qualities found in the poetry of every age: "the moments in it when we are thrilled by the indefinable spell of strangeness wedded to beauty, when we are startled by the unexpected vision of mystery beyond the circle of appearances that wrap the dull commonplace of daily usage" (ix). In this sense a work of classic art like the *Odyssey* contains "romantic" sections. On the other hand, the word is used to refer to a definite historical movement of modern Europe. More generally uses the term in the second sense "as a convenient term for what I take to be a dominant tendency and admitted ideal of the modern world" (xii). As we might expect, the ultimate distinction between the two uses of the word romantic lies, in his view, in the recognition of dualism.

If I had to designate very briefly this underlying principle which gives to historic romance a character radically different from the mystery and wonder of classic art, I should define it as that expansive conceit of the emotions which goes with the illusion of beholding the infinite within the stream of nature itself instead of apart from the stream [In other words, such romanticism is a form of naturalism]. The question raised finally is thus one of dualism: Is there, or is there not, some element of man's being superior to instinct and reason, some power that acts as a stay upon the flowing impulses of nature, without whose authoritative check reason herself must in the end be swept away in the dissolution of the everlasting flux? (xiii)

Thus, More's complaint against historic romanticism, in any of its forms, is that in its essence it is "a denial of classical dualism and an illusory substitution of the mere limitless expansion of our impulsive nature for that true infinite within the heart of man, which is not of nature and whose voice is heard as the inner check, restraining, centralizing, and forming" (234).

According to More, historic romanticism came into being with Blake and Rousseau and was systematized by the Schlegels, but the spirit at work in these men had a much earlier origin. For the source of romanticism we must go back to the remote beginnings of our era, to the mingling of Oriental and Occidental civilization which followed Alexander's invasion of Asia, and more particularly to the confluence of Eastern religion and Western philosophy. Eastern religion emphasized the vast and the vague, the infinite. Greek philosophy, on the other hand, had a repugnance for the infinite and dwelt upon the concrete and upon control. Oriental thought had no clear conception of the ego, whereas Occidental thought did. It was the great work of the first Christian centuries "to merge the Oriental and Occidental conceptions of infinity and personality together in a strange and fruitful union." The Occidental sense of ego merged with the Oriental sense of vastness and vagueness during the Roman Empire, and "to this alliance, if to any definite event in history, we may trace the birth of our sense of an infinite, insatiable personality, that has brought so much self-torment and so much troubled beauty into the religion and literature of the modern world" (*SE,* VIII, 26). The place where this alliance was consummated was Alexandria. This city on the delta of the Nile became the chief center and workshop for a widespread revolution in sentiment which manifested itself in movements like Neo-Platonism and Gnosticism. In the "farrago of superstition and philosophy" which comprised the teachings of Valentinus, an Alexandrian of the second century, More detects what he thought to be the real heart of what after many centuries would be called romanticism (29-30). Romanticism was thus early introduced into Christianity, and with Christianity descended to our own days. Some aspects of the true Christian faith remained and prevented the world from falling completely into Alexandrianism. Indeed, romanticism as we know it today, says More, "arose only after the purer Christian faith and the authority of the classics had given way together to the tide of naturalism which set in strongly with the eighteenth century" (31).

This tide of naturalism gave birth to rationalistic science as well as to romanticism, and according to More, the two sprang up together and have grown side by side. In one respect they embrace radically different temperaments—on this side the man who deals with facts and tends to a hard materialism or a dry intellectualism, on the other the man of sentiment who dreams and loses himself in futile reverie—but their point of contact is clear: "Those limitless forces which were raised into the scientific hypothesis of a self-evolving, or rather self-creating, universe are the exact counterpart in outer nature of those limitless desires or impulses in the heart which are the substance of the romantic illusion" (*SE,* VIII, 234). In other words, More objected to romanticism as a form of sentimental and emotional naturalism which is in essential agreement with scientific naturalism in this respect: "both types fail to recognize in man any element

54

belonging to a different order from the rest of nature. Nature and human nature are one. For the scientific naturalist man in his entirety is the product of, and determined by, the same forces which the physicist and biologist study. For the sentimental naturalist man is one with nature through feeling and impulse in which rather than in reason his essential humanity and innate goodness consist."[13]

In short, More believed the whole aim of romanticism was "to magnify the sense of individuality to a state of morbid excess, wherein the finite and the infinite should be dissolved together in formless reverie" (SE, VI, 37). Such a dissolving of the finite and infinite into each other is, of course, a denial of dualism, and therefore romanticism is at bottom monistic. In opposition to it he places classicism. At the heart of the true classicism, he says, is the fixed belief in a dualistic concept of the world: the one and the many. The "one," or what he calls "the infinite," is the absolute principle of self-concentration that makes for unity. The "many" is exactly the opposite; it is the limitless expanse of impulse and desire that he usually calls "the flux."

An important part of classicism is tradition, which he defines as "the experience of society" (SE, VIII, 255). It is the romanticist who magnifies the sense of individuality to excess; on the other hand, it is the humanist "who takes into positive account the value of tradition as a complement to the limitations of the individual, and who regards the present as a small but integral part of the long experience of the human race" (NSE, III, 12). The humanistic critic described in his essay on "Criticism" (SE, VII, 213-44) is forever "checking the enthusiasm of the living by the authority of the dead," and his doctrine "is still the command to follow the well-tried path of common sense."

More does not mean that tradition *creates* standards; to suppose that it did, he says, would be to fall into the pseudo-classical error of regarding age as a criterion of excellence. But tradition, which is the experience of society stored up in what may be called "the objective memory," may be evidence that certain philosophical principles, patterns of behavior, or works of art embody qualities that we should appreciate, and that we have every reason to use as criteria for judgments and choices. Tradition is not absolute or infallible and therefore, says More, men are prone to cry out that there is no tradition. He answers this charge by saying "no intelligent man supposes that tradition is a scale fixed once and forever in all its *nuances* of valuation; but it is a simple matter of history, nevertheless, that a long tradition of taste does exist, wavering and obscure on its outskirts, growing steadier and more immutable as we approach its centre" (*NSE,* I, 12). The humanist strives to absorb this tradition and his aim is always "to hold the past as a living force in the present" (*SE,* VII, 237). Notice that More says "a living force;" this is different from merging the present in a sterile dream of the past. He had a strong suspicion that the historical canons of Taine and Arnold would result chiefly in using "the past too much as a dead storehouse of precepts for schoolmastering the present" (243). In remembering the past, the race must exercise the principle of selection as well as retention. This involves "the weighing of cause and effect, by the constant and active assumption of the past in the present, by which the events of life are no longer regarded as isolated and fortuitous moments, but are merged into a unity of experience" (242). The imagination is a vital tool in this endeavor; indeed, says More, "its deepest and noblest function lies in its power of carrying what was once seen and known as a living portion and factor of the present, and there is no surer test of the quality of a man's mind than the degree in which he feels the long-remembered past as one of the vital and immediate laws of his being" (*SE,* IX, 19).[14] Institutions, in turn, are "symbols and efficacies of the imagination, which swallow up the individual man in involuntary actions and then render back to him his life enriched by manifold associations, and whose traditional forms are the hands of the past laid caressingly on the present" (*SE,* IX, 176). Elsewhere More recognized that the influence of some aspects of the institutional past were the opposite of caressing.

Thus, for More, tradition, as a major element of classicism, has value for the artist, the critic, and men in general, if it is reasonably winnowed and sifted. And to his way of thinking, tradition's greatest value lies in its relationship to faith.

In that power of the past to impose itself on the heart as a thing no longer subject to decay lies the natural bond between tradition, or memory in its transcendent sense, and faith which is the faculty of beholding the eternal beneath the transient. There is no surer sign of lessening faith than the tendency to turn, for a fulfilling of the present, from the possession of what has been to an uneasy hankering after a future which is no more than a glorification, as it is the descried product, of change itself. (*SE,* VII, 133-34)

This last statement leads naturally into the final consideration of this chapter: More's views on humanitarian reform involving innovation and a departure from the traditional.

Humanitarianism

Another persistent theme in More's body of writings is antihumanitarianism. Several of his books and essays concentrate on humanitarianism and references to it run all through his writings alongside pronouncements on literature, politics, and morality. His intense concern with the subject may be partially explained by the fact that he lived in the world of the social gospel in which humanitarian reforms of all sorts were in their enthusiastic beginnings. But a more pertinent explanation lies in the fact that he considered humanitarianism to be the application of romanticism to the fields of sociology and religion. It is one more manifestation of man's failure to recognize and understand the consequences of his inner dualism. According to More, humanitarianism is a misguided sympathy which causes the individual to seek his

57

humanity by submerging his identity in the mass of humanity rather than emerging through purpose and self-control to a genuine humane self-realization. It can provide no hope against the threat of ungoverned change posed by the flux or the many (as opposed to the inner check or the one) because it is but another aspect of the absorption in change: "an attempt of the individual to flow, so to speak in the direction of every emotional impact from the world. It contains no power of resistance or principle of restraint, but tends on the contrary to make man a more helpless prey of the ever-encroaching flood" (SE, VII, 267). Thus, from More's point of view, humanitarianism is the opposite of humanism.

It is important to understand the distinction More made between humanism and humanitarianism. Those who are harshest in their criticism of More's opposition to humanitarianism usually fail to take this distinction into consideration. They attack a particular statement by More on the subject of humanitarianism without looking closely at what he means by the term or how it fits into the total context of his humanism. He did not mean to be "a foe of charity and human kindliness and justice and institutions that mitigate the hardship of man's fate."[15] He quarreled with humanitarianism when it places "the element of enthusiasm above judgment, of emotion above reason, of spontaneity above discipline, and of unlimited expansion above centripetal control" (SE, XI, 82); in this form it "loses sight of judgment in its cry for justice. It ceases to judge in accordance with the virtue and efficiency of character, and seeks to relieve mankind by a false sympathy [or by arousing extravagant hopes which do not take into account mankind's proneness to rapacity]. Such pity merely degrades by obscuring the sense of personal responsibility. From it can grow only weakness and in the end certain decay" (JL, 297).[16] It was what he considered to be the negative side of humanitarianism, therefore, which vexed More's soul, and not its portion of human love and concern. "Sympathy, creating the desire for even-handed justice," he says, "is in itself an excellent motive of conduct, and the stronger it grows, the better the world shall be" (*SE,* IX, 211). But sympathy prefixed by the word "social" (as it commonly was in his day) takes on dangerous connotations. And social sympathy erected into a theory which leaves out of account the responsibility of the individual and seeks to throw the blame of evil on the laws and on society is debilitating to a true humanism. "The whole effect of calling sympathy justice and putting it in place of judgment is to relax the fiber of character and nourish the passions at the expense of reason and the will" (*SE, IX,* 211). This kind of social sympathy is based on the naturalistic level of sentiment whereas "the only potent social sympathy," according to More, "is that which will come of itself from a common reverence of something above man—without that you will have endless talk about sympathy and a growing dissociation of men, ending in war and anarchy."[17]

Again, therefore, we find dualism to be at the heart of things. For More it is the only basis for a sound ethical and sociological theory and practice. The brotherhood of man cannot be realized on the naturalistic level of feeling and sentiment. The notion that it can is the humanitarian fallacy to which More repeatedly objects. He believed that "just as surely as a man who bases his conduct on sentiment rather than on character and knowledge will weaken his resistance to prejudice and passion, just so surely a false humanitarianism will not only fail to bring about the brotherhood of mankind, but will make a people more sensitive to the gusts of international hatred" (*SE,* IX, 239). He pointed out as a historical fact that with the increasing vogue of fraternal sympathy, wars have actually increased in frequency and destructiveness.

Thoreau said, "There are a thousand hacking at the branches of evil to one who is striking at the root, and it may be that he who bestows the largest amount of time and money on the needy is doing the most by his mode of life to produce that misery which he strives in vain to relieve."[18] These were More's sentiments exactly, and his attitude toward humanitarianism was probably shaped to some extent by the doctrine of self-reliance espoused by Emerson and Thoreau, about whom he wrote essentially favorable essays. He, along with these two American transcendentalists, responded to the note of self-reliance in Carlyle's writing. Speaking through his persona, Philip Towers, More says he was always rather repelled by Carlyle's "noisy voluminousness," but "one message at least he had to proclaim to the world,—the ancient imperishable truth that man lives, not by surrender of himself to his kind, but by following the stern call of duty to his own soul. Do thy work and be at peace. Make thyself right and the world will take care of itself. There lies the everlasting verity we are rapidly forgetting" (JL, 296). In contrast to this ideal of self-reliance and responsibility is the humanitarian who, says More, in practice, if not in speech, denies all the spiritual insight of the race and seeks to lower the ideal of mankind to a "fool's commonwealth of comfort in this world" (JL, 83). More, of course, was suspicious of any movement or philosophy which purposely, or unintentionally, tends to lower the ideal of mankind and lose sight of the importance of individual responsibility. For example, he was critical of the vague and "expansive" humanitarianism of the New Deal, says J. D. Spaeth, "not because he was insensitive to the plight of the impoverished or blind to the struggle of the underprivileged, but because he was suspicious of a democracy of the Heart that repudiated the aristocracy of the Intellect and while remembering the forgotten man, forgot the memorable man."[19]

At one point in *The Jessica Letters,* Towers-More divides humanitarians into two classes—those who have no imagination, and those who have a perverted imagination:

The first are the sentimentalists; their brains are flaccid, lumpish like dough, and without grip on reality. They are haunted by the vague pathos of humanity, and, being unable to visualize human life as it is actually or ideally, they surrender themselves to indiscriminate pity, doing a little good thereby and a vast deal of harm. The second class includes the theoretical socialists and other regenerators of society whose imagination has been perverted by crude vapours and false visions. They are ignorant of the real springs of human action; they have wilfully turned their faces away from the truth as it exists, and their punishment is to dwell in a fantastic dream of their own creating which works a madness in the brain. They are today what the religious fanatics were in the Middle Ages, having merely substituted a paradise on this earth for the old paradise in the heavens. They are as cruel and intolerant as the inquisitors, though they mask themselves in the formulae of universal brotherhood. (*JL,* 270-71)[20]

What More really finds wrong with both kinds of humanitarians is that each holds to "the comfortable doctrine that men are by instinct all seeking the welfare of some one else" (*SE,* X, 63). In other words, they fail to recognize the evil in human nature. "Total depravity may have been Christian and mediaeval," he says, "but total goodness can find no authority in the classical writers of Greece and Rome, and is, in fact, the mark of modern humanitarianism as distinguished from Renaissance humanism" (*SE,* VI, 218). Part of the premise of More's dualism, we must remember, is the reality and persistence of evil; it is not something to be slurred over. One of the dangers of humanitarianism, according to More, lies in its tendency to externalize evil from the individual. This leads to a shirking of individual responsibility which in turn poses a serious threat of social disintegration. For this reason, says More, "we are bound, in any clear-sighted view of the larger exigencies of the relations of man with man, to fortify ourselves against such a pervasion of the institutions of government as would adapt them to the nature of man as he ought to be, instead of the nature of man as he actually is, and would relax the rigour of law, in pity for the degree of injustice inherent in earthly life" (*SE,* IX, 140).

A major part of his criticism of humanitarianism is that it stresses the material well-being of others—not to mention ourselves—to the exclusion of concern for their spiritual needs. In a word, it is a form of materialism. Humanitarian reformers denounce the evils of wealth, but in the end, More insists, their plans are simply the extension of the same ideal from the few to the many, "a substitution at best of the ideal of comfort for the ideal of material power." He acknowledges that socialist reformers look to the proper distribution of wealth as merely a first step which is to be followed by some greater spiritual reform.

But as a matter of fact the spiritual ideal is at present a nebulous hypothesis; the creating of universal comfort is the actual aim and ideal held before the eyes. It is well in itself, but the present day exaggerated insistence on it arises from the absence of other ideals. . . . It [humanitarianism] is the flower of materialism, if you will; but it is still materialism, a mere dilution of the more concentrated ideal of wealth. The upholders of it look upon it as a propaganda against the ideal of wealth; they are in reality fostering what they seek to overthrow.[21]

Thus, according to More, humanitarianism, by presenting materialism to the world in the disguise of a sham ideal, is really playing into the hands of those who find in the accumulation of riches the only aim of life, and is in fact the chief obstacle in the path of any genuine reform. "Because men to-day have no vision beyond material comfort and the science of material things," says Towers-More, "their aims and actions are divided between the sickly sympathies of Hull House and the sordid cruelties of Wall Street" (*JL,* 299).

More ends his essay on Plato (*SE,* VI, 321-55) with a description of the man who understands the dualistic vision of true Platonism; in other words, he is describing his concept of the true humanist. In addition to some other characteristics, he lists these which are relevant to the subject at hand and which I quote as a conclusion to this discussion: "He [the ideal humanist] will be no humanitarian, casting the responsibility of his sins upon some phantom perversion of society and looking for redemption to some equally phantom work of social sympathy. He will feel the compassion of the world; but he will be convinced that the fateful struggle for him, as for each man, lies within his own nature and is for the possession of himself."

Conclusion

It is this body of philosophical concepts and attitudes—these first principles—presented in the foregoing sections which constitutes the basic continuity of More's criticism. He is predominantly a judicial critic whose method consists in applying his own philosophy or his own view of life to the works of a writer, and in approving or condemning them by this standard, or by portioning out the proper balance of praise or blame. He had a passion for the realities of human nature, and his dualistic concept of human consciousness is the central point around which his interpretations of various human ideals and endeavors revolve. His views on politics, religion, and morality; his attitudes toward science, romanticism, classicism, humanism, humanitarianism, deism, rationalism—all have their ultimate source in that dualistic premise. Some critics have derided More's use of dualism as a norm for classification and judgment as a "cosmic rule" for measuring literature. More smiled at the term "cosmic rule," but he admittedly was seeking a firm standard for evaluating literature and interpreting the history of thought, a standard which recognizes man for what More believed him to be: an intelligent moral creature of free-willed responsibility distinct from other forms of life. More's critics may quarrel with his basic premises, but they cannot very well deny that his philosophy is consistent within itself.

The chapters that follow examine how More brought these first principles to bear on his study of the thought of English-speaking people during the last four centuries. It has been necessary in this chapter to isolate the principles from their context of supporting examples; this, in a way, is unfortunate, but it is the only way to summarize them and show their interrelationship. I hope the lack of context is remedied in the following chapters, in which specific examples of More's thinking and conclusions are presented as a synthesis of the historiography which results from More's application of his principles to particular ages and individuals.

CHAPTER THREE

The Renaissance

The Spirit of the Renaissance

More viewed the Renaissance as a seminal period for the English people. We might expect that since he was so fond of classical languages and literature, he would have felt much in tune with the spirit of the Renaissance and its revival of classical learning. But this was not the case. The revival of classical learning and the proliferation of knowledge were fortunate, of course, but More thought they were accompanied by a certain spirit of unrestrained expansiveness. This he distrusted, suspecting that there was something incongruous and even wrong about it. The medieval world may have been benighted in many ways, but it recognized the importance of some kind of check or restraint on man's expansive passional nature. The Renaissance, in many ways, seemed adverse to such restraint.

While visiting Florence in 1925 and viewing the artistic products of the Italian Renaissance, More was intrigued by the incongruity he sensed in some of the religious art. He said he could understand the Gothic and Oxford and Greece and Rome, but he was "balked before a people who built San Marco and developed the Dominican discipline, and then adorned the cells with the pictures of Fra Angelico. What were the thoughts of the monks before those sweet, fragile angels and madonnas?" He concluded that "the whole Renaissance is something of a mystery, a kind of glinting and ephemeral transition that must fill a thoughtful mind almost with alarm."[1] The alarming element for More was the idea of beauty without character behind it. During this visit, he said that he could not find the connecting link between the religion of the Middle Ages, or indeed of Christianity generally, and the peculiar beauty of the late fourteenth and fifteenth centuries. He went to see Bernard Berenson, at Berenson's request, and put the problem before him, but got no answer. "With all his subtlety," says More, "he had not felt the incongruity at all. I was uneasy in Italy for this reason."[2]

It was not just Italian Renaissance art, however, that made More uneasy, but the age itself—the age in England as well as in Italy. He says at one point in an essay on Beaumont and Fletcher that we have difficulty comprehending many of the persons who speak upon the Jacobean stage because we have the same difficulty with the more typical men and women who were playing the actual drama of the age. People like Henry VIII, Mary Stuart, James I and his whole court, with its Bacon, its Buckingham, its Lady Essex, have never been made comprehensible, says More, and will probably remain a "bewildering medley of passions" (SE, X, 23).

Barrows Dunham, who as a student had known More, says that because of his moral bias, his "redoubtable conscience," More "could not much like the Renaissance, a time when people began to enjoy things without a sense of sin."[3] There is a good deal of truth in this rather playful comment because as More outlines the general transition from the Middle Ages to the Renaissance, the central thread of that transition was a rejection of the supernatural scheme and a reliance on the concept of the basic rightness of human nature which can "expand indefinitely" (SE, VI, 218-19). More suggests that the appearance of new feelings regarding expansiveness in the Renaissance was, "after due reservations are made for the insoluble complexities of history," the result of "the failure of the Catholic Church to supply a central law of character in place of its decaying discipline" (SE, X, 25). During the Middle Ages the Church had, on the whole, tended to discredit reliance on man's own inner control and to substitute in its place outer conformity, and "when ecclesiastical authority was broken by knowledge and scepticism, the soul was left with all its riches of imagination and emotion, but with the principle of individual responsibility discredited and the fibre of self-government relaxed" (SE, X, 27).

More acknowledged that the age of the Renaissance was enormously complex, but he seems to have been preoccupied with the notion that a central characteristic of that age was a breakdown of control, both moral and aesthetic, which led to an undisciplined expansiveness in the field of art; the emphasis was on the eternal flux of things, the passions, rather than on the restraining influence of the higher will, the inner check. This preoccupation on More's part is clearly indicated in his treatment of the drama of the period, specifically Shakespeare and Beaumont and Fletcher.

The greatness of Shakespeare was by no means lost upon More, but he did have some reservations about that greatness. These reservations were connected with what More saw as a lack of a coherent, ordered vision of life underlying Shakespeare's works.

We may find the whole gamut of human emotion in Shakespeare, but we begin to darken counsel with words when we undertake to construct out of the medley of his plots any coherent vision of life such as exists in Milton or Homer or Dante or Aeschylus. Other dramatists have resorted for their tragic thesis to some definite philosophy, whether of their own eliciting or of the age. . . . Shakespeare proceeds otherwise: simple passion is his theme, and his tragic exaltation is obtained by magnifying passion until it assumes the enormity of a supernatural obsession and the bearer is shattered by the excess of his own emotion. (SE, II, 21-22)

Thus, according to More, as the stuff of life presented itself to Shakespeare, "broken and unarranged, so he reflects it in his magnifying mirror—a tale full of sound and fury, signifying nothing" (SE, II, 23). In other words, Shakespeare had a tendency, born of the Renaissance spirit, to portray human passion in all its chaotic diversity without processing and ordering it sufficiently. J. Duncan Spaeth, in his "Conversations with Paul Elmer More," quotes More as saying that

Shakespeare's German commentators have read into him their own metaphysical and ethical abstractions. Shakespeare had no profound or unified view (theory in the Platonic sense) of the immutable laws governing human life and conduct. . . . But his power to word every slightest shade of human thought or emotion and his superb command of the music of English speech explain and justify his unfading influence. . . . His color as well as his music is the touch that makes him kin to the whole world of Romantic Art. Form and motion of form are clearly defined, intelligible, classic. Color is illusive, impressionistic. The Greeks were preeminent in their imitation of form. The Renaissance artists excelled in color.[4]

We merely deceive ourselves, says More, if we go to Shakespeare for any philosophic systematizing of life or any reshaping of the material of experience into a world of supreme artistic or ethical significance. "What we do get from him is a sense of boundless life. Other men have suffered and enjoyed privately, but in him were brought together all the passions of mankind; he is the master of human experience"(SE, II, 26). But although Shakespeare is the "master of human experience" and is "cumulatively overwhelming," More still thought him to be "savage and barbarous in both language and action," and said that the tragedy of English literature is that " 'so great a genius so little disciplined' should have had such an influence upon it."[5]

To the reader of our decade this distrust of the Renaissance and these strictures regarding Shakespeare seem peculiar. And it should be noted that in this case the negative aspects of More's views are emphasized by our focusing on his detective work in identifying key attitudes of the age. But we must recognize also that he viewed this age from a perspective rarely shared today. He possessed a familiarity with the literature and thought preceding the Renaissance that few people nowadays possess. Shakespeare is our foremost classic.

We compare everything with him. More was in a different position: he compared Shakespeare with the writers of classic antiquity. And we must remember also his bias toward those writers, a love for the Greeks that lasted throughout his life. His last visitor before he died found him reading *The Odyssey* in Greek, with a French translation at his side.[6] He preferred Homer over Shakespeare because of an assumption that the function of literature is not only to portray human passion and the variety and depth of human experience but to produce moral order and perhaps even religious peace.

More thought the lack of discipline he saw in Shakespeare to be characteristic of the Elizabethan Age. In an essay on Elizabethan sonnets, in which he takes most of the Elizabethan sonneteers to task for rather mechanically imitating the ideas, forms, and style of earlier Italian sonnet writers, he points to the Elizabethans' failure to develop skill in controlling form.

England has always lacked art, and the lack was greater perhaps in those licensed days than at any subsequent period. Give the greater men of that age an exquisite fancy to dandle or some swift emotion to utter in lyric form where the first impulse of genius is sufficient; let them have some overriding passion or extravagant humour to unfold in a drama whose looseness of structure imposes no restraint, and they will bring forth effects incomparable for freshness and penetrating beauty. But put on them the habit of stricter art, bid them confine their expression to a mould where form and conscious style are essential, and immediately they sprawl and are helplessly confounded. (*SE,* II, 16)

The source of this failure in discipline and control, in More's view, was the general tendency toward expansiveness characteristic of the Renaissance. The large inspiration of these poets and playwrights came "before the critical sense of the land was out of its swaddling clothes" (*SE,* III, 71). Critical restraint did produce a certain aridity in the eighteenth century, he admits, but think what might have happened if the Elizabethans had had a Boileau to teach them restraint and control.

Shakespeare might have been taught "to prune his redundancies, to disentangle his language at times, to eliminate the relics of barbarism in his denouements." Likewise the lesser dramatists might have been compelled "to simplify their plots and render their characters conceivable moral agents." Spenser might have been constrained "to tell a story." In short, "We should have had our own classics, and not been forced to turn to Athens for our canons of taste. . . . It is not too much to say that the absence of such a controlling influence at the great expansive moment of England is a loss for which nothing can ever entirely compensate in our literature" (*SE,* III, 72).[7]

In his essay on Beaumont and Fletcher (*SE,* X, 1-40), More, by focusing on these two playwrights, makes clear his interpretation of the primary thought currents of the age. He credits these playwrights with developing tragicomedy into the well-marked genre of the romantic drama, the influence of which, direct and indirect, he says has been "incalculable." But there are faults inherent in this genre which bother More, who is always so concerned with the moral-aesthetic implications and ramifications of even the slightest elements in a piece of literature. "Ethically" these faults "are so involved in the obscure currents of the age that their real source and gravity are likely to be overlooked, and aesthetically we have become more or less blunted to them by long familiarity" (5). For More, these faults, both from the ethical and aesthetic standpoint, stem from a submission to the flux of human passions, a failure to recognize and incorporate in the plays that inner controlling and ordering force which is the higher element in human nature and which is chiefly responsible for making art comprehensible. For example, More finds the motivation and characterization of Evadne in *The Maid's Tragedy* "incoherent," a mere series of alternating passions. The whole woman is difficult, if not impossible, to grasp and comprehend—she is no woman at all, "unless mere random passionateness can be accounted such" (6-9). The same random passionateness and moral inconsistency, he says, is to be found in Fletcher's *Valentinian:* "If there is anything in reputable literature more revolting to the ethical sense (as the Greeks conceived *êthos*) than the conclusions of that play, I cannot now recall it" (9). After dwelling at some length on these two plays, he says he has done so because "they offer examples, though glaring ones indeed, of the sort of moral inconsistency that is characteristic not only of their plays, but of the whole drama of this later period." It may be possible for a reader to reconcile the inconsistencies of contradictory passions in these plays, "but the dramatist himself gives us no such ease, and one cannot read many of these plays without feeling that the fault lies deeper than any mere crudeness of literary procedure, that it touches, in fact, the very conscience of the writers and of the people who encouraged them" (11-12).

In order to explain the nature of this fault, More compares three ways the passion of love has been treated dramatically—in Euripides' *Hippolytus,* Shakespeare's *Romeo and Juliet,* and the Beaumont and Fletcher plays already mentioned. His main point regarding *Hippolytus* is that the tragedy lies not in the passion itself but in the character who succumbs to it. "More particularly Phaedra, the protagonist, does not appear as a mere personification of a passion, but is by many touches represented as a person existing apart from the passion that assails her. Deep in her bosom lies the *aidôs,* the sense of honour, modesty, reverence, the inner check whose office is to oppose a restraining force upon inroads of excessive or unlawful emotions, and which forms the elemental basis of that mysterious entity called character" (14). Note particularly "inner check" and "character" in this context; both are significant words in More's critical lexicon. In short, More believes Euripides' play to be "essentially moral" because the tragic pity and horror are based on the distinction between passion and "the inner citadel of character." Shakespeare, on the other hand, made love the central theme of *Romeo and Juliet* and "painted it with a luxuriant beauty and a deep understanding. . . . but he has done an ill thing in bringing this fair passion wantonly, or ignorantly, to a tragic end, and has shown thereby that to this extent he stands on a lower moral level than his Greek predecessor" (15-16). The quarrel of Capulet and Montague might well have served to shape the plot of the play, and by offering resistance to the course of true love might have accentuated its blissful end; "but to make this purely external circumstance the cause and source of tragedy is to pass from the realm of moral cause and effect into a region where emotion is accidental and bears no relation to character. A truer ethical sense would have brought the drama to a happy end, or would have drawn its tragic pathos from some conflict of passion within the same breast, or, more profoundly, as Euripides has done in the *Hippolytus,* from the opposition of character and victorious excessive passion" (16).

More thinks it is quite typical of early Elizabethan tragedy that, "if the action is examined, it will be found to omit the essentially moral element and to bring before us a personified passion rather than a character overcome by passion." In his greater tragedies, says More, Shakespeare "stands quite apart from his age, rising above it by the very strength in him of this moral sense which was so generally weak in his rivals." In *Macbeth,* for example, he belongs with Aeschylus and Euripides. "Though romantic in detail and in complexity of form, and though, it must be admitted, sometimes barbarous in the handling, the greater plays of Shakespeare are in their substance profoundly classic" (17).

The main characteristic of Beaumont and Fletcher's treatment of love is the "random passionateness" already mentioned. In contrast to this, More speaks of "that profounder pleasure of the imagination which springs from the intimate marriage of the emotions and the understanding;" this, he says, is lacking in the plays of Beaumont and Fletcher. Intellectual comprehension and moral judgment flow together, he adds, and the trouble with a play like *The Maid's Tragedy* is that "its incomprehensible tangle of the passions weakens to a certain extent the sympathetic echo of each within us, and in the end leaves an indistinct and blurred impression in memory" (20-21).

For it must be observed that moral judgement and literary criticism here go hand in hand. There is no doubt much to condemn in Beaumont and Fletcher from the direct standpoint of public decency; but, on the other hand, they are full also of moral sentiments magnificently expressed. The real moral indictment under which they lie is rather the more central charge that in ignoring that element of our being which stands apart from the passions as a governing power, they loosed the bond of character, removing from conduct the law of cause and effect and leaving human nature as a mere bundle of unrelated instincts. (20)

That is the moral judgment, says More, and the aesthetic criticism "is but the same thing in different words."

According to More, Puritanism, which warred against drama in the seventeenth century, wrought many evils with its extremes, but it did do a service by bringing into relief the conception of character, thus rendering literature again both moral and comprehensible. Perhaps the Anglican Church might have been able to effect this restoration without the excesses of Puritanism; nevertheless, "when we pass from Beaumont and Fletcher to Milton, and even to Bunyan, we are bound to acknowledge that something new and of inestimable value to art has come to the surface" (28). And from Milton's and Bunyan's day "almost to ours" (the break occurring with modern literature is treated in a later chapter) this feeling for character has been a major possession of English literature and has made it, "despite deficiencies of external form and frequent poverty of thought," a great literature; and this possession was "the undeniable gift of the Puritan conscience" (29).

The Religious Imagination

The growth of knowledge and skepticism which More identifies as the source of the expansiveness of the Renais-

73

sance dramatists became the basis for the dominating idea of the seventeenth century. The two aspects of that idea, according to More, were rationalism and science, the twofold notion that man's whole conception of the universe must be reconstituted along the lines laid down by abstract reason and physical science. This was the beginnings of modern naturalism which would have such far-reaching consequences in the centuries to follow. From the many workers who laid the foundations of science, More selects three as being variously typical: Bacon as the prophet of the dominating idea, Descartes as its theorizer, and Aldrovandus, the Italian naturalist, as its practical exemplar. "All three were conscious of the radical break with the past involved in the new idea" (SE, VI, 160). Bacon advocated beginning anew, starting from the immediate perceptions of the senses; Descartes, similarly, deliberately set about sweeping his brain free from the cobwebs of tradition; and Aldrovandus saw the necessity of rewriting the whole book of natural history from actual observation. Thus, the new science of this age brought into sharp relief the dualism of the natural and supernatural, secular and religious, of science and faith. It provided a baffling dilemma for the men of this age, and the key term More uses in analyzing how the major writers met the challenge of this dilemma is "the religious imagination."

More is not very precise in defining what he had in mind by the term religious imagination; indeed, from what he does say about it, it appears incapable of being defined very precisely. He suggests that it is similar to, if not the same as, the poetic imagination. At one point, he mentions that Coleridge defined it as the faculty "by which we unite the broken and dispersed images of the world into an harmonious poetic symbol" (SE, VI, 167). What More seems to be getting at is some kind of faculty residing in man's higher nature by which he is able to blend in a very meaningful way the past and tradition with the present and the individual. The recognition of such a faculty and the exercise of it were extremely important during the seventeenth century when the new science was breaking down ecclesiastical dogmas regarding man and his relationship to the universe and casting doubt on the very validity of the traditional concept that man possesses a higher, superrational nature capable of imposing a genuine order on the eternal flux of sense impressions. In nearly all of More's essays on the writers of this period the significance of the religious imagination is expressed or implied. A good example of this is his treatment of Sir Thomas Browne.

More begins his essay on Browne (*SE,* VI, 154-86) by pointing out that he, more than most writers, was influenced by that dominant idea of his age; but the significance of Browne is that while by intellect he was a force in the forward movement of the new science, by temperament he was a reactionary. This is well illustrated, says More, in Browne's treatment of witchcraft in the treatise on *Vulgar Errors,* being primarily an antiquarian amassing of citations and only secondarily a scientific exposing of error. There is an ambiguity in Browne's method here which goes beyond a mere uncertainty in correcting individual errors. It is symptomatic of a larger ambiguity of the age: "It was not merely the shackles of tradition in matters external which the new scholarship would throw away; it would invade the ancient sanctuaries of the heart also, and for the humility of religious faith substitute its own pride of investigation" (164). The consequences of that movement were apparent even to the men who were engaged in forwarding it. Some of them foresaw and dreaded what seemed to them a limiting of man's higher life by the rationalizing tendency of science. Thus, in the middle years of the seventeenth century, before the dominion of Newton and Locke, there were a number of writers who revolted against the tyranny of science, either by denying its dictates or accepting them and twisting them to different conclusions.

Pascal sought to avert the danger by a revival of Augustinian doctrine tempered with the intuitions of the imagination. Henry More undertook to involve the ancient sombre faith together with the coming optimistic deism within a cloud of Neo-Platonic mysticism. Bunyan belonged to the extreme wing of Protestantism which disguised its participation in the new philosophy and its lessening spirituality by a rigid discipline of intellectual and moral dogmatism. (165)

Browne, in his *Religio Medici,* undertook to establish himself in a safe compromise, which amounted to putting religion and science into separate compartments of his noetic life. More is basically sympathetic to Browne's method and says, "In effect his work takes its place, a splendid place, among the innumerable protests of the imagination against the imperious usurpations of science" (166).

More is sympathetic to Browne's method because it involves a recognition of dualism, the belief in a force outside the material realm. "If the spirit were to maintain its liberty against the encroachments of a fatalism which would reduce the circle of a man's life to a mere wheel spinning for an hour in the vast unconscious mechanism of the world, it must be by the assertion of another principle distinct from and unmoved by the levers of physical energy" (166). More concedes that Bacon, and more definitely Descartes, has granted this immaterial law, but they left it in "the sphere of the lofty inane, with no hold upon the heart and actions of men, with no answer to the cry of the bewildered conscience, with no root in human experience—an empty fragment of the reason or a sop to quiet the barkings of the Church" (167). In contrast to this empty rationalism, Sir Thomas Browne exercises the religious imagination. In their investigation of the laws of nature, the new men of science and reason in Sir Thomas Browne's day "did not sufficiently recognise that these solid-seeming phenomena are but the shadow, too often distorted and misleading, of the greater reality which resides within the observer himself, and obeys its own law. In their haste they lost the power of subjecting the less [*sic*] to the greater reality, of associating the outer with the inner, and thus of finding through the many that return to the one"

(167). Sir Thomas Browne, on the other hand, through the religious imagination was able to recognize the inner reality and, amid the changing forms of the Many, keep his eye fixed on the One.

Always there is present the sense of something other and different lurking beneath natural law and peering out at the observer with strange enticements; and this to him was the great reality. He was one of the purest examples of the religious imagination severed from religious dogma or philosophy; dualism with him takes the form of an omnipresent and undefined mystery involving, and sometimes dissolving, the fabric of the world. (172)

There is a danger, More admits, that this kind of romantic wonder which sets itself above the systematic intellect might degenerate into all kinds of "lawless and sickly vagaries," as we have in fact seen it do, he says, in later times. Indeed, already in Browne's works we can see a lack of solid content, an occasional lapse into pure emotionalism; yet they are saved in the end by the writer's "sturdy regularity of life and by the great tradition which hung upon the age" (173). In short, More sees in the work of Sir Thomas Browne "no harsh opposition of spirit and matter, but an attempt to interpret and estimate the law of nature by the law of man's inner life" (173). This is the kind of humanism he could admire.

More's essay on George Herbert (*SE,* IV, 66-98) is another which indicates rather clearly More's attitude toward the age in general and toward the religious imagination in particular. The starting point for this essay, as for so many of More's essays, is the review of a current edition of a writer's works, in this case, *The English Works of George Herbert* edited by George Herbert Palmer (Boston, 1905). In his evaluation of this edition, More suggests that Professor Palmer has failed to exercise adequately the "historic sense," that faculty of vision which pierces through the transient modes of an age and discovers what that age has attained of essential and permanent truth. This failure has caused a lack of sympathy with the period on Professor Palmer's part, causing him to be apologetic for Herbert's religious emotion, as though it were "something outworn and outgrown, something comprehensible to the man of to-day only by deliberately narrowing his larger spiritual interests to a lesser sphere" (69). It becomes clear in the remainder of the essay that More is not only warmly sympathetic with the spiritual searching of the age and with Herbert's religious emotion, but that he considers the religious sense which men like Herbert possessed to be one of the truly great characteristics of the seventeenth century.

In discussing the development of Herbert as a poet, More mentions the influence of John Donne, "One of the few real turning-points in our literature" (74).[8] The style and manner of Herbert's poems are marked repeatedly by Donne's influence, says More, but what is more significant, that influence goes deeper than just style and manner. "Donne's life had suffered a division such as was regular enough in those days, however suspicious it may appear to us." He was wild in his youth and then turned to religion. "It was a course quite familiar to his contemporaries, corresponding to the sharp cleavage in their minds between secular and sacred things" (76). More suggests that this aspect of Donne's life served as a lesson for Herbert: "For him there should be no such division as that which made two different poets of Donne; he would clothe his verse in the 'Venus livery' of the early Donne and the other Elizabethans, but it should be the Venus Urania; he would be the love-poet of religion" (78). This essay was written before More used the term religious imagination, but it is apparent from the way he describes Herbert's blending of sacred and profane ideas that he saw Herbert exercising the same faculty which enabled Sir Thomas Browne to meet another aspect of that central cleavage in human thought and experience which dominated the age.

In explaining the unifying power of the religious imagination in Herbert's career, More is very careful not to exaggerate the harmony of that career. He demonstrates that Herbert was fully aware of life's problems and experienced his full share of depression and bewilderment. For More, such an awareness is an admirable quality. Part of the true dualistic vision of human experience is the recognition of the reality of evil, that the life of man necessarily involves a certain amount of unhappiness and struggle. More was consistently unsympathetic to any literature or philosophy which attempted to gloss over the real problems and conflicts involved in human existence. For instance, his major criticism of Fanny Burney is that "her satire skates over the surface of life with unfaltering dexterity." She did not react to "the troublesome problems of existence. She seems to have passed through the world without experience and without questioning"(*SE*, IV, 60). People of this sort More often refers to as "sentimentalists," but Herbert "was no mere sentimentalist, but a man of subtle understanding" (82-83).

Toward the end of the essay, More quotes this statement by Professor Palmer regarding George Herbert: "For the most part he is concerned with the small needs of his own soul." More criticizes this comment as being "like a taunt thrown ungraciously at the ideas of a great and serious age" (92). And although he is writing here at a period relatively early in his career, before he had gravitated to his frankly Christian position, he points out how important concerns of the individual soul are and says "it is one of the glories of Herbert's age that it introduced into poetry that quick and tremulous sense of the individual soul. Religion came to those men with the shock of a sudden and strange reality, and we who read the report of their experience are ourselves stirred, willingly or rebelliously, to unused emotions. Do you know, in fact, what most of all is lacking in the devotional poetry of recent times? It is just this direct personal appeal" (92-93). Religion, he goes on to say, has changed since that time "from the soul's intimate discovery of beatitude to the dull convention of sermons" (94). "He speaks of God like a man that really believeth in God," said Baxter of Herbert, and this, suggests More, is no small matter. He ends his essay by saying of Herbert's work, "all of us may profit from its pages if we can learn from them to wind ourselves out of the vicious fallacy of the present, and to make our own some part of Herbert's intimacy with divine things" (98).

What More believed to be "the vicious fallacy of the present" is the subject of chapter 7, but what he meant by "intimacy with divine things" can be further clarified by considering his treatment of some other writers of the seventeenth century.

More acknowledges his admiration for the poetry of Milton numerous times in his writing, but unfortunately he never wrote an extended essay on Milton and his work as a whole. There is a brief essay on the theme of *Paradise Lost, (SE, IV)* and one not much longer on "How to Read *Lycidas*" (*NSE,* III). It is possible, however, to learn a good deal about More's general attitude toward Milton and how this great Puritan fitted into his age even from these two short essays; for even when More is treating a single work by a writer, he tends to make some comment on the character of the man as a whole and how his thought is related to the main spiritual-intellectual currents of the age. From one standpoint, Milton posed a special problem for More: he admired the poetry but not the man—"how can one so combine detestation and love? how can one make so complete a separation between Milton the destroyer of Church and State, and Milton the artist?" (*NSE,* III, 192). One of the ways by which More makes this separation is through a distinction between the way the religious imagination operates in Milton's poetry and the way it operates in his prose. Milton, he asserts, was a "supreme artist" in poetry, but not in prose. "What I would insist on is that the very style of his prose has a close relation to the fact that when he passes from imagination to theory his voice is not that of his people but of an exasperated individual" (189). What More means by this is that when Milton is creating poetry, he is expressing a kind of universalized experience; but when he is writing a plea for freedom of divorce, he is just giving vent to his own private passions. More says that if he hesitates to accept Milton's prose style as the norm of good English, it is not on the grounds of Eliot's "dissociation of sensibility;" "Rather I should maintain that Milton's failure, so far as he failed, was owing to something essentially un-English, or only partially English, to something belonging to his individual temperament, which passed into his philosophy of life and diverted a noble love of liberty into a morbid and isolating passion" (186-87). By inference, we may assume that, in More's view, Milton exercised the faculty of religious imagination—that power to see the One in the Many, to blend the individual with the universal—in his poetry but not in his prose. In his prose, the unique English element of character is lacking. After discussing this weakness in Milton's prose, More makes this comment, fitting Milton into his age:

The seventeenth century, with all its greatness, is an age of frustration, filled with fine promises that, except in the field of science, came to no fruition, replete with noble utterance that somehow failed to convince. In the Church, in the State, in society, the one thing needed and not found was a commanding genius that should have been indeed the voice of England. It is the tragedy of the time that he [Milton] who had the genius so to speak should have wasted his energies in querulous complaints against what was, and in the future was to show itself, the true spirit of the land. In a word that spirit may be described precisely as liberty, not license, as centrality, not dissent. (189-90)

Perhaps it is wrong to dwell so long on what More saw as Milton's failings, because despite these, More says, "Milton came nearer than any other man of England, nearer than Shakespeare, to combining the law of limitation with the law of enthusiasm,—which is only the great law of the imagination."[9] And although the bitterness of Milton's disappointed soul breaks into his prose at times and debars him, in his total effect, from being accepted as the voice of England, he is still left with "the high credit of having raised in *Paradise Lost,* to the honour of his native land, the one monumentally successful product of that humanistic culture of the Renaissance in which originality of genius and faithfulness to the classical tradition are combined in perfect union" (*NSE,* III, 201).

The most explicit treatment of More's concept of the religious imagination is to be found in his essay on Bunyan (*SE,* VI, 187-213). In order to understand how More fitted Bunyan into the spiritual-intellectual currents of this period, it is helpful to contrast his treatment of this late-seventeenth-century Puritan with his treatment of Beaumont and Fletcher, dramatists of the early years of the century. There are two points of contrast that are particularly instructive here. First, according to More, Beaumont and Fletcher failed to distinguish clearly between character and passion—this is what marks them as romantic rather than classical. In contrast to this, Bunyan's portrayal of the human soul as a city besieged by devils "springs from the same perception of the dualism of character and passion as that which guided Euripides in his treatment of Phaedra and Aphrodite" (*SE,* X, 30). But despite this, Bunyan has "exasperating limitations," and this leads to the second point of contrast. Whereas Beaumont and Fletcher ignored the higher element in our being which is apart from and acts as a governing power over the passions, thus removing the law of cause and effect from moral conduct, Bunyan and his party went to the other extreme of working out a sterile conception of legalism in the sphere of moral conduct and religious belief.

This contrast serves to point up More's ambivalent attitude toward the Puritans in general. On the one hand, he believed it was the Puritan conscience which had been the wellspring of that note of character which, to him, was the great distinguishing mark of English literature. But on the other hand, he was repelled by the Puritans' insensitivity to the power of imagination and their tendency to break with tradition. The two sides of this attitude are clearly presented in this essay on

Bunyan. For example, after pointing out the intensity of Bunyan's consciousness of sin and concern for pleasing God, More suggests that in his writing there is "a denial of the religious imagination . . . which lies against almost all the writing of his school, and which has marked it surely for death" (*SE,* VI, 189). "It is a rule from which there is barely, if at all, escape, that those who forget the past are in their turn forgotten. Now the lack of imagination among the Puritans showed itself in contempt of the arts and in many other manifest ways, but in none more clearly than in their violent break with the continuity of tradition" (190).

As a way of illustrating what he means by the connection of imagination and tradition and displaying the weakness at the heart of Puritanism, More contrasts Bunyan with Pascal, asserting that Bunyan "is a product of transition" and will have less meaning for men as time goes on, whereas Pascal is likely to be remembered increasingly "as one of the pure voices of faith."

What is the cause of this distinction? Is it not, again, due just to the presence or absence of what may be called the religious imagination? For Pascal the community of generation with generation by tradition makes easy the conception of mankind as spiritually one instead of an innumerable company of repellent personalities; for him, too, the sacramentarian offices of the Church introduce a certain irrational and saving element into dogma. The door is left open for the healing ministry of ignorance (the knowing that we cannot know) and for the superstitious eye of love. In this twilight of humility moves the imagination, leading the soul upward on ways beyond the calculation of the reason. Morality is not weakened, but becomes a discipline and not an end; it is taught to be the handmaid instead of the mistress of the spirit. (203)

In his characteristic manner, More, after discovering Bunyan's lack of religious imagination, becomes vitally interested in the implications of this failing—what are its consequences? The consequences, according to More, are that Bunyan (and the Puritanism he represents) is the forerunner of "the rational mood which is fundamentally a denial of religion" (204).

In his linking of Bunyan with rationalism, More displays a typical characteristic of his interpretation of intellectual history: the perception of a fundamental similarity lying below the surface of two apparently contradictory minds or philosophical schools. We might ordinarily place Bunyan and Puritanism in sharp contrast with the line of Bacon, Locke, and Newton, but More says we shall miss the significance of Bunyan if we forget that he belongs to that line, "and that his exasperation of the moral sense is the working out of their conception of legalism in the religious sphere as contrasted with Hooker's earlier and Blake's later vision of law through the imagination" (193). Speaking of Bunyan and his party, More says, "The extreme individualism of their creed must not be dissociated from their incapacity for that mystical self-annihilation in the divine, and the multiplied sects of seventeenth-century England were a direct consequence of the deadening of spirituality in legalism" (192). "It was inevitable, therefore, that when their enthusiasm and their conviction of sin died away they should be found to have prepared England for the natural religion of the eighteenth century" (193). Here, then, is one of the links More sees between the seventeenth and eighteenth centuries, between Puritanism and Deism. As paradoxical as it may seem, seventeenth-century Puritanism, with its notion of total depravity and a burning hell for sinners, is a relative of eighteenth-century rationalism, with its notion of the inherent goodness of man and its disregard or denial of consequences beyond the grave—they both belong to the same family of rationalism. "The mind of man swings like a hanging pendulum, and Rousseau's faith in the essential goodness of human nature, with its implied denial of infinite consequences altogether, was the inevitable and equally exaggerated reaction [to Puritanism]. The Puritan and the Rousseauist stand at the two opposite poles of rational sin" (196-97).

More's treatment of Henry Vaughan placed in juxtaposition to this interpretation of Bunyan and Puritanism should serve as a revealing final example of More's attitude toward the religious currents of this age. More confesses that Vaughan is for him one of those poets who, "by virtue of some affinity of spirit with our own, appeal to us with an intimacy that takes our judgement captive; we go to them in secret, so to speak, and love them beyond the warrant of our critical discernment" (NSE, I, 143). Why does More admire Vaughan? For one thing, Vaughan, in contrast to Bunyan, displays "the touch of imagination from which the Puritan conscience revolted, and, so revolting, shut itself off from the future communion of the wise" (SE, VI, 202). The "victorious iconoclasm" of the Puritans was ruthlessly sweeping away "all the comfortable traditions which stayed the inherent restlessness of man's soul, all the symbols which had trained the imagination to take its due share in the act of worship" (NSE, I, 154-55). Vaughan clung to those traditions and symbols. Probably most appealing to More is Vaughan's dualistic vision of life. There is an obvious dualism in Bunyan's work, but that dualism, according to More, consists of the conception of life as a debate between two moral abstractions: man the personification of absolute evil and God the personification of absolute righteousness. Such a conception oversimplifies things and aids little in the struggle of individual experience. Vaughan's dualistic vision, on the other hand, consists of a recognition "of the sorrow and discontent that are caused by no accidental evils of an age but are inherent in the very conditions of mortal existence" (155). But this recognition does not make him essentially gloomy and depressing because "the joy in him still overrides the gloom, the joy that came to him, as it can only come to a man then or at any time, from lifting his eyes out of these shades and flickering lights to the radiance of another sun, and to the possession of a peace that is not of earth"(156). This is the note which Vaughan and his contemporaries sound in their moments of inspiration and which makes the religious poetry of the period, "despite its mass of fumbling attempts, something unique in English literature." Faint echoes of this note can be detected in Whittier and Newman and Francis Thompson and other nineteenth-century poets; "but the glorious courage and assurance, the pure joy, the full flight against the sun, you will meet nowhere in England since the [Puritan] Revolution, with the new politics, brought in the grey reign of naturalism" (156).

The Ethos of the Restoration

In light of More's admiration for the religious imagination, it is not surprising that he found the ethos of the Restoration uncongenial He did not write very much on the literature of the Restoration but in his essay on Aphra Behn (*SE*, X, 69-97), his basic attitude toward the period is rather clearly delineated.

He thought the drama of the period was "more hidebound by convention" than any other outstanding literary movement, and possessed a vicious character (75-76). He could not accept these playwrights as Charles Lamb professed to accept them, claiming that it is pleasant now and then "to take an airing beyond the diocese of the strict conscience." More says such an airing might be pleasant "if it weren't for the odour!" (78) Likewise, More cannot accept Montague Summers's plea that the writers of this period have been done an injustice by being confounded with the characters they created. He admits that this error is common enough and easy enough, "but however true it may be that a good author may create bad characters, it is also true that we ought to hold him to account for the moral atmosphere, so to speak, in which he envelopes his characters. It is a nasty thing to take complacence in creating a nasty world, and there's an end on't" (78). "Those who, like Charles Lamb, find a note of exhilaration in the very perfection of this immorality, are playing paradoxically with their own innocence"(82). More also will not be convinced that the Restoration playwrights were portraying vice in order to forward the cause of virtue: "No doubt these purveyors of amusement felt the twinges of conscience at times, and tried to flatter themselves by posing as the moral censors of the age; but I strongly suspect that their prior sentiments were in part uttered in pure self-defence, with a good tinge of hypocrisy"(81).

In his treatment of Restoration wit, More's penchant for tracing causes and effects in the broad stream of human thought is again revealed. From an ethical standpoint, he sees Restoration wit as belonging to a brief period of transition and sets about distinguishing it from what preceded and followed. The tone of Restoration wit resembles the tone of comedy before the Civil War, he says, but there are significant differences which overshadow this resemblance. "In the earlier writers the darkness of evil is made hateful by an implied or explicit contrast with the light of a traditional ideal of virtue. The ideal may not be very certain, it may be almost lost, so that ethical judgement fades away into the license of rollicking fun; but it is not denied as a convention, and it can be found lurking somewhere in the background, if not in full sight" (85). The gloomy failure of the Commonwealth tended to discredit that ideal and caused the Restoration wits to reject it. Therefore, there is no light of a traditional ideal in their writing playing off against the darkness of evil and making it hateful.

More believed that in general the ethos of the Restoration wits was not so much a license of high spirits as a complacent cynicism. This explains the link he sees between the Restoration and the period which followed, because "out of this cynicism the drama of sensibility, preluding the rise of a whole new literature, came as a natural reaction, but it introduced an error as vicious in its consequences as that against which it revolted" (87). The error that More has in mind here is the Rousseauian concept of the noble savage, or in other words, the doctrine of the natural goodness of man.

It was the creed of the wits [of the Restoration] that mankind as they saw it in civilized society was thoroughly vicious; yet all the while another creed, the deistic belief in the universal goodness of Nature herself, was growing stronger and gathering converts. Out of this contrast of the literary and the deistic creeds, both rooted in the discredit of virtue as a conscious self-discipline, what could be more inevitable than just such a fancy of the purity and excellence of man in his natural state, untouched by the vitiating hand of civilization? Thus the idea of the noble savage arose as a sort of halfway stage between the mockery of the wits and the sentimentalism, or sensibility, which was finally to usurp dominion over literature. (94-95)

Conclusion

More's writing on the Renaissance is confined to only a few essays; and in these, he is primarily interested in defining what he sees as the peculiar underlying spirit of that era—the spirit of expansiveness and incipient naturalism. He is less interested in pointing out what was precious and salutary about the Renaissance than he is in pointing out certain less obvious tendencies which marked an unfortunate break with the past and which produced gradually unfolding consequences during the following centuries—consequences which have generally constituted loss rather than gain for humanity. Specifically, he is concerned with showing that the Renaissance de-emphasized the notion of the self-disciplined individual soul responsible to a power transcending nature, while at the same time emphasizing the belief in man's unlimited power, within nature and unaided by supernatural checks or guidance, for expanding knowledge and improving human welfare.

The seventeenth century was of special interest to More because he viewed it as the most dramatic moment in the conflict of our dual nature. It was during this age that the revolt from classical dualism began. And this revolt precipitated the battle between humanism and naturalism which, in More's opinion, has determined the course of intellectual history for the last four centuries. At the beginning of the seventeenth century, and always in the background throughout the age, was the dualistic vision, the orthodox view of man as a being conscious of reason and impulse in the natural order and supernatural insight above them: on the one side the great flux of nature, embracing in its endless activity man's passionate nature and the phenomenal world, and on the other the restraining power above and beyond nature. During the course of this century there were a number of forces acting in opposition to this dualism. For one thing, the age so wasted itself in religious wars that all religion fell into disrepute and an age of naturalism followed. For another thing, the new science, reflected in men like Bacon (More always singles out Bacon for special opprobrium as the father of naturalism), was disproving certain ecclesiastical dogmas and indirectly casting doubts on others, placing such emphasis on empirical methods as to discredit knowledge acquired through revelation or religious intuition. Also, iconoclastic Puritanism broke with tradition and caused in England a division between the imagination and practical sense, placing them in irreconcilable camps, the practical-sense party becoming the people of dullness, and the imagination party being "divested of all the magnificence of morality" (SE, X, 141). All of these forces had particular consequences for the age which followed, and these consequences are treated in the next chapter. More's own statement best sums up the period: "The irremediable fault, default one might say, of the age was that it never attained to a clear and untrammelled definition of the superrational insight upon which its faith was based" (SE, VIII, 228).

CHAPTER FOUR

The Eighteenth Century

The Battle of the Wits

It was a "terrible mischance," More believed, "which in the days of the Stuarts divided the imagination and practical sense of England into irreconcilable camps, and separated the loyalty to symbols of authority so far from the actualities of force" (*SE,* X, 135). And this separation, he believed, maintained its character into the next century. Therefore, he viewed the battle of the wits during the early eighteenth century as "no causeless or merely bookish event," but as a manifestation of the great political war of the land, and that political war, in turn, was a manifestation of the conflict between very fundamental philosophies regarding human nature and experience.

According to More, the battle of the wits—the literary warfare engaged in by such people as Swift, Pope, Addison, Gay, Prior, Arbuthnot, Mary Wortley Montagu—"grew inevitably out of the ruinous divisions, as it echoed the drums and tramplings, of the previous century; and if ink now flowed instead of blood, the contest was hardly the less venomous for that, or the consequences less serious" (135). He suggests that on the one hand, "Bolingbroke's vision of the Patriot King was a reassumption of the faith of the Cavaliers, and as it was a product of the imagination divorced of practical sense, we see its working out in the follies of George III and the loss of an empire." And on the other hand, "Walpole's policy was essentially a continuation of the empire of Cromwell, and as it failed to make place for the imagination in its practice, we see the result in the gradual lowering of England's ideal life" (135). This searching for antecedents is typical of More. He always sees an individual literary movement within the continuity of the history of ideas.

Wit is an important concept in More's interpretation of the eighteenth century. By wit he had chiefly in mind the main characteristics of the literati who gathered about the court of Queen Anne and went into opposition on the coming of George I. But as we might expect, he did not think these wits were an entirely new type. He traces their progenitors back to the men who came up to London in the days of Queen Elizabeth, attracted there by the playhouses, "and bringing with them plentiful baggage of genius with a small portion of learning" (*SE,* X, 240-41). The Jacobean drama found material in their descendants, "the merry rogues who used their 'understanding, travel, reading, wit,' as money in the purse for buying the joys of the town." During the Restoration the tradition split in two: those who catered to the court ("These men refined the licence of Fletcher into a philosophy of licentiousness"), and those who in Swift's words wallowed in the "thick sediment of slime and mud." Reading these latter, says More, one gets the notion "that wit is a convention in which scandal, drunkenness, and lechery take the place of faith, hope and charity—but the greatest of these is scandal" (242). He identifies Tom Brown as the leading spokesman for this group. As early eighteenth-century literature tended more and more to forms of cynicism and satire, wit became almost synonymous with malice. But there was something else needed for the "devil's brew" to give this malice "the true ring of the wit of Twickenham."

That final ingredient was politics. Once that was added, England had what More refers to as "the select band who were fighting the battle against dullness from the headquarters of Pope and Mary Wortley Montagu at Twickenham, who by their genius raised wit to be one of the triumphs of our literature, as, at its worst, it is one of the disgraces" (248-49). He likens the dizzy battle of wits during the Queen Anne period to a medieval tournament. The combatants are divided into two main parties, but in such a way that each knight is rather free to follow his own personal feud. The political division of Whig and Tory constituted the general battle lines, but there were times when politics were lost sight of in the antagonism between genius and dullness or even virtue and vice.

More's attitudes toward the wits are rather predictable, given the basic principles of his critical philosophy. First, in light of the "law of measure," it is not surprising that he was repelled by wit in its extreme forms, where it becomes little more than licentiousness or scandal mongering. Also, because of his ethical bias, it was natural that he should be troubled by the fact that in the warfare of wit the honors went too often to the ablest and not to the most honorable.

The best aspects of the literary style of the wits, in fact of the eighteenth century generally, he found very appealing. His own literary standards were in many ways close to those of this age. He extolled temperance, restraint, decorum, and common sense; he formed his taste by a constant reference to tradition. It is understandable, therefore, that he should have loved the literature of that age, the style of which he thought "distinguished for precision, unfaltering directness, and a kind of splendid clearness" (SE, VI, 215). He believed that style had changed enough since those times that readers of his day might have difficulty in appreciating the eighteenth-century voice. "The fact is that not many readers to-day can approach the verse of the eighteenth century in a mood to enjoy or even understand it. We have grown so accustomed to over-emphasis in style and wasteful effusion in sentiment that the clarity and self-restraint of that age repel us as ungenuine; we are warned by a certain *frigus* at the heart to seek our comfort elsewhere" (SE, III, 2).

According to More, "malice is an essential ingredient of what we mean by 'wit' " (*SE,* X, ix). What he apparently means by malice in this context is the intent to vex somebody. He seems to think that, in this sense, malice is not without redeeming aspects. In fact, he says that "nothing would be a more wholesome tonic for our modern surfeit of sentimentalism than a little of the saving grace of malice" as it might be served up by a Swift or Pope. "Malice is an excellent medicine for self-complaisance in the artist; it is a good purgation also for cant and humbug in high places" (ix-x). Thus, he admired the early-eighteenth-century satirists, from one standpoint, because they were engaged in putting down mediocrity, complacency, and humbug. His sympathies, of course, were with the Tories, and he felt that the fall of the Tories in 1714 produced serious consequences for English literature. He says he knows of "no more distressing fact" in English history than the situation which, "at the critical moment of 1714, set almost all the notable men of letters on the losing side—all of them, I should say, with the exception of Addison and Steele, for Defoe at least served Harley and fell with him" (*SE,* X, 136). He seems to identify these writers of the losing side with genius as opposed to dullness, with imagination as opposed to a practical sense devoid of imagination, with the aristocratic principal as opposed to the democratizing principle in art. For example, he sees in Pope's *Dunciad,* beneath the motives of personal satire, "the passionate warfare of the losing party of wit against the triumphant party of practical common-sense" (137).

Another characteristic of wit he found congenial was the recognition of dualism implied in the type of satire being written. Deism, with its sympathy for mankind, its doctrine of the innate benevolence of man, and its rejection of the old theological notion of absolute evil, went against the spirit of wit and satire, which are based on a concept of man being all too easily susceptible to meanness, folly, dullness, and venality. More does not subscribe to the notion of man's total depravity, but he says "it may as well be recognized that, without some lingering suspicion of the eternal deceitfulness of the heart and some malicious glee in the unveiling of the deceit, no man shall feel at home in the old battle of the wits" (*SE*, X, 140). This says a good deal about More himself who seemed to be perfectly at home in that battle.

The next section explains More's attitude toward deism; but it is useful here to point out that he saw deistic optimism running parallel with the cynical movement and in the end supplanting it. The coexistence of these two tendencies— "the one drawing on the essential selfishness and baseness of human nature, the other treating evil as a mere accident in the make-up of the world and leading on to the school of sympathetic sentimentalists" (*SE*, X, 111)—was in itself a curious anomaly, he says, but it became something more than an anomaly when it showed itself in a single writer. And in his view this was the case with Pope, who in the same years could write both the *Dunciad* and the *Essay on Man*. From More's point of view, this inconsistency is "flagrant and inexcusable." "It troubles me in my admiration of Pope—for I am bound to admire his genius, and somehow I cannot help loving the man too—this troubles me, I say, more than all the atrocious intrigues of his vanity" (112).

He finds no such inconsistency in Swift and explains the difference between these two great wits in terms of their different approaches to satire. Pope vented his spleen at individual men rather than at human nature itself, and this preoccupation with individuals "left the door open, in a way, for adopting Bolingbroke's deistic attitude of benevolence when it came to dealing with human nature in general" (113). Swift, on the other hand, directs his satire devastatingly toward human nature itself, not individuals. He loved individuals, but he dwelt bitterly on the shortcomings of mankind in general. And again, it was the reverse suffered by the Tories in 1714 which constituted the focal point for the divergence of these two satirists. "So the event [the political reverse] that carried Pope into the shallows of deistic evasion lifted Swift's cynicism to a perfect philosophy of hatred, and made of him the true logician and master spirit of wit" (119).

Stuart P. Sherman, who, after being aligned for a time with the New Humanism, forsook it and criticized it, wrote that More

values the writers of the Restoration chiefly for their wickedness. It is such good ammunition to use on the humanitarian enthusiasts and the whitewashers of human nature. He can forgive Pope his virulent personal satire, but not his deistic optimism. He praises Swift above Pope for his consistent adherence to the representation of his fellows as "the most pernicious race of little odious vermin ever suffered to crawl upon the face of the earth." He requires, or thinks he requires, the Yahoos as hideous caryatides to uphold the towering superstructure of his aristocratic political and social philosophy.[1]

This statement is an exaggeration, but its essential insight is probably true.

In the final analysis, the real significance of the battle of wits for More's interpretation of history lies in the fact that although that warfare was a temporary thing, in one sense it is still going on, and will not end until the differences of human nature are reconciled. "Men in this living age, always a few, are still fighting for the rights of the mind against a dull and delusive materialism, for the freedom of the imagination against a prosaic tyranny, for a pure and patient ambition against a fatuous self-complacency" (SE, X, 148). To these the triumphant satire of the eighteenth-century wits is a perpetual encouragement.

The notion of the religious imagination, which More found so important in the seventeenth century, is absent among the wits because men of their age had reacted against the religious turmoil of the preceding century, and under the influence of science and rationalism, were tending toward the rationalistic religion of deism. But More seems to recognize something akin to the religious imagination in the satire of the Tory wits. Their order and control and acceptance of tradition resembles the ordering and organizing powers of the religious imagination. Therefore, in More's terms, the battle of the wits is a modified version—a transitional step—of the larger warfare between human nature striving to fulfill its higher potential through the imagination and human nature which denies that higher potential or nullifies it by permitting the practical sense to overpower the imagination.

A Compliant Brotherhood

Like most students of intellectual history, More considered rationalism to be the dominant philosophy of the eighteenth century. This main current of the times, he said, "on its surface carried religion and science and literature in a compliant brotherhood" (*SE,* VIII, 230). In the area of religion it "denied, or at least minimized, all that is mysterious and escapes the net of logic, and in science regarded the world as a vast machine which can be perfectly expressed in a mathematical equation. Literature followed the lead and became rational and pseudo-classic" (229). His portrait of this compliant brotherhood of rationalism is examined in this section.

Rationalism in the field of religion took the form of deism. He accounts for the origins of deism in the following way. In medieval times the concept of the last judgment and of an avenging God were very clear but were meliorated by the Church "with its substitution of temporal penances and pardons and an interposed Purgatory in place of the terrible paradox of irrevocable judgment." The Reformation, and particularly Calvinistic Puritans, tore away those "veils of compromise" and brought man face-to-face with the awful abstraction he had created. "The result was for a while a great hardening and strengthening of character, salutary indeed after what may be called the almost hypocritical compromise of Catholicism; but in the end human nature could not endure the rigidity of its own logic, and in revolting turned not to another compromise but to questioning the very hypothesis of its faith." This reaction from the intolerable logic of the Puritans was deism, "in which God was stript altogether of his judicial and moral attributes and reduced to a kind of immanent, all-benevolent force in nature" (*SE, IX, 200*). Also contributing to the growth of deism was the fact that Calvinistic Protestantism, unlike the Anglican and Roman creeds, looked to the Bible as the sole source of revelation and made the individual mind the judge of what the Bible teaches rather than submitting individual judgment to the authority of the Church. "Now it is clear, if the reason of the individual is to determine the meaning of revelation, that reason is the ultimate authority, and the step to rationalism is easy and inevitable" (*SE, VIII, 56*). Rationalism is increasingly apparent in the seventeenth-century religious controversialists, says More, and the deistic rationalism of the eighteenth century was a direct outgrowth of that Protestant rationalism of the preceding century.

The rationalism of deism served to cast enthusiasm out of divinity. In More's view this was not unfortunate in itself, but the pity is "that so much of the true inspiration had to be ejected with the false" (*P, 285*). This narrowed religion. As an example, he cites this statement by Bolingbroke, who thought his predecessors had made the basis of religion far too wide: "Men have no further concern with God than TO BELIEVE THAT HE IS, which his physical attributes make fully manifest; but, that he is a rewarder of them who diligently seek him, Religion doth not require us to believe, since this depends on God's MORAL ATTRIBUTES, of which we have no conception" (*SE, IX, 201*). According to More, deism, by taking from religion the notion of supernatural rewards and retribution, left no place for the undeniable existence of evil in the world. This produced far-reaching consequences because "with the idea of an avenging deity and a supernatural test there disappeared also the sense of deep personal responsibility; the very notion of a radical and fundamental difference between good and evil was lost. The evil that is apparent in character comes to be regarded merely as the result of the restraining and thwarting institutions of society as these exist—why, no one can explain" (201-2). According to this way of thinking, man is inherently good, and the superficial variations displayed in his behavior are caused by the degree of his freedom to develop. We should condemn no man. "In place of judgment we are to regard all mankind with sympathy; a sort of emotional solidarity becomes the one great virtue, in which are included, or rather sunk, all the law and the prophets" (202).

It should be obvious, then, why More was so antagonistic toward deism. In his eyes it was but another form of rationalistic monism. The deists denied the kind of dualism which he considered to be the foundation of a sound view of man's nature and a sound basis for his behavior. On the one hand, this rationalistic approach to religion denied the supernatural realm of experience, and on the other, denied the reality of evil within the human heart. Both of these notions are essential to the dualistic vision. Also, deism, by ignoring the essential reality of evil, opened the gate to a kind of social sympathy which minimized the importance of free-willed responsibility. This in turn paved the way for the rise of that kind of humanitarianism which he found so abhorrent. Moreover, deism tended to emasculate religion by separating it from the emotional, imaginative, intuitive elements which he believed were so vital to the true religious experience. He thought that deists like Bolingbroke fostered the politico-religious concept that "religion was imposed more or less deliberately on the people by their masters as an instrument of government" and served as a "salutary and necessary fraud" (*NSE,* III, 120-21). This kind of sterile and utilitarian concept of religion More found repulsive. Religion should spring from a perception of man's dual nature and should aid him in living according to the dictates of his higher nature as they are interpreted by intuition and the religious imagination.

The repudiation of the dualism in the human consciousness which he found at the heart of deism, was, in his opinion, a distinguishing characteristic of the age. "It is not exaggeration to say that the consciousness or unconsciousness of this dualism is the most fundamental mark of division among men. Herein lies the distinction between civilisations, between faith and reason, between religion and rationalism, between piety and morality, between genius and talent. The stoic deism of the eighteenth century was singularly blind to this dualism" (*SE,* VI, 146-47). But it was not deism alone that was blind to dualism. The dominating ideas of this age "all imply a denial of that sense of dualism which hitherto had lain at the base of religion and philosophy, and . . . lacking this sense they seem always to be shirking certain of the more troublesome problems of life. The artificiality of that literature has become a proverb" (221).

There is an interesting ambivalence about More's attitude toward the eighteenth century. While being in complete sympathy with the style and what might be called the voice of the age, he can at the same time relentlessly attack its dominating spiritual-intellectual ideas. This ambivalence can be explained, at least in part, by the fact that he applied his yardstick of dualism to art as well as life. In terms of art, the eighteenth-century writers in general exercised the inner check over the flux of impressions and passions. In other words, they were conscious of dualism and complied with that consciousness in the proper way. Thus, from the standpoint of dualism, he could commend the formal excellence of their literature, while at the same time condemning many of their religious and philosophical ideas and attitudes.

A few selected examples should serve to illustrate how the notion of dualism functioned in More's criticism of eighteenth-century writers.

In his essay on Thomas Gray's letters (*SE,* X, 255-76), he points out that Gray did much reading and note taking, but he seemed to lack real purpose; and this, suggests More, was the source of his constant, though not severe, melancholy. Gray had a stirring imagination which, "though it was suffi- ciently strong to prevent him from finding content in merely feeding the appetite of an insatiable curiosity [i.e., he did feel moved to write poetry], was yet not powerful enough or steady enough to give him a real purpose or to lift him to the serener heights of unworldliness" (266). He was a religious man, but "there is no sign that he found any deep source of consolation in his faith or that the drama of the Anglican service meant anything to his imagination" (266-67). We should perceive that what underlies More's point here is his belief that "the serener heights of unworldliness" can only be reached when one has a clear conception of dualism and is able through the higher will or religious imagination, or whatever term we use for the faculty, to come in direct contact with the ideal world that exists concurrently with the physical world and yet apart from it. The situation with Gray was that "he had too much of the romantic imagination for the dull satisfactions of pedantry, too little of the religious imagination to create for himself a life of peace in the ideal world" (271).

The central theme of More's essay on George Crabbe (*SE,* II, 126-44) is Crabbe's recognition and appreciation of man's unique nature. His point is that Crabbe does not confuse man with the natural world around him. "It was man, and the moral springs in man" that really concerned Crabbe, and "even when he submits his art to minute descriptions" of nature "there still lurks this human ethical instinct behind the scientific eye" (132). Crabbe, in other words, observes the distinction between law for man and law for things that is so central in More's conception of humanism. Unlike Wordsworth and others among the Romantic poets, Crabbe's attitude toward nature is not that of "an emotional pantheism which uses the outer world as a mere symbol of the soul" (133). After quoting a descriptive passage from Crabbe's po- etry, he says, "All this is the furthest possible remove from vague reverie; it is a bit of amusing psychology, tending to distinguish more sharply between man and nature rather than to blend them in any haze of symbolism" (134). In addition to commending Crabbe for his recognition of the difference between law for man and law for things, he also praises him for his understanding of the primacy of individual will and responsibility and for not minimizing the evils inherent in human life: "He is at bottom a true Calvinist, showing that peculiar form of fatalism which still finds it possible to magnify the free will, and to avoid the limp surrender of determinism. Mankind as a body lies under a fatal burden of suffering and toil, because as a body men are depraved and turn from righteousness; but to the individual man there always remains open a path up from darkness into light, a way out of condemnation into serener peace" (138). This, of course, is the dualistic vision.

In accounting for the fact that Crabbe, "a poet of such great, almost supreme powers," should fail "to preserve a place in the memory of critics" (141), More says that our attitude toward nature has changed profoundly since the advent of Shelley, Wordsworth, and the other great Romantic poets. We now demand of the poet not only a minute and almost scientific acquaintance with nature but also "a certain note of mysticism, a feeling of some vast and indefinable presence beyond the finite forms described, a lurking sense of pantheism by which the personality of the observer seems to melt into what he observes or is swallowed up in vague reverie" (142)—such as we find in Wordsworth's "Tintern Abbey" and Shelley's "Ode to the West Wind." Crabbe had more than his share of science, says More, "but for reverie, for symbolism, for mystic longings toward the infinite, he had no sense whatever. It is quite true, as Goethe declared, that a 'sense of infinitude' is the mark of high poetry, and I firmly believe that the absence of this sense is the one thing that shuts Crabbe out of the company of the few divinely inspired singers" (143). But More goes on to qualify this statement by saying that the sense of infinitude, as it is found in the great classic writers, "is something far more sober and rational than the musing of the modern spirit—something radically different from the ecstatic rhapsodies of Shelley's *Prometheus Unbound*; and Crabbe's very limitations lend to his verse a brave manliness, a clean good sense, that tone up the mind of the reader like a strong cordial" (143).

There is a basic difference then, in More's view, between Wordsworth's and Crabbe's attitude toward nature; and there is a similar difference in their treatment of humanity. In Wordsworth's poems we find the concept of "humanity betrayed by circumstances and corrupted by luxury, but needing only the freedom of the hills and lakes to develop its native virtues; humanity caught up in some tremulous vision of harmony with the universal world; it is, in short, the vague aspiration of what we have called humanitarianism, and have endowed with the solemnities of a religion" (144). If this is necessary to poetry, says More, then Crabbe is undoubtedly "unpoetical."

In him there is no thought of a perfect race made corrupt by luxury, no vision of idyllic peace, no musings on humanity as an abstraction, but always a sturdy understanding of the individual man reaping the fruits of his own evil-doing or righteousness; his interest is in the individual will, never in the problem of classes. His sharply defined sense of man's personal responsibility coincides with his lack of reverent enthusiasm toward nature as an abstract idea, and goes to create that unusual atmosphere about his works which repels the modern sentimentalist. (144)

It seems necessary at this point to make a digression and reiterate a point made in my introduction. It is a manifest injustice to focus on a particular aspect of one of More's essays, ignoring the wealth of illustration, appreciative response, and rebuttal contained in the essay as a whole. The justification I offer is that this method enables me to bring into clear relief basic relationships and patterns of continuity which, it is hoped, should enrich the reading of individual essays as well as the essays taken as a collective body. It is hoped, for example, that the above points regarding Crabbe—More's emphasis on the dualism of man and nature, on free-willed responsibility, on the reality of evil, and on the negative consequences of romantic reverie and sympathy for man in the abstract—serve to illuminate these same basic attitudes and assumptions as they appear in varying forms throughout More's criticism; and particularly, at this point, as they serve to explain his spiritual-intellectual history of the eighteenth century.

An interesting contrast to his interpretation of Crabbe is his interpretation of Bishop Berkeley. As already noted, he thought that Crabbe maintained the dualistic vision and therefore his work remained "classic" rather than "romantic." It was quite the contrary with Berkeley. "He was in many respects, notably in the restraint and measure of his language, very much a man of his age and of the neo-classical school that ruled it; but there burned within him, nevertheless, an enthusiasm belonging to a different school altogether, and linking him with that hidden spirit which all through the eighteenth century was preparing for the revolution of the nineteenth" (*SE*, X, 220). (This "hidden spirit" is discussed further in a later section.) His essay on Berkeley (*SE*, X, 189-222) is perceptive and worthy of a more lengthy consideration, but the conclusion to the essay alone should serve the purpose here. The main thrust of this conclusion is that Berkeley's philosophy failed to recognize that old duality in the human consciousness.

By dissolving the outer world into personality, and by depriving phenomena of their objective material reality, his logic did more than any other writing of the day to break down the distinction between the law of man and the law of things. In his attempt to spiritualize nature he was really preparing the way for the conversion of naturalism into a bastard sort of spirituality. So it is that Berkeley's metaphysical thesis seems to me to reach through the years, and to connect itself with the later literary revolt against rationalistic compression on the one side, and against the truer inhibitions of religion on the other side, in favour of the free, oftened [*sic*] unbridled, expansion of the emotions and what else we regard as the elements of personality. (221-22)

In short, in its rejection of classical dualism and its emphasis on personality, Berkeley's work bears the sure mark of the coming romanticism. Also contrasting with Crabbe's views is Berkeley's treatment of evil and free will. "If the world is only the ideas emanating from the mind of a personal creator, what of evil? . . . And what of the individual human wills and their power of creating ideas?" (218).

The eighteenth century is commonly viewed as mainly an age of classicism or neoclassicism. More, who had very definite ideas regarding what constitutes a true classicism, would qualify this notion. At the heart of the true classical spirit is the apprehension of man's dual nature. The dominant philosophy of this century was a rationalism that rejected the superrational which is coupled with man's higher nature. Therefore, the writers of this age, lacking a true sense of dualism, were "pseudo-classical" rather than classical. More acknowledges that such a literature "in itself has many comfortable excellences" (*SE*, VIII, 229-30), but clearly he thinks these are lesser excellences. He also points out that any comment on this pseudoclassic literature "should not fail to distinguish the truly Augustan circle of Butler and Johnson and Reynolds and Goldsmith and Burke, whose humanism, like that of Horace, contained, not so much explicitly as in solution, the higher insight which the philosophy of their age was so busily hiding away. They contained, that is to say, some marks of true classicism as contrasted with pseudo-classicism" (23).

Unfortunately, More never wrote extended essays on any of the members of this "truly Augustan circle." His admiration for Johnson, however, is expressed incidentally throughout his writing, and these references give us some idea of what he considered to be the classical elements in Johnson. In a letter to a friend More explained,

To me the central fact of the man Johnson is so big, so over-powering, that his minor faults, which are many, sink into—shall I say, esthetical?—insignificance. That personality of his, that mysterious inexplicable something, is itself one of the great-est facts in literature. . . . You see how this fact of character or personality, outweighs with me all other matters. Hence perhaps my undue leaning on the side of ethical criticism. Critically to me that great question is how the imagination deals with this fact. In classical literature it seems to me to have dealt with it supremely well; in romantic literature generally not at all well. Hence the common saying that classical literature is strong in judgment whereas romantic literature is strong in imagination al-ways seems to me a crude error.[2]

More once mentioned to his sister Alice that he had read Boswell's *Life of Samuel Johnson* ten or twelve times and found that "it never palls." In puzzling over what it was about Johnson that enthralled him, he concludes, "Perhaps he at-tracts me by his combination of humble fear before God and pride before men. At any rate, he is one of the few who speak in a language I completely understand—as do Newman and Henry More and Henry Vaughan and Trollope."[3] Johnson's "humble fear before God and pride before men" appeals to him because it reveals a vivid personal experience of the deceitfulness of the human heart and the consolations of reli-gion. This is the same thing he responds to in Newman and the others; and such an experience is at the heart of the dualism within human consciousness.

I have minimized More's appreciative response to this age because it is outside the scope of this study; but it should be noted, at least in passing, that he found the literature of the eighteenth century very congenial, and he found much in it to praise. This serves to establish a fact that should not be forgotten: as is the case with most critics, More's personal tastes and emotional responses are not always consistent with the cold logical development of his basic premises and funda-mental assumptions. My main concern is with his history of ideas, and despite his fondness for much eighteenth-century literature, from the standpoint of his critical philosophy, the main currents of thought during this period were pernicious. The compliant brotherhood of rationalism would have a baleful influence on the next century.

Rousseau and the Drift to Humanitarianism

A primary strand of continuity found in More's spiritual-intellectual history is what he refers to as "the drift to humanitarianism." His essays describe a slow drift in human thought from medieval religion to humanitarianism, which he views as the dominant element in modern religion. Indeed, humanitarianism with its correlative belief in the essential goodness of man is, for him, really a secularization of medieval theology. This process of secularization—in simplest terms—took the following course. The religion of the Middle Ages was based on the longing for personal justification and supreme bliss; the Church, claiming the authority of revelation, spelled out how such ends were to be achieved. As this longing passed into the freer emotional life of the Renaissance, it began to change, or rather the concept of how the longing could be satisfied changed. As the supernatural scheme of redemption became overshadowed by the rationalism of natural religion, the confidence in man's ability to satisfy God easily passed into the belief "that human nature, being essentially right, has within itself the power to expand indefinitely, without any act of renunciation, toward some far-off, vaguely-glimpsed 'divine event' " (*SE,* VI, 219). Thus a kind of social sympathy, wherein the ideal is that all enjoy equally the things of this world, took the place of individual striving to please God through renouncing the things of this world in favor of the less tangible things of a higher world.

The center of focus in this drift to humanitarianism is Rousseau, "who gathered up in himself the floating ideas of his age, and, by simplifying them to a portable creed and infusing into them the carrying power of his own great personality, made them the chief formative influence down to our own times" (*SE*, VI, 214). For More, Rousseau is the great pivotal figure of the eighteenth century, indeed of the last four centuries. In beginning his essay on Rousseau (*SE*, VI, 214-41), he says that "the intellectual life of to-day has its source in Rousseau more than in any other single man" (215). A summary of this essay, coupled with what we already know of More's first principles, should make clear why Rousseau, in More's eyes, was such a significant figure.

Although More's historiography is primarily concerned with the development of thought in England, he makes excursions into other countries when he feels that a writer of another country has significantly influenced, or been influenced by, English thought. Such is the case with Rousseau. Rousseau, in More's view, was thoroughly a child of his age, and both the age and Rousseau in particular were strongly influenced by England; there is a continual recurrence of English names in Rousseau's works. "Intellectually, he has little that is original; his deism, his passion for liberty, his doctrine of instinctive goodness, are all avowedly from over the sea, and even his minor ideas can, for the most part, be traced to various predecessors" (223). In analyzing the revolution of the eighteenth century, More, acknowledging his oversimplification, says that "the guiding principles and the original dynamic impulse of the age came from England, that the translation of these into a homogeneous social law was the work of France, and that their conversion into a metaphysical formula was finally accomplished by Germany." The starting point of this movement, "the caldron, so to speak, in which this great fermentation began, was the turbulent England of the seventeenth century" (215).

Such were the influences which shaped Rousseau's philosophy. The most significant characteristics of that philosophy, as More distinguished them, are now considered. In a letter to Stuart Sherman, More says that the notion of human nature underlying Rousseau's concepts of "The Social Contract" and the *volonté générale* "is clear and has had an entirely unambiguous influence, is indeed to-day responsible for much that is dangerous in our educational and political practice, its influence of course being due in large measure to the fact that it expressed with marvelous eloquence the ruling sentiment of the age." That concept of human nature "is simply that a man's temperament is the fundamental element of nature, is of itself totally good and needs only to be released from restraint to be totally good in act."[4] This concept places intuition over reason, and although More on many occasions, as we have seen, champions a certain kind of intuition over reason, it is not the kind of intuition advocated by Rousseau. He illustrates the distinction by comparing Rousseau with Edmund Burke and Sir Joshua Reynolds, both of whom, as previously noted, were closer to More's ideal of the classical dualist than most men of their time.

He [Rousseau], equally with Burke and Reynolds, appealed to intuition as a power having greater authority than reason. But the intuition of Burke and Reynolds was as different from the intuition of Rousseau as Burke's political doctrine was different from the Rousselian doctrine legitimately developed in the revolution. To Burke intuition was a centripetal and restraining force pointing to an ultimate unity, as opposed to impulse and temperament and instinct, in the lower use of the word. It meant subordination of reason to superrational intuition. That, ultimately. In general he spoke in the language of Reynolds, contrasting abstract logic with "accumulated experience" and "habitual reason." Now, to Rousseau as I see him . . . intuition meant the guidance of temperament, impulse, individual emotion. It was centrifugal and abhorrent to restraint. It certainly cannot be expressed by "accumulated experience" and "habitual reason."[5]

It scarcely seems necessary at this point to call attention to the fact that reflected in this passage are most of More's first principles: his admiration for the unifying powers of the higher intuition or imagination, as he sometimes calls it; his concern with the restraining influence of the inner check; his respect for tradition; and his recognition of the disruptive forces of man's lower nature.

Rousseau's concept of human nature determined his theory of education as it is developed in *Emile*. And the thesis of this book, says More, has worked, and is still working, like a poison in the blood of society. "To make instinct instead of experienced judgment the basis of education, impulse instead of control, unbridled liberty instead of obedience, nature instead of discipline, to foster the emotions as if the uniting bond of mankind were sentiment rather than reason," seems to him "so monstrous a perversion of the truth as to awaken abhorrence in any considerate reader" (230-41).

His quarrel with Rousseau's concept of human nature and theory of education has its source in the question of dualism. More, of course, thought that Rousseau ignored the genuine dualism at the center of human consciousness, but this is not to say that Rousseau's philosophy is devoid of a dualism of its own. Indeed, More says that Rousseau taught a dualism which recognized the reality of evil. Evil, he says, was such a serious thing for Rousseau that he felt it with "the whole weight of his emotional being" (226). But this evil has its source not within the individual himself, as the promptings of an erring Augustinian natural man, but within his relationship to society. Rousseau "was driven to the idealisation of his own personality, and of every personality in so far as he projected himself into another, as good, and of other personalities, in so far as they are hostile to him and limit or pervert his native proclivities, as evil. Hence the dualism of the individual regarded in the state of nature and in the state of society, of the one and the many without the old accompaniment of the infinite and the finite" (225). Thus Rousseau's dualism is not a dualism within the human consciousness, between a higher and lower nature in man; it is the dualism of the individual in opposition to society.

At the center of the drift to humanitarianism as More unfolds it is the development of the apparently conflicting

110

tendencies of self-interest and sympathy. "Nothing," he says, "is more curious throughout the seventeenth and the first half of the eighteenth century than the way in which the contradictory notions of essential evil and essential goodness alternate with each other, sometimes in the same writer" (219). To the dominant moralists of the seventeenth century (e.g., Hobbes in England and La Rouchefoucauld in France) the basis of human nature was a pure egotism. But also existing during the same period, in contrast to Hobbes's position that men always struggle with one another for self-interested power, were the Levellers and Diggers with their notion of natural sympathy. "In this opposition between Hobbes's notion of the natural condition of man as one of warfare, and the humble effort of the Diggers to restore mankind to a primitive state of equality and fraternity, one may see foreshadowed the ethical theories of self-interest and benevolence which were developed in the next century" (*SE*, VIII, 156-57). But there was an element which separated the men of the seventeenth century from those of the eighteenth. "Above the idea of nature hovered, more or less distinctly, the idea of a supernatural power" (157). But this sense of the divine passed out of most eighteenth-century thinking, he says, chiefly through the instrumentality of Locke, who, without expressly denying the existence of a supernatural world, gave a clear psychological basis for the naturalistic philosophy which had been struggling for existence through the seventeenth century.

Rousseau, like his English predecessors, starts with the motives of self-interest and sympathy, but gives them a different direction.

He saw, as did Hobbes and Hume, that property depends on the mutual concessions of self-interest, but he saw further that on this basis alone society and traditional morality were in a condition of unstable equilibrium, were in fact founded on injustice and not justice at all. He perceived no relief from this hazardous condition except through counteracting self-interest by the equally innate and human force of sympathy, which was somehow to be called into action as the *volonté générale,* or mystical will of the people, embracing and absorbing the wills and desires of individuals into one harmonious purpose. (*SE,* VIII, 168)

More, of course, did not think that sympathy was a force sufficient in itself to combine the endless oppositions of self-interest. In fact, he thought that, at bottom, Rousseau's "double motive of self-love and sympathy was one thing, and not two" (*SE,* VI, 237). He thought that Rousseau would probably admit that, "to a certain extent, sympathy, as the faculty of putting one's self in the place of another, is a phase of *amour-propre,* in so far as we are led thereby to convert the pain of others into fear for ourselves and the joy of others into hope for ourselves." But he did not recognize "the cognate truth that when the condition of others is conceived in a causal relation to ourselves this order is reversed. That is to say, if the pain or loss of another in any way contributes to our own advantage, we rejoice in it, even when the feeling of uneasiness remains more or less consciously present; and contrariwise with the joy or gain of another which effects our own disadvantage" (237–38). Here is the essence of More's complaint against social sympathy. Because of the ambiguous character of sympathy, it can never take the place of discipline and justice in regulating the affairs of man; "as it is at best an extension of self-love, so it is always, when interests clash, in peril of unmasking as downright selfishness. A little honest observation of the actual working of Rousseauism in modern society would confirm this opinion only too cruelly" (238).

Probably enough has been said to indicate quite clearly just how Rousseau fits into More's history of ideas, but several brief examples of the influence he attributes to Rousseau may be instructive. First, he says that Rousseau's vital personality and the way he impressed his private emotions on the world made him "the father of romanticism and of a morbid individualism that seeks to hide itself under the cloak of a collective ideal" (237). That same vital personality influenced modern religious attitudes. "As the creed of Christianity came to the Middle Ages coloured by the intense self-absorption of St. Augustine's *Confessions,* so the new faith has flamed up from the *Confessions* of Rousseau" (236). "Rousseau has, more than any other one man, given us our religion of to-day, but it is a religion of the State, and not of God" (234); he wrought a change from theology to sociology. More can see things as diverse as Nietzschean philosophy and socialism growing out of Rousseauism. Both of these, he says, grew out of Rousseau's dualism of society and the individual with its correlative minimizing of personal responsibility. Both seek, "through the application of natural science to human affairs and through the resulting free development of man's natural instincts, one in the direction of egotism, the other of sympathy" to solve the antimony of the individual and society. It is generally known what a bugbear Rousseau was for Irving Babbitt (*Rousseau and Romanticism*); obviously, Rousseau is one of the subjects on which More and his good friend from Harvard were in accord.

The Quarrelsome Twins of Rational Science and Irrational Romanticism

Although the neoclassical school and rationalism apparently dominated the eighteenth century there were hidden forces at work all through this age preparing for the revolution of the nineteenth century. "At every turn one comes upon traces of these subterranean currents," says More (*SE,* IV, 216); and as examples he cites John Wesley's preaching of the immediate dependency of the soul on God; the visions of Emanuel Swedenborg, who came from Amsterdam to London in August 1771; and Macpherson's pseudotranslations from the Gaelic. "Cynical men of the world, such as Horace Walpole," says More, "and masters of traditional learning, such as Thomas Gray, felt the influence of these subterranean streams and showed it in their works" (217).

He views Walpole as an important representative of the age; in fact, in his essay on Walpole he quotes with approval this statement: "The history of England, throughout a very large segment of the eighteenth century, is simply a synonym for the works of Horace Walpole" (*SE*, IV, 257). The reason Walpole is such a characteristic representative of his times is that "his taste wavered uncertainly between the official classicalism of the age and the new stirrings of romance, even where politics did not intervene to warp his judgment. . . . To unravel his opinions would be to track the whole shifting literary movement of the age" (257). The dichotomy in Walpole's writing can be seen in the fact that although his style is neoclassical, commonly the ruling passion of his characters is "an overweening, undisciplined imperiousness of will, turned in upon itself and producing an egotism which only increases its insolence at the approach of death" (265). (Compare a romantic character such as Byron's Manfred.)

Thomas Gray is another figure who More notes particularly as embodying the two contradictory phases of the age.

On the one side of his character, in his mordant, cynical attitude toward the persons of the University with whom he lived and in his faculty of sharp critical phraseology, Gray belongs with the wits and continues the tradition of Pope and Swift. On another side, shown more completely perhaps in his verse but indicated also in the descriptive passages of his letters—as in the occasional touches of sentiment and in the enthusiastic acceptance of Ossian—he stands with the new creators of romance. (*SE*, X, 275)

This composite nature of Gray's mind may be one of the contributing causes "of a certain inefficiency in his genius," suggests More, and may have separated him from the Augustan circle of which Johnson was the deity, but it also explains in part "the fascination of the man and of his Letters."

Thus, Walpole and Gray reflect the influence of the "subterranean forces" of the age, "but only a genius entirely innocent of the schools and of the world," says More, "could have been so acutely sensitive to all these vaguely comprehended forces; only such an one could have surrendered himself to be for them a spokesman so single-minded in purpose as to have seemed to his own generation, if indeed not to ours also, a babbler and a maniac" (*SE,* IV, 217). That genius was William Blake.

More uses Blake at one point as an example to illustrate his apparently paradoxical notion that rationalism and romanticism have a common source. As noted at the end of the preceding chapter, according to More the events of the seventeenth century served to usher in an age of naturalism. He is using the term in his own particular way to indicate the philosophy which acknowledges both the reason and the instincts or emotions as belonging to the nature of man, the philosophy which subsumes all of man's characteristics under nature while denying a supernatural source for any of them. This philosophy, he says, left the door open to a revolt against the tyranny of one element of nature over the other.

Accordingly, almost with the beginning of rationalism we see springing up, timidly and uncertainly at first, various forms of appeal to pure instinct and unrestrained emotion. This voice of insubordination first became clear and defiant and fully self-conscious in Blake; and the message of Blake, repeated in a hundred various notes, now tender and piercingly sweet, now blurred by strange rumblings of thunderous madness, is everywhere a summons to the perfect freedom of instinct and primitive emotion and a denunciation of the control demanded by reason or by authority of any sort. (*SE,* VIII, 230-31)

This freedom of emotion and denunciation of control suggests the expansiveness which More saw as one of the principal characteristics of the Renaissance, and interestingly enough, he devotes considerable space in his essay on Blake (*SE,* IV, 212-38) to connecting this romantic of the late eighteenth century with the Elizabethans. (As seen in the next chapter, he makes a similar connection in his treatment of other romantic poets, most notably Keats.)

But he feels that in the final analysis Blake's work "is not so much an attempt to revive an earlier art as a personal revolt against the present. He sought above all that immediacy of impression which it was the chief aim of the age to avoid" (227). More sees Blake as "a voice crying in solitary places" against the established education and society of the times. "That was an age sufficiently easy to comprehend," he says, "because it had formed for itself so clear an ideal. Its aim above all was to avoid immediate contact with realities, to interpose some layer of philosophic experience between a man's soul and the emotional shocks of life" (215). There was feeling enough, he admits, as the tearful annals of the sentimental school prove, and there was adequate efficiency, but both the heart and will were trained to act in accord with approved formulae. In contrast to his age, Blake had his mind on immediate impressions, directly on the particular incident and its application to himself—this in direct contrast to a writer like Gray who was concerned more with the traditional experience of mankind and its generalized expression.

More is quite clear in fitting Blake into the age, but it is more difficult to determine just how he felt about him in this regard. Most of Blake's ideas were manifestly contrary to his first principles, yet he does not attack Blake very rigorously. The treatment is gentle, almost sympathetic, compared with the treatment a romantic like Shelley receives at his hands. He does say that Blake's method "when carried to its extreme is more disastrous to poetry than the most rigid convention of the century" (229), and he concludes by disparaging Blake's "charms of self-deception," saying that we usually "fall back on poets who accept fully the experience of the human heart. We find something closer to our understanding, something for that reason wholesomer, in men like Wordsworth and Goethe—perhaps even in the more formal poets of Blake's own age" (238). But, nevertheless, he seems more open and tolerant toward Blake than one familiar with his antiromanticism might expect.

Perhaps there are two reasons for this. First, he could admire Blake's tendency to confront experience with directness and immediacy. More was consistently antagonistic to lapses of common sense during which rational systems or conventions are established that fly in the face of concrete experience. His whole concept of dualism is founded on the premise that experience, when not distorted by rationalistic preconceptions, amply testifies of its validity. Secondly, he saw something admirable in Blake's dedication to the imagination. The concept of imagination is central in More's view of art, politics, and religion, and thus he can say of Blake's *Prophetic Books,* "here, at least, is no compromise with the imagination. The business of the poet, he held, was to cleanse the eyes so as to discern the eternal ideas of Plato, not as the mere deduction of dialectic, but as real and palpable existences" (231). This goal approaches that of the "religious imagination" which More admires when manifest in any age.

But what Blake saw as the poet's goal must not be confused with what he himself as a poet achieved. More believed that Blake, in his revolt against reason, certainly gave impetus to the romantic movement, but this revolt seen as "spiritual speculation" (a term More borrows from Swinburne) has made romanticism the source of endless illusions.

In the field of the imagination the school of Blake at the last carried victory with a high hand over the pseudo-classic and humanistic writers, and the nineteenth century opens upon a world pretty well divided between the quarrelsome twins of rational science and irrational romanticism. In so far as the romantic imagination yields to the self-sufficiency of instinct and emotions it implies a real revolt from rationalism; it is in a way even more hostile to rationalism than the classic use of the imagination, for classicism never involved a rejection of the reason, though it differed from pseudo-classicism by leaving the door open to an intuition above reason. But the peculiar tone of romantic writing comes not so much from the mere revolt against pseudo-classicism as from the illusion that this revolt is a return to spiritual insight. (*SE,* VIII, 232)

117

In other words, the imagination is a necessary instrument for obtaining spiritual insight, but it serves this end only when it manifests itself through a restraining check and a law of concentration within the flux of nature, and not when it makes itself known as the mere endless expansion that ensues upon the denial of any restraint whatsoever. Thus More's primary criticism of the romantic imagination, as it emerges with Blake, is that "in place of the higher intuition which is above reason it would commit mankind to the lower intuition which is beneath reason" (*SE,* VIII, 233). Therefore, in his opinion, Blake, because he failed "to accept fully the experience of the human heart," exerted an influence "not among the greater romantic writers of the early nineteenth century, but among the lesser men—Rossetti, Swinburne, and their school—who in one way or another have shrunk from the higher as well as the lower realities of life" (*SE,* IV, 238).

The transition between the eighteenth and nineteenth centuries, between neoclassicism and romanticism, reminds More of the middle sixteenth century.

The great passions that had been generated by political and religious upheaval lingered on, but, being deprived of their normal sustenance, worked themselves out in monstrous idiosyncrasies of character, which gradually subside into whims of an ever milder temper. In both ages the imagination, feeling the want of restraint, imported a model of poetic regularity from abroad and then, at the end, rebounded into an excessive romanticism. Surrey and Wyatt are as close a parallel to the school of Pope as Spenser and Sidney are to the school of Shelley. (*SE,* IV, 263)

He admits, however, that such comparisons are "as dangerous as they are seductive." Each age is unique, despite the repetition of general patterns. It is safer, he says, to consider the liberated passions which marked the transition into nineteenth-century romanticism as "an exaggerated illustration of traits that have always prevailed more or less in English society and literature." What happened at the end of the age under consideration here is that the "devastating materialism" of late eighteenth-century philosophy produced a change in ideals.

> The veritable feeling for the otherworld and for spiritual values was lost, while at the same time the new school, stirred with vague aspirations, was not satisfied with a simple and, in its way, wholesome naturalism. Above all these prophets of the romantic movement, as we designate it, revolted from the restrictive rules of an art which was neither classical nor innocently naturalistic, but pseudo-classical, and which had developed from one side of the Renaissance. They too perceived that no great art was possible without escape from the levelling tyranny of natural law, and, being unable to transcend nature, seeing indeed no higher reality into which nature could be raised, they sought freedom by sinking below nature. (*NSE*, I, 37-38)

This process, he says, ironically leads not to liberation but to less and less freedom.

According to More, therefore, the naturalism of the eighteenth century, encompassing as it did both reason and emotion or instinct, contained the seeds of both rationalism and romanticism. By the end of the century these seeds had grown into "the quarrelsome twins of rational science and irrational romanticism," and the interaction of these twins is the central subject of the next chapter, which continues to emphasize More's sense of ideological continuity.

CHAPTER FIVE

The Nineteenth Century

The Romantic Revolution in England

There are times, says More in his preface to volume VIII of the *Shelburne Essays,* when a general drift of ideas is so dominant that a critic can be pardoned if he slights some of the distinguishing marks and sounder aspects of a particular writer or work in order to focus on the larger relations of that drift of ideas. And the critic is to be pardoned all the more in doing so when, to his mind, the ideas appear to be carrying the world toward the desolation of what he holds dear. The romantic movement seemed to him to be just such a drift toward disintegration and disease. A summary of his antagonism toward romanticism has been presented in chapter 2. The purpose here is to fit that antagonism into the continuity being traced and to consider specific examples that illustrate it. In considering these examples, it is well to keep in mind the justification offered above. It is obvious throughout his essays on the Romantic poets that he felt a pressing need to make clear why the romantic movement, despite the sound aims and true insights of some of its leaders, had ended by playing into the hands of the enemies of man and his happiness.

He recognized romanticism as a humanist movement in the sense that it pretended to restore a balance and was a protest against imbalance. But, as illustrated in the last section of the preceding chapter, he thought romanticism failed to check the dehumanizing tendencies of the age, and merely substituted a sentimentalized naturalism for a mechanistic naturalism. The peril of the romantic movement, he thought, "lies in the fact that with its return to seventeenth-century enthusiasm it retained the eighteenth-century acceptance of nature, but now without restriction, thus leaving to itself no inner check" (*SE,* VII, 13). The great writers of the seventeenth century distrusted human nature as possessing tendencies toward ruinous evil. "But along with this fear of undisciplined nature, went a belief in the efficacy and virtue of certain supernatural emotions, in an infinite appetite that was not wild and indetermined—in enthusiasm" (11). The following age, under the impact of deism, brought about a complete reversal of this position: "Nature was used almost without deviation as a synonym of reason; and strong emotion, or enthusiasm, was condemned as contrary to nature and perilous" (11). In short, romanticism revolted against this bridle on emotion and enthusiasm, but at the same time, retained the naturalism which accompanied it—the concept that every part of man is encompassed within nature. Therefore, romanticism was not a true humanist movement, because it ultimately denied man's unique separateness from the rest of nature and the power of limitation or control this separateness implies. According to More, then, the underlying principle that gives romanticism (taken as a historical movement) a character radically different from classic art and humanism is "that expansive conceit of the emotions which goes with the illusion of beholding the infinite within the stream of nature itself instead of apart from the stream" (*SE,* VIII, xiii). At another point he deprecates this distinctive romantic trait as "a morbid egotism which is born of the union of an intensely felt personality with the notion of infinity as an escape from limitations" (36).

He thought that all the poets of England's romantic movement were affected by that "expansive conceit of the emotions" mentioned above; however, their practice was modified by other principles. "Wordsworth proclaimed it in his worship of the 'impulse from the vernal wood,' but with an admixture of Puritanic asceticism which made of it a kind of passive discipline. Byron possessed with it a saving self-reproach and cynicism. In Keats it was qualified by an aesthetic humility which rendered him in the end curiously docile to tradition" (*SE,* VII, 13). Only in Shelley does it attain to a nearly pure form. Shelley's philosophy always is "the voice of enthusiasm, of unreasoned emotion" (14). A brief survey of the essays on these poets should clarify and make more concrete the generalizations which have already been made regarding More's antiromanticism.

The essay on Wordsworth (*SE,* VII, 27-48) does not question the value of this poet's greater works in themselves; they have their assured place, he says. But he does question the value of Wordsworth's "chosen and cherished habit of life which is supposed to lend a prophetic power to his meanest words" (30). What he has in mind here is the poet's contemplative reverie in communion with nature. The "one impulse from a vernal wood" stanza "is good verse," he says, "but literal folly. Nor does it yet appear a fact that idle revery in the fields is better for a man's soul than the discipline of Plato or Jesus" (*SE,* V, 166). When Wordsworth, dismayed by the outcome of the French Revolution,

turned for solace to the quiet of the fields and the sublimity of the hills, he carried into that communion all the enthusiasm which an earlier age [particularly the seventeenth century as noted above] had reserved for the religion of the supernatural and which the deists in their satisfaction with natural religion had deliberately and completely shut out from their consciousness. In thus obliterating the distinctions of the reason [thereby denying a higher reason which operates in a realm separate from nature] Wordsworth introduced into the worship of nature the great pathetic fallacy which was to bewilder the minds and hearts of poets for an indefinite period. (*SE,* VII, 258)

Thus More distrusted Wordsworth's essential philosophy of nature. He saw the illusion of the nature worshipper and the deception of the humanitarian springing from the same substitution of reverie for judgment. He says, "there is something hollow and at bottom false in that blessed mood of revery by which we are laid asleep in body and become a living soul at one with the motion and the spirit of the wide-expanded world." There is a good deal to be said for solitude and life in the country, "but to go out into scenery as 'a dedicated Spirit,' to cultivate a chronic habit of admiration, to hang upon the seasons' every mood for the sake of harvesting the 'gentle agitations of the mind,' to prod the imagination deliberately that no day may lack its 'matins and vespers of harmonious verse,' in a word to make a poetical business of nature—this will never do" (42). But More's objection to Wordsworth's nature philosophy goes deeper than the fact that it makes a poetic business of nature. After quoting the lines about "a presence that disturbs me" from "Tintern Abbey," he says, "I would not deny the exquisite charm of such a feeling towards nature; nevertheless, even at its best and purest, pantheism is a kind of halfway house, and no abiding place for the spirit of man. He who stops there will find himself after a while turned out upon the common highway, obliged to journey forwards to belief in a frankly personal deity, or backwards to an avowed atheism" (*CW*, 283-84). In a note to this passage he adds that the former was the path taken by Wordsworth.

He concludes the essay on Wordsworth by reasserting the value of judgment and interaction with men over nature reverie. But he qualifies his objections to Wordsworth by saying that "his reproach is not, like Shelley's, a question of essential falseness, but of exclusion on the one side and of exaggeration on the other;" and he says, "all of us may drink in fresh courage and renewed vigour from seasons of wise passiveness." Many years after this essay was written, More took up the phrase "wise passiveness" as part of a modification of his evaluation of Wordsworth. J. D. Spaeth recounts a walk he took with More on a beautiful evening in early spring. After listening to More comment on the beauty of nature around them, he said, "You almost persuade me that you shared Wordsworth's 'impulse from a vernal wood.' " More smiled and answered, "I think I shall have to retract some of the harsh things I have said about Wordsworth, if the Lord spares me."[1] That retraction was never put into the form of a published essay, but in 1931 More wrote to Robert Shafer: "As for my own early criticism of Wordsworth, I simply confess that it is one example out of many where I have said things that ought not to have been said or, more particularly in this case, left unsaid the things that ought to have been said."[2] What he thought ought to be said he had outlined in an earlier letter to Shafer in which he disapproves of Babbitt's rigorous criticism of Wordsworth on the grounds of the notion of "wise passivity." He distinguishes between mere passivity and wise passivity, saying that Wordsworth fluctuated between the two but his work, taken as a whole, was dominated by the latter.[3] And this wise passivity opened the mind to the perception and influence of divine purpose in nature. It appears that More, in his later thought, came to view Wordsworth's wise passivity (which he considered the focal point for any understanding of the poet) as, in its highest expression, closely connected with the religious imagination. Wordsworth, in other words, was not entirely without some kind of inner check to balance his romantic expansiveness.

It is appropriate, and not without significance, that of all the Romantic poets, More edited an edition of Byron's poetry.[4] The appropriateness and significance lies, of course, in the fact that Byron is the least "romantic" of the major Romantics. And More was one of the first to point this out. In an essay published in 1898, titled "The Wholesome Revival of Byron," he emphasizes the classic elements in Byron's work, defining classical in this context as "a certain predominance of the intellect over the emotions, and a reliance on broad effects rather than on subtle impressions; these two characteristics working harmoniously together, and being subservient to human interest."[5] He likes the way Byron used his intellect to produce simple controlling ideas. In *Manfred,* for example, "we feel that a single and very definite idea has been grasped and held throughout; and we in turn receive a single and definite impression, which we readily carry away and reproduce in memory." In contrast to this, the central idea of Shelley's *Prometheus Unbound* is difficult for us to grasp and retain because it "has been diverted and refracted through the medium of a wayward imagination, and is after all an illusion of the senses" (803). More thinks that Byron's broad brush strokes account for some of the strength of his achievement. For example, he asserts that nowhere in English literature, outside of Shakespeare, can we find "the great passions of men set forth so directly and powerfully as in Byron, and on this must rest his final claim to serious consideration" (807). But his broad strokes also account for some of his major limitations: "Had his genius possessed also the subtle grace of the more romantic writers, he would have been classical in a still higher and broader sense; for the greatest poets, the true classics, Homer as well as Shakespeare, have embraced both gifts" (803). Here is the humanistic principle of balance—the law of measure—making itself felt this early in More's career.

He defends Byron against charges of immorality. This may be surprising to those who have categorized More as a prude. There is no denying the rigidity of his Puritan conscience, and at the same time, he does not deny the moral lapses in Byron's life, but he defends him on the grounds that he clearly knew the difference between right and wrong even when he did the wrong. In evaluating his own ruinous life, Byron saw the cause in "his lack of self-restraint and his revolt from conventions." In contrast to this is Shelley, who in all that he did, said his wife, "at the time of doing it, believed himself justified in his own conscience." This inner falsehood More found more deadly than the spoken lie. "There is no such insidious disease in Byron's mind" (808).

In contrast to Wordsworth's "lack of native vitality," Byron displays a "superabundance of vitality" (*SE,* VII, 32). And in contrast to Wordsworth's vague worship of nature, Byron manifests a tighter grip on realities. Byron was too much a child of his age to escape "the longing for mystic fellowship with nature," says More, but even so there is in him "a firmness and a directness of utterance which distinguish his work from the more flaccid rhapsodies of his romantic rivals."[6] In his essay on Wordsworth, More compares "Tintern Abbey" with some stanzas from Byron's *Childe Harold,* admitting the superiority of Wordsworth's lines in terms of rapturous beauty and the power to awaken in the reader the full emotions felt by the poet. But when it comes to the underlying ideas, he is not so sure Wordsworth wins the prize. His suspicions regarding the nature philosophy of Wordsworth's poem are considered above. What he sees in Byron's lines is a turning to nature, not in order to submerge the will in some kind of mystic communion with it, but in order to "cultivate the higher will to refrain and lift [the] mind above nature into a serene communication with itself and with its God" (*SE,* VII, 37-40). In other words, he can admire Byron's poetic treatment of nature over Wordsworth's because "at bottom Byron's sympathy is not with nature, but with man, and in the expression of this sympathy he displays the sturdy strength of classic art."[7] More's attitude regarding romantic nature poetry and his affinity for Byron are both clearly indicated in this excerpt from an editorial he wrote for the *New York Evening Post:*

This romantic poetry . . . no longer bears any relationship to actual life. We have grown sick to death of those that go out to admire dutifully the mountains and streams; we distrust the pretty singer of birds and flowers; and the decadent merchant of sentimentalities evokes only a smile or a tear. Our age is critical and reflective, prosaic perhaps. What we need is a return to something akin to that solid school of the eighteenth century which dealt with men and the moral responsibilities of men. In-

127

stead of a "renascence of wonder" we long for a little common sense. Our fancy is surfeited while our intelligence starves. Nothing would be more wholesome [cf. the title of More's essay on Byron, "The Wholesome Revival of Byron"], nothing would come with a greater shock of surprise, than a good stinging satire on the sharp intellectual manner of Pope.[8]

Probably because he saw Byron's work as closely related in spirit to "the accepted canons of the past" (*SE,* III, 167) and believed that Byron looked upon life "from the old point of view" (169), he considered *Don Juan* to be the high point of Byron's poetry. He liked its flavor of the eighteenth-century satirists whom he so much admired. But he is quick to point out in his essay on the poem (*SE,* III, 166-76) that we make a sad mistake if we regard it as a mere work of satire. Its scope and significance, he says, go beyond that of many other great works of satire. "It does in its own way present a view of life as a whole, with the good and the evil, and so passes beyond the category of the merely satirical" (171). It becomes apparent as he continues the essay that the "view of life as a whole" that he mentions here is the dualistic view. And because of this total view of life, he classes the poem with "the more universal epics of literature rather than with poems that portray only a single aspect of life" (171). As already noted, More believed that the great poets all took a somber view of the world—somber in the sense that they recognized man's very real limitations along with his potentialities. Byron, he says, "is conscious of the same insight into the illusive spectacle" (172). But we must not suppose that because the heroic poems of old were touched "with the pettiness and sadness of human destiny," that their influence was supposed to be narrowing or depressing. Indeed, their very inspiration was derived from "the fortitude of spirit struggling to rise above the league of little things and foiling despairs. . . . There lay the greatness of the heroic epos for readers of old,—the sense of human littleness, the melancholy of broken aspirations, swallowed up in the transcending sublimity of man's endurance and daring" (172-73). He summarizes his evaluation of Byron's accomplishment in *Don Juan* in this way:

Out of the bitterness of the soul, out of the wreck of his passions which, though heroic in intensity, had ended in quailing of the heart, he sought what the great makers of epic had sought,—a solace and a sense of uplifted freedom. The heroic ideal was gone, the refuge of religion was gone; but, passing to the opposite extreme, by showing the power of the human heart to mock at all things, he would still set forth the possibility of standing above and apart from all things. He, too, went beyond the limitations of destiny by laughter, as Homer and Virgil and Milton had risen by the imagination. And, in doing this, he wrote the modern epic. (176)

Thus, More sees the poem as, in one sense, not half but wholly serious, because "it takes so broad a view of human activity and because of its persistent moral sense" (175). And he rates Byron over other Romantic poets who either fail to recognize man's true condition or else fail to recognize the higher will and the control over expansiveness which are necessary for him to overcome it.

The controlling idea that runs through More's essay on Keats (*SE*, IV, 99-128) is that his poetry, in spirit and subject, is closely related to the Elizabethan Age. In particular, Keats shared "that same faculty of vision in his mind which, like theirs [the Elizabethans], beheld the marriage of the ideas of beauty and death" (102). As already noted, More distinguished the expansiveness of the Elizabethan Age from the order and restraint of classic art. Therefore, Keats, being aligned with the Elizabethans, is not Greek in artistic spirit, as some have supposed. Consider, for example, the theme mentioned above of the marriage of the ideas of beauty and death. The Greeks, too, had a version of this theme. However, its interest for them lay "in its ethical associations, and the Powers of beauty and death were minor agents only in the great moral drama moved by the supreme unwritten laws"

(115). Keats, on the other hand, in his treatment of this theme, is preoccupied with its aesthetic associations rather than its ethical associations.

Keats could learn much about style from the Elizabethans, says More, but he could not learn taste from them; "here where he most needed guidance they seemed rather to sanction his lawlessness." The circumstances with the Elizabethans were different, however, from those with Keats: "When a language is young and expanding, the absence of restraining taste is not so much felt, and liberty is a principle of growth; whereas at a later stage the same freedom leads often to mere eccentricity and vulgarisms. So it is that in Keats's language we are often obliged to distinguish between a true Elizabethan spontaneity and a spurious imitation that smacks too much of his London surroundings" (104). The London flavor of Keats's Elizabethanism was amplified by the fact that, in his early impressionable years, the natural qualities of his mind were reinforced by Leigh Hunt and B. R. Haydon "with what may be called a kind of bastard, or cockney, Elizabethanism" (108).

Keats's Elizabethanism fell short of the true Elizabethanism on several counts. For one thing, despite "the superb zest and beauty" of Keats's poetry, which is reminiscent of the early dramatists, there is little of "the rich humanity and high passions that for the most part fill the Elizabethan stage" (122). Although by his "depth and sincerity" he differs from certain other writers of the century who dealt with the theme of the conjunction of beauty and death (William Morris, for example), "he is still far from the brave furor and exultation of the great passages in Marlowe" (121). Furthermore, he fell short of a "profounder vision of disillusion" possessed by the Elizabethans, though he does approach near to it in the sonnet, "When I Have Fears" (107). This profound vision of disillusion is apparently the kind of vision mentioned above in connection with Byron, which Byron possessed but the Romantics in general lacked. More suggests that Keats himself was aware that the motto of his faith, "Beauty is truth, truth beauty," was only a partial and imperfect view of the reality, and his letters were filled with "vague yearnings for a clearer knowledge." Unfortunately, however, "when he came to put his half-digested theories into practice, he turned, not to the moral drama of the Greeks or to the passionate human nature of the Elizabethans, but to the humanitarian philosophy that was in the air about him; and, accepting this, he fell into a crude dualism" (123). That dualism was "an exquisite sense of the luxurious" (Keats's phrase) on the one side, and the idea of doing some good in the world on the other.

In summary, although More greatly admired the poetry of Keats, as usual he felt a compelling necessity to fit his work into that great current of thought which so much fascinated him, and in doing so he was forced to point out that Keats was drifting in an eddy of romanticism which flowed away from the humanistic ideal. This is not to say that he was not a great poet. At the same time More measures a writer against the ideal and finds him wanting, he recognizes that all must fall short of that measure, and we must cherish them for the qualities they do possess.

More's essay on Shelley (*SE,* VII, 1-26) is primarily concerned with the long, "supposedly-philosophical" poems, of which he is highly critical because he finds nothing of value in Shelley's "alleged philosophy." He praises the short lyrics, saying that when Shelley is expressing personal joy or sorrow, love or regret, "his genius suffers no let or thwarting; it is even strengthened by that romantic acceptance of emotion" (22). But it is an entirely different matter with the longer philosophical poems. He asserts that Shelley was powerfully affected by the prevailing forces of the age and that his character and poetry suffered "a certain perversion" from this influence. The forces which affected him so much were "revolution and romanticism." Revolution need not necessarily have a perverting effect on a poet, says More—witness Milton.

But with Shelley revolution meant the fluttering of an opaque and dizzying flag between the poet's inner eye and the truth of human nature. He was peculiarly the child of his age, betrayed by his own feminine fineness of nature, and lacking that toughness of fibre, or residue of resistant prose, which made Byron and Wordsworth followers but not altogether victims of the ever-despotic Hour. With a child-like credulity almost inconceivable he accepted the current doctrine that mankind is naturally and inherently virtuous, needing only the deliverance from some outwardly applied oppression to spring back to its essential perfection. With Rousseau the perverting force had been property. With Shelley it was more commonly personified as Jehovah or Jove. (6-7)

In More's opinion, Shelley's philosophy "is chiefly unliterary, destructive, that is to say, of that self-knowledge out of which the great creations and the magnificent joys of literature grow." He does not mean to say that Shelley was by nature "base or sensual or cruel"; on the contrary his life displays "many acts of instinctive generosity." "Nevertheless, there was some flaw at his heart, some weakness of overweening self-trust, which exposed him to the most insidious poison of the age, and in the final test left him almost inhuman" (8). Shelley's major flaw was his tendency to accept "each emotion as it arose in his breast" as justified in itself, "without pausing to consider its causes or consequences" (10-11). Frequently much is made of Shelley's Platonism, but More, a Platonist himself, feels that Shelley's flaw caused him, along with the other romanticists, to misinterpret Plato's Ideas and their relationship to the imagination. The romanticist "sees clearly enough that Ideas are the property of the image-making faculty, but treats them as if they were somehow created by a purely spontaneous power *ex nihilo,* and so deprives them of eternal and authoritative validity" (P, 193). More believed, on the other hand, that the imagination does not create the Ideas out of something residing merely in the individual; rather, the imagination is the faculty of perceiving something external to the individual, though perhaps acting within him at the same time. That something external, something higher, is the realm of Ideas, or Forms.

He may have mellowed in his appraisal of Wordsworth over the years, but his antipathy toward Shelley apparently never abated. As late as 1928 he said he believed "that the divorce in Shelley between character and ideals has been, so far as it is typical, a danger signal of national degeneration morally and artistically" (*NSE*, I, 121).

Thus he interprets the major figures of England's Romantic Age. This survey certainly does not do justice to the subtleties of his arguments, his evidence and refutation, nor to the sensitivity of his appreciative responses; but it does clarify his sense of the continuity of human thought. Coleridge is conspicuously absent from this survey simply because More wrote no essay on him. However, it is possible to make some likely conjectures regarding what his treatment of Coleridge might have been. The following sections show how More viewed romanticism as a vital force throughout the century even though it underwent certain transformations.

The Philosophy of Change

More of the *Shelburne Essays* are devoted to the literature of the nineteenth century than to the literature of any other period. This makes it impossible, in a study of this sort, to give detailed consideration to particular essays. But, because of the emphasis here on general currents of thought, the omission of such detailed consideration, though regrettable in terms of presenting the breadth and total value of More's criticism, does not hinder a recognition of the continuity in his criticism, not as an end in itself, but as a step toward a broader understanding and appreciation of his work. Therefore, the treatment of Victorian literature which follows centers on More's philosophical theme in dealing with the period. Individual authors and works are treated only briefly and are primarily used to clarify or support generalizations regarding that theme.

The theme is set forth most explicitly in "Victorian Literature" (*SE,* VII, 245-69), which is the nucleus for a number of
other essays. The ideas expressed in it are developed with
greater or lesser completeness in separate essays on most of
the figures named in it and on other figures as well—on
Wordsworth, Morris, Swinburne, Browning, Whitman,
Tennyson, Newman, Carlyle, James Thomson, and Huxley.
He begins "Victorian Literature" by emphasizing the impact
of Darwinian evolution on the thinking of the nineteenth
century. This new law, he asserts, "left no place for a power
existing outside of nature and controlling the world as a
lower order of existence, nor did it recognize a higher and
lower principle within nature itself, but in the mere blind
force of variation, in the very unruliness to design or government, found the source of order and development" (248).
Thus, for those influenced by Darwin's thesis, the law of
change became sufficient in itself to explain the nature of
things; in the organic sphere it became the correlative of the
law of motion in the inorganic sphere. The work of Malthus
and Arnold, of Newman and Spencer, is imbued with this
spirit of change. Indeed, says More, this "philosophy of
change" is to be seen on every hand: Darwinism in science,
impressionism in the arts, the theory of development of doctrine in religion, pragmatism in philosophy, laissez faire in
economics, and the elective system and emphasis on scientific
studies to replace the old emphasis on classics and humanities
in education.

The chief literary accomplishment of the Victorian age,
according to More, was the unifying of science and poetry; in
other words, the establishment of an uneasy peace between
the "quarrelsome twins" mentioned in the last chapter. Science was a dominating intellectual force of the age, "and the
point of contact of science with literature is just this law of
change" (250). As science tried to reduce the flux of the
natural order to scientific law, poetry gave emotional expression to the same flux. All through Victorian literature is clear

evidence of the effects of the philosophy of change on the substance and form of English verse. Though it is paradoxical, he points out, the effect of science upon literature and art has been to promote romantic impressionism. This comes about because the philosophy of change at the heart of science, when carried into literature, acknowledges no principle of taste superior to the shifting pleasure of the individual.

More identifies the influence of the philosophy of change upon the poets of this age in the following way. To Whitman's eye the universe was "a strange and motley procession of shifting forms, at which he gazed undismayed, calling upon no passing appearance to stay for an instant and deliver its meaning" (SE, VII, 259). Swinburne, like Whitman, is a poet "of vast and confused motion" and in his poetry there is "the same thronging procession of images which flit by without allowing the reader to concentrate his attention upon a single impression" (SE, III, 118), and particularly in his later work, "the rhythm lacks resistance; there is no definite vision evoked out of the rapid flux of images; the thought has no sure control over the words" (105). To William Morris also the world was "a swift-moving succession of forms, glinting now with iridescent colours and breathing entranced melodies, with always the haunting fear in the observer's mind that if for one moment they should pause in their headlong flight they would vanish irrevocably into the void: life is many-hued, intricate motion; rest is death" (SE, VII, 259). Christina Rossetti's poetry reveals "a spirit always refined and exquisite in sentiment, but without any guiding and restraining artistic impulse; she never drew to the shutters of her soul, but lay open to every wandering breath of heaven" (SE, III, 124). Speaking of the pessimism of James Thomson's writing, he says, "What is it more than the poetic imagination stung to frenzy by the scientific conception of universal motion? . . . This is the ground which pessimism seeks always for its building" (SE, V, 192). Such pessimism is produced from a lack of spiritual insight and is connected with "the notion of man as an integral part of nature, subject wholly to natural law, and with the terror which arises when a heightened self-consciousness, without the stay of healthy animal instincts, finds itself confronted by the vision of all-involving motion and permutation. So necessary for the soul is some place of stability outside of nature's vortex that, if no other place is allowed, it will make its account with death" (194). George Meredith was deeply immersed in the spirit of the times, "and there is no poet or prose-writer in English who more speaks and exalts the belief in humanity as completely involved in the process of natural growth. . . . He has written out his reading of life in *The Woods of Westermain,* and the heart of his reading is at the end of his glorification of change as the wonderous renovator and revealer: 'Change, the strongest son of Life, / Has the Spirit here to wife' " (*SE,* VII, 262).

The philosophy of change, of course, runs counter to More's humanistic dualism, particularly as that dualism manifests itself in the opposition of the inner check and the flux of experience. Therefore, those who are caught up with the philosophy of change are especially liable to the danger of ignoring or denying such a dualism. This, according to More, was the case with Browning. In "Why is Browning Popular" (*SE,* III, 143-65), he refers to "a certain philosophy" which had its beginnings "in the naturalism of Rousseau and the eighteenth century," but the flower of which belongs wholly to the nineteenth century (160). And that flower is manifestly the philosophy of change, which in Browning "took the disguise of a buoyant revelling in the mere conflict and tumult of life without any formal restraint upon its multiform activity. His joyous acceptance of the world and his optimistic assurance that all things will of themselves work out right have passed with many for spiritual insight, whereas in reality his appeal to the present is due to his blind courage in waiving the critical check of the spirit of permanence" (*SE,* VII, 259-60). Browning imposed his philosophy on his writing from the outside, while at the same time failing to accept "the simple and pathetic incompleteness of life," but rather trying "with his reason to reconcile it with an ideal system" (*SE,* III, 161). Nowhere in his "rhapsody" is there "a hint of any break between the lower and the higher nature of man, or between the human and celestial character" (163). Therefore, "there is no tragedy, properly speaking, in Browning, for the reason that passion is to him essentially good" (161-62). What his philosophy really offers is a kind of short cut to spirituality; this accounts partly for its popularity. "The secret of his more esoteric fame is just this, that he dresses a worldly and easy philosophy in the forms of spiritual faith and so deceives the troubled seekers after the higher life" (163).

Of course the philosophy of change was not welcomed enthusiastically and without reservation by all the poets of the age. Obviously there is another aspect of Victorian poetry that must not be ignored.

As no age, even the most self-satisfied, is entirely itself, but carries with it the memory of all that has gone before, so these singers of the flux are troubled at times by echoes of a past experience. Now and again a line, a note, will slip in that recalls the old desire of changeless rest and of the consummation of peace. It might even be more exact to say that the poets of the century as a whole do not so much give utterance to the unhesitating acceptance of the official philosophy as they express its ever growing predominance. (*SE,* VII, 260)[9]

Thus the most characteristic voices of the age were the two, Tennyson and Arnold, "who felt most poignantly and sang most clearly," though in diverse ways, of the transition from the old to the new.

In Tennyson the two fields were placed side by side, and More believed "it is a sign of a certain lack of hardness in his mental fibre that he never seemed to perceive their mutual antagonism" (261). He felt that the gist of Tennyson's faith, and what made him the spokesman of the age ("Tennyson is the Victorian Age" [64]), was his completion of evolution by a theory of indefinite progress and by "a vision of some magnificent consummation wherein the sacrifices and the waste and the pain of the present were to be compensated somehow, somewhere, somewhen—who shall say" (82). And this reconciliation of faith and science, "this discovery of a father near at hand within the inexorable law of evolution, this vision of an eternal state to be reached in the progress of time—all this is what we call the Victorian compromise" (83). This explains how, at one moment, Tennyson could be "the conscious laureate of science and evolution and of a self-evolving change moving to some far-off divine event," and at another moment, "the prophet of insight, singing the mystery of the timeless, changeless spirit." But Arnold's intellect was made of a tougher fibre that prevented him from accepting such a compromise. "Emotionally he was about equally susceptible to the prevailing currents of his day and of the past, and their intimate fusion produced a strange uneasiness of mind and heart, leaving him at home neither in this world nor the other" (261). This uneasiness is expressed in his famous complaint, "which is in a way the confession of his generation," made at the Grande Chartreuse:

> Wandering between two worlds, one dead,
> The other powerless to be born,
> With nowhere yet to rest my head,
> Like these, on earth I wait forlorn.

More suggests that an examination of the spirit of compromise that made Tennyson the official poet of the age will reveal that it rests finally "on a denial of religious dualism, on a denial, that is, of the consciousness, which no reasoning of philosophy and no noise of the world can ever quite obliterate, of two opposite principles within us, one bespeaking unity and peace and infinite life, the other calling us to endless change and division and discord. Just this cleft within our nature the Victorians attempted to gloss over" (86). [10]

Taking Tennyson's spirit of compromise as a focal point, More saw diverging lines of development radiating from it. William Morris, for example, he speaks of as "the representative of one of the diverging lines from Tennyson's early Victorian compromise" (*SE,* VII, 95). "You may sink your plummet into his mind, but you will touch no bottom; there is no solid core; all is movement and flux, save this sense of beauty, which was itself largely a matter of flowing rhythm" (101-2). He never felt the moral compromise of the age. In More's opinion, there is little real humanity in Morris: "His sense of moral values is of the most rudimentary sort, and the law of cause and effect, which we associate with the moral law, scarcely exists for him" (116). "There is nothing immoral in his work; but of morality in it we do not think at all, save as another term to distinguish the beautiful from the ugly" (102).

In direct contrast to Morris in his scheme of Victorian thought is Carlyle, who did not accept the philosophy of change as others did and who, therefore, was diametrically opposed to the main currents of belief that swept the age. Science, and particularly evolution, fostered the notion that morality was based on "the evershifting quicksands" of custom and superficial social conventions. But Carlyle "perceived in the phenomena of life only thin cobwebs, wherethrough Death and Eternity sat glaring, whereas the moral law alone was unchangeable, founded on the everlasting rock of truth" (*SE,* I, 95). This sense of the illusions in human existence coupled with the sense of the eternal stability of moral law produced in Carlyle the extraordinary union within one man of "the spirit of the Hindu seer and the Hebrew prophet."

The central figure in More's treatment of the philosophy of change is Thomas Huxley. In Huxley he found an antagonist to his form of humanism who was as formidable as, if not more formidable than, Rousseau. The name of Huxley crops up repeatedly throughout More's writings. Perhaps this is partly to be explained by the fact that he grew up during a time when America was experiencing the greatest impact from Darwinian evolution; but a fuller explanation is to be found in what Huxley represented for him: he was the prophet of the philosophy of change, the spokesman of philosophical science in its most pernicious form, the preacher of naturalism and a rationalistic monism; in short, an archenemy to religious dualism. Huxley "more than any other man stood in the nineteenth century for the triple power of positive and hypothetical science and of philosophical science in the form of naturalism" (*SE,* VIII, 208).[11]

He saw concealed in Huxley's total work "an insoluble ambiguity." Huxley had a passion for truth, but at the same time, was "one of the master sophists of the age" (210-11). There is sophistry in the term "agnosticism" which he coined: "Indeed, an agnostic might briefly and not unfairly be defined as a dogmatist in attack and a sceptic in defence, which is but another way of calling him a sophist" (212). The tracks of this sophistry lead straight to "that confusion of positive science and hypothetical science and philosophical science which is, perhaps, the most characteristic mark of the last century" (211). In essay after essay Huxley will be found "maintaining on one page the self-limitations of positive science and on another page passing from hypothesis to dogmatic philosophy, here rebuking those who confound the domains of scientific and spiritual law and there proclaiming science as a support of what he deems true religion" (203). In short, More's criticism of Huxley is that he made "a false extension of the procedure of science [with which More had no quarrel] into a philosophy of naturalism [with which More never ceased to quarrel vigorously]" (217).

In a note to his discussion of skepticism in the second volume of *The Greek Tradition,* More gives a summary of the extent to which Huxley, as a genuine skeptic, remained within the legitimate bounds of science, and the extent to which he launched into metaphysics. In his practical work as an observer of nature and experimenter and classifier of observations, Huxley was a pure skeptic (using the term in the technical philosophical sense). Likewise in his acceptance of Hume's analysis of causality and distinction between science and metaphysics he was a true skeptic,

But when he goes on to make cause and effect an absolute and universal law of nature . . . when he declares that Darwinian evolution is "no speculation but a generalization of certain facts;" and, further, that "the materials of consciousness are products of cerebral activity," that we are pure "automata," that all causation is of a material, mechanical sort, and that "man, physical, intellectual, and moral, is as much a part of nature as purely a product of the cosmic process, as the humblest weed," then he slips from scepticism and genuine science, to rationalizing and pure metaphysics. (HP, 344n)

Because of the dominance of the philosophy of change, there is, according to More's way of thinking, something lacking in the Victorian poets. Because they "bowed down in the temple of the idol of Mutability," some deeper satisfaction or assurance is wanting in their work that will not be regained until "we have looked once more within our own breasts and learned that there is something in human nature besides an indefinite congeries of changes" (SE, VII, 265). "The adventurous soul who to-day against the reigning scientific and pragmatic dogma would maintain no vague and equally one-sided idealism, but the true duality of the one and the many, the absolute and the relative, the permanent and the mutable, will find himself subjected to an intellectual isolation and contempt almost as terrible as the penalties of the inquisition, and quite as effective in producing a silent conformity" (268). One cannot help but feel that he is speaking here of his own experience. He once described himself as one of the least read and most hated of writers.

The Religious Spirit

Whereas Huxley was More's mortal enemy in the great battle of human thought, Newman was an admired ally and kindred spirit. A portrait of Newman hung in his study, and in that visage he saw reflected the marks of a great spiritual struggle: "visionary hope," "the perplexity of an inner conflict," and "the sweetness of self-surrender" (*SE,* VIII, 73). He once remarked his affinity toward Newman in a letter to his sister. This passage is worth quoting at some length because in addition to illustrating his attitude toward Newman, it also reveals once again his basic notions regarding human thought and experience.

Newman's whole life was a protest against the modern invasions of materialism and epicurean scepticism, and in that respect he seems often to be speaking words that I should speak myself if I had his power of lucid expression. His sense of the illusion of this world also comes very close to me. . . . I can sympathize too with Newman's desire for a clear voice of authority and for some escape from the limitations of our individual experience. "Truth," he said, "is wrought out by many minds working freely together." That is my notion of the long tradition of philosophy, in so far as philosophy remains true to human nature and does not go awhoring after the strange gods of Plotinus and Kant. But when Newman jumps to the conclusion of a Church which has in its charge the revelation of clear absolute truth, then I draw back. We have no such precision of knowledge, no such guide, no such visible monitor. There is where the philosopher needs a courageous heart—to preserve his reverence for the hidden truth which is involved in clouds of ever-shifting error. With all that my notion of the traditional experience of humanity is not so very far from Newman's idea of the Church. He has come to mean more to me, on the whole, than any other writer of the past century.[12]

It should be apparent from this passage why More was so interested in Newman. It is also important to note that More, for most of his life, was close to the Anglican Church himself; he found it a congenial kind of Christianity.[13] Late in his career he collaborated on a book about Anglicanism.[14] This passage also indicates why he, though leaning as did Newman before his conversion toward the most Catholic type of Protestantism, never seriously considered becoming a Roman Catholic.[15]

142

In his view, Newman's "perhaps was the most religious spirit of the past century" (*POD,* III), and his conversion "was, undoubtedly, the most important religious event of England in the nineteenth century—so much, after all, do the struggle and destiny of a great individual soul outweigh in significance the unconscious or undeliberate movements of masses of men" (*SE,* VII, 53-54). Therefore, when More writes of religion during the nineteenth century, he usually focuses his attention on Newman and the Oxford Movement of which he was a part.

The Oxford Movement, according to More, "was part of the great romantic flood that swept over Europe, and owed more to Germany than the men of Oxford were aware of, but was still primarily English" (*SE,* VIII, 431). Two impulses, which were in reality one, were at the origin of the movement, he says, illustrating once again his concern with continuity. First, "Religion had lagged behind the rest of life in that impetuous awakening of the imagination which had come with the opening of the nineteenth century; it retained all the dryness and lifeless cant of the preceding generation, which had marked about the lowest stage of British formalism" (*SE,* III, 223). Newman and his friends at Oxford attempted to find a substitute within the Church of England for the fervor of Wesleyanism and Evangelicalism, which fervor they thought was salutary but without anchor in that form of the religious imagination that accompanies a humble reverence for tradition. Without such an anchor, they thought, it was "a kind of emotional effervescence from a utilitarian rationalism and must in the end serve only to strengthen the sway of irreligion" (*SE,* VIII, 41). The second impulse was the shock of the Reform Bill of 1832. This bill promised to open the way for liberalizing and democratizing tendencies which threatened to lay hold of the Church and use it for utilitarian ends. The leaders of the Oxford Movement "sought to go back beyond the ordinances of the Reformation, and to emphasise the close relation of the present forms of worship with those of the first Christian centuries; against the invasions of the civil government they raised the notion of the Church universal and one" (*SE,* III, 225).

Although More recognized the Oxford Movement as a part of the flood of romanticism, he saw its emphasis on the religious imagination as a link with tradition and its resistance to liberalizing and democratizing tendencies as a wholesome check on the main currents of romanticism. Therefore, he could sympathize with Newman's struggle for a reasonable *via media,* and he admired his genius as a master of language in being able to convey to the reader "some derivative notion of the reality of that noetic sphere of which he himself was, apparently by birthright, a citizen. In this gift, and not in philosophic argument, where in truth Newman was not strong, resided his royal prerogative over the souls of others."[16]

But in More's view, this prerogative was apparently lost when Newman converted to Catholicism. More felt that Newman's surrender to Rome was "a pathetic mistake" that caused a promising career to lapse into obscurity. While it is true that Newman wrote his *Apologia* and *Idea of a University* and other noteworthy works after his conversion, "yet withal it is hard to avoid the conclusion that in a purely literary way something was lost to him when he severed himself from the tradition in which his imagination and feelings were so deeply rooted" (*SE,* VIII, 64), and "for all who draw their spiritual sustenance from English literature, that event was, if not the silencing, at least the muffling, of a magic voice" (65). Newman's conversion, suggests More, had its source in "a certain lack of the highest faith and of that sceptical attitude towards our human needs upon which faith must ultimately rest" (76). In other words, his courage failed him in facing the great uncertainties which faith must resolve, and he "bowed down to the Demon of the Absolute" (*CF,* 205), meaning he joined the Catholic Church, which provides all the answers from an absolute source and does not

144

require of the believer the full effort of finding truth on his own. "Say what one will, there was something in Newman's conversion of failure in duty, a betrayal of the will. In succumbing to an authority which promised to allay the anguish of his intellect, he rejected the great mission of faith, and committed what may almost be called the *gran rifiuto*. In the agony of his conversion and in his years of poignant dejection there is something of the note of modern romanticism intruding into religion" (*SE,* VIII, 77).

More points out two alternative choices that were open to Newman rather than conversion to Catholicism. One was to reject Christian mythology and external forms and rise to "that supreme insight which demands no revelation and is dependent on no authority, but is content within itself." The second was to stay with the national worship of Anglicanism "as a symbol of the religious experience of the people," breathing into it the fervor of his own faith and "waiting reverently until by natural growth his people were prepared, if ever they should be prepared, to apprehend with him the invisible truth without the forms" (74). This later choice, incidentally, is very close to the one More made for himself.

In More's scheme of historiography, therefore, Newman represents a force in contradiction to the main currents of the age. Newman was fully aware of the dualism at the bottom of human life: he recognized the illusionary nature of the material world and accepted the concept of a realm of Ideas outside of nature. He believed in the primacy of the religious imagination linked with tradition as a source of authority outside the individual experience. He may have fallen short of what More considered to be the highest and most courageous kind of faith—most of us do, as More was well aware—and he may have become rather romantic about his conversion; but in the end he remains in More's eyes an admirable representative of classical humanism during an age dominated by a romantic naturalism.

Morality and Fiction

More's notions regarding the relationship between ethics and aesthetics are clearly reflected in three essays on Victorian novelists: "The Praise of Dickens" (*SE,* V, 22-44), "George Gissing" (*SE,* V, 45-65), and "My Debt to Trollope" (*NSE,* I, 89-125). The views expressed in these essays demonstrate once again the continuity of his fundamental principles and premises, and they also expand the historical continuity of nineteenth-century thought as he interpreted it.

In the essay on Dickens, More relates that when he was living in the seclusion of Shelburne the only novels available to him were a complete set of Dickens in the village library. "One day, being hungry for emotion, I started on these volumes, and read them through—read as only a starved man can read, without pause and without reflection, with the smallest intermissions for sleep. It was an orgy of tears and laughter, almost immoral in its excess, a joy never to be forgotten" (*SE,* V, 43). Some years later when he read the novels again more slowly, weighing their effect, he found the pleasure rather meager. He concluded that the first way had been the right way to read Dickens. These incidents have implications regarding the nature of More as a critic: he had considerable sensitivity to and appreciation for literature of many kinds, but always following the appreciative response came the thoughtful examination of ideas to ferret out sources, consequences, and ramifications, and finally the measured judgment of the moral significance of the work in question. In the case of Dickens, he is unstinting in his praise of the novelist's genius, and it is obvious how much pleasure the world of Dickens afforded him; but, as we might expect, there are certain ways in which Dickens fell short of More's standards.

In terms of style, he sensed in Dickens's work a lack of restraint. He defines style as

that rare gift of words, that union of simplicity and freshness, which lends a charm to writing quite independent of the ideas or

146

images conveyed. . . . Manifestly, there must be no false emphasis, no straining for effect beyond the needs of the time and place, no appearance of uneasiness, but quiet assurance and self-subordination. The law of style may be defined as the rule of Apollo: Nothing too much; it is the art first of all of dealing frankly with the commonplace and the trivial without being common and mean. . . . nothing can take the place of the law of fitness and balance. (*SE, V*, 23-24)

Clearly, says More, Dickens lacked style in this sense. And coupled with this lack of fitness and balance in style, he perceives a lack of modesty and propriety in Dickens's character that carries over into his work: "Neither suffering nor prosperity brought him the one gift denied at his birth, intellectual *pudor,* and the absence of that restraining faculty passed, as how could it help passing, in his work" (32-33). This produces "a strain of vulgarity" that runs through his fiction.

Even with his moral bias More can appreciate "the superb irresponsibility of Dickens's world, and the divine folly of his characters" (26), and the democratic nature of his genius. He has some reservations about this last quality, however. In particular, he objects to the fact that Chesterton's critical study of Dickens[17] implies "on every page that great art is always, like that of Dickens, democratic" (26). More remarks that in all the living literature of the past the predominant note has been aristocratic rather than democratic. He acknowledges that a democratic soil is necessary: "The demand for simple uncontrolled emotions, for clear moral decisions meting out happiness to the good and misery to the evil . . . the call for immediacy of effect and the direct use of the material of life—all this is the democratic soil from which literature must spring. Without this it lacks sap and the comfort of sweet reality" (28). But, paradoxically, though this emotional root alone gives life, it cannot of itself maintain life.

The preservative of letters, what indeed makes literature, is the addition of all those qualities that, for the sake of comparison, we may call aristocratic,—the note of distinction which is concerned more with form than with substance, the reflective faculty which broods over the problems of morality, the questioning spirit which curbs spontaneity, the zest of discrimination which refines broad effects to the nuance, the power of fancy which transforms the emotion into ideas. In a word, the aristocratic element denotes self-control, discipline, suppression. (29)

According to More, discipline and suppression Dickens never acquired, and he therefore had no measure for the grace and ease that are born of voluntary self-discipline. This accounts for the absence in Dickens "of that kind of tragedy which involves the losing contest of a strong man with destiny and his triumph through spiritual discipline" (33).

A quality making for great art that More thought Dickens did possess was a sense of artistic distance. Because he could "stand with the powers above" and not be finally implicated in his theme, he was able to turn it into an abiding and satisfying expression of the zest of life. George Gissing, on the other hand, was not able to rise above the "misery" he described, and "all his marvellous understanding of the human heart and his chastened style do not quite save his art in the end" (54). Gissing wrote from his own deep experience, and although he was unable to cultivate artistic distance, his account of the world of the poor and oppressed has the one thing that More feels is commonly lacking in these pictures—the profound sense of morality. "Through all these graphic, sometimes appalling, scenes one knows that the writer is still primarily concerned with the inner effects of poverty, and his problem is the ancient, insoluable antinomy of the one and the many, the individual and the mass" (56). (It is "the inner effects of poverty" which More feels the humanitarians frequently fail to take into proportionate consideration.) The philosophy of capricious circumstance rules over Gissing's world as a whole, but when he touches on the individual, the law of morality (meaning for More free-willed responsibility) often makes itself heard. At such times the sure insight of the artist asserts itself, and he orders his people not as automatons, but as characters moved by their own volition, and, though it may be in unaccountable ways, reaping as they have sown.[18] The knot of fate and free-will is not always disentangled, there is no conventional apportioning of rewards and penalties such as Dickens indulged in at the end of his novels; but always, through all the workings of heredity and environment, he leaves the reader conscious of that last inviolable mystery of man's nature, the sense of personal responsibility. (57-58)

In More's opinion, it is "the deep-rooted convention of moral responsibility," such as he sees reflected in Gissing, that raises English literature, "despite its deficiencies of form and ideas, to be the first of modern literatures" (59). But the convention of moral responsibility is not adequate in itself. The greatest art, he clearly indicates, would combine both the free outlook or aesthetic distance of Dickens and the moral insight of Gissing. And in his view this combination is most nearly realized in the novels of Anthony Trollope.

Trollope was one of those authors to whom he responded in a special way. Like Henry Vaughan and Dr. Johnson and Newman he spoke in a language that evoked a sympathetic echo deep within More's emotional and spiritual being. More felt that he was discharging an obligation when, rather late in his career, he acknowledged "My Debt to Trollope." In this appreciative essay, he defends Trollope on two sides: on one side against those critics of More's day who, influenced by the aesthetical insurgence of the closing century, speak for the dehumanization of art and complain against Trollope's overt manipulation of the narrative and his habit of moral teaching; and on another side against critics like Henry James who charge that Trollope is without ideas of any sort.

As for Trollope's overt manipulation of his narratives, More simply states that, for his part, he is willing "that the mover of the puppets should step forth openly now and then upon the scene and tell me how he is manipulating the strings" (NSE, I, 102). He insists that the pleasure of artistic illusion is not broken by the interruption of such authorial comment, but rather is enhanced by it.[19]

Some of More's statements regarding the relationship of ethics and aesthetics quoted in this study have come from this essay on Trollope.[20] They may be summed up in the notion that, by the nature of the relationship between art and life, a writer cannot help teaching, whether he wishes to or not. Granting that Trollope is a writer who wishes to teach, how shall he proceed? More answers this question by what he calls "the canon of poetic justice." If truth to life forbids an author from being too open in distributing rewards and penalties, then he must have recourse to more indirect means.

He must by cunning suggestion carry our thoughts into those secret places of the heart where, beneath all the distractions of blind events and the defensive crust of vanity, our conscience dwells face to face with those everlasting laws. . . . Unless the poet or novelist, oftener by hint than by open declamation, can centre our judgment of his characters upon those high laws and by them ultimately move and control our emotions, he is at the last, however rich his talent and refined his method otherwise, no true artist but a mountebank of letters. (105-6)

More asserts that the theme pervading all of Trollope's fiction is the ethical. Trollope may lapse from time to time, as Thackeray does, into eighteenth-century sentimentalism, "as if morality were synonymous with a natural and undisciplined goodness of heart"; but for the most part his code is of sterner stuff: "No one of our greater novelists, unless it be George Eliot, saw more clearly than he the inexorable nexus of cause and effect in the moral order, or followed more relentlessly the wide spreading consequences of the little defalcations of will, the foolish misunderstandings of sympathy, the slight deflections from honesty, the deceptive temptations of success, the failures to make the right decision at critical moments, the ruinous corrosions of passion and egotism" (98). What Trollope held to be desirable and presented as worthy of respect "was the slow and unostentatious distinction that comes normally to strength of character and steadiness of purpose, checked by the humility of religious conviction" (119). Can we wonder why More was so fond of Trollope?

To the charge that Trollope is without ideas he answers by pointing out instances of the novelist's treatment of political and religious ideas, and, of course, the ethical ideas already mentioned; but the crux of his defense rests on what he considers "the faultless adjustment of character and circumstance" in Trollope's novels. He insists that this adjustment (Matthew Arnold, he says, would call it the "criticism of life") is precisely the method by which the novelist should display his realization of ideas. Some critics identify thought with "fussy activity of mind," says More, but for him "the right identification of thought is rather with the perception of truth, and there is no truth more important or profound or more difficult of attainment than that which concerns the adjustment of character and circumstance. The idealism of Plato means at bottom no more than this" (112).

His view of Trollope is epitomized by this remark made to a friend after reading one of Trollope's novels: "There's a man for you, and, in an unobtrusive fashion, ethics and aesthetics and a philosophy of life."[21]

Foreign Voices

More's spiritual-intellectual historiography is primarily concerned with the thought of the English people, but as noted in the case of Rousseau, he does make excursions into other countries to consider writers who have had a marked connection with the development of English thought. In his consideration of nineteenth-century literature and opinion, there are three foreign voices—one French, one German, and one Russian—that he believed are especially important, and he devoted a rather lengthy essay to each: "The Centenary of Sainte-Beuve" (*SE,* III, 54-81), "Nietzsche" (*SE,* VIII, 145-90), and "Tolstoy; or, The Ancient Feud Between Phi-

losophy and Art" (*SE,* I, 193-224). These essays warrant
consideration in this study in a special way, because in each
of them More's manifest purpose is to connect these authors
with the spiritual-intellectual continuity of the age. Sainte-
Beuve he sees as an embodiment of the religious and intellectual currents of the century; Nietzsche and Tolstoy he sees as
divergent spokesmen in that development of humanitarianism which is a major trend in his scheme of history.

Alongside of the portrait of Newman in his study hung a
portrait of the great French critic Sainte-Beuve. Stuart Sherman called More "our American Sainte-Beuve," and many
have repeated this appellation. His admiration for the
Frenchman is clear in his essay, and a number of passages
indicate similarities between the two men.[22] In rather typical
fashion he begins the essay by sketching the main characteristics of French thought from the eighteenth century to Sainte-
Beuve's time. In the wake of the French Revolution the old
humanitarian passion remained side by side, he remarks,
with a profound distrust of the popular heart; innumerable
schemes of socialism were hatched; skepticism grew; romanticism made itself felt; and science steadily developed strength.
Sainte-Beuve was more or less intimately concerned with all
these movements. And because of the varied twistings of his
interests and alignments, he more than any other single man
"summed up within himself the life of the nineteenth century" (*SE,* III, 60).

This can be seen, for example, in the area of religion. In
his earlier years Sainte-Beuve was a sincere seeker after religion, but he was held back at the last moment from joining
any particular sect "by some invincible impotence of faith."
And in this desire for religion joined with an incapacity for
faith, he was the image of the times. "What else is the
meaning of all those abortive attempts to amalgamate religion with the humanitarianism left over from the eighteenth
century, but a searching for faith where the spiritual eye had
been blinded?" (61). Sainte-Beuve, in a kind of desperation,

threw himself upon the Jansenism which contained the spirituality the other creeds missed; but "he was too much a child of the age to breathe in that thin air, and fell back on all that remained to him,—inquisitive doubt and a scientific demand for positive truth. It is the history of the century" (61-62). In such statements More shows himself capable of using but at the same time transcending Taine's historical method.

What he admired in the criticism of Sainte-Beuve was the way he pointed out excess, overemphasis, and self-indulgence in his portraits; the way he emphasized the principle of restraint; his love of the golden mean; his distrust of unchecked human nature; in short, his innate sense of proportion that brought him to see the dangerous tendencies of the day—exaggeration and egotism. More found the springs of Sainte-Beuve's critical art in "his treatment of literature as a function of social life, and his search in all things for the golden mean" (79). There we find his strength, but also his limitation, because if he fails anywhere it is with "those great and imperious souls who stand apart from the common concerns of men," the men of inspiration who stand outside the pale of ordinary social life. More uses this point to make a revealing contrast between French and English literature. French literature is preeminently social in its strength and weakness, emphasizing discipline and taste. On the other hand, the glory of English literature "lies in the very field where French is weakest, in the lonely and unsociable life of the spirit, just as the faults of English are due to its lack of discipline and uncertainty of taste" (81). Because, in these terms, Sainte-Beuve is essentially French, "indeed almost inconceivable in English," he is immensely valuable in attaining a more balanced perspective on English literature.

The main concern of "Nietzsche" (*SE*, VIII, 145-90) is the answer Nietzsche gives to the question of the relation of self-interest and sympathy. As background to this answer, More gives a rather extensive survey of the fluctuating growth of self-interest and sympathy since the seventeenth century (155-69). The main points in this survey are already considered in connection with Rousseau and the drift toward humanitarianism.[23] What he desires to illustrate is that the problem to which Nietzsche gives so absolute an answer had been clearly posed in the seventeenth and eighteenth centuries.

Nietzsche's answer to the problem, of course, is a total rejection of sympathy. In the last analysis, More points out, Nietzsche's Superman "is merely a negation of humanitarian sympathy and the socialistic state of indistinguishable equality" (182). Nietzsche's protest, in his own words, is against "sympathy with the lowly and the suffering as a *standard* for the *elevation of the soul.*" More, as we might expect, is willing to acknowledge that much of Nietzsche's protest against the excesses of humanitarianism was sound and well directed. "But the cure Nietzsche proposed for these evils was itself a part of the malady. The Superman, in other words, is a product of the same naturalism which produced the disease it would counteract; it is the last and most violent expression of the egotism, of self-interest, which Hume and all his followers balanced with sympathy as the two main springs of human action" (184). Thus, he asserts that in Nietzsche's boasted transvaluation of values—"the change from the morality of good and evil depending on supernatural rewards to the non-morality of the purely natural Will to Power" (181)—was in reality "a complete devaluation" that left him more deeply immersed in the nihilism that he exposed as the prime evil of modern civilization. "With Hume and the romantic naturalists he threw away both the reason and the intuition into any superrational law beyond the stream of desires and passions and impulses" (187-88). In other words, More's complaint against Nietzsche is that he did not see that true development in a conscious being can only come by a choice among natural impulses, which implies a controlling power above them, a power that may thus be properly called supernatural. He did not see that true character comes only with prohibition, and that without prohibition there is no will in any sense of the word, but surrender, and in the end dissipation and death. In short, Nietzsche carried naturalism to its extreme, and thereby showed its inherent fallacy.

The harsh contrast between sympathy and egotism found in Nietzsche is, in More's opinion, "an inevitable consequence of naturalism become romantic" (186). Such a union permits the coexistence of extremes, and this is a sign of its decadence. He cites as example the paradoxical closeness of Nietzsche's *Zarathustra* and Whitman's *Leaves of Grass:* "Nietzsche denounces all levelling processes and proclaims a society based frankly on differences of power; Walt Whitman, on the contrary, denies all differences and glorifies in absolute equality: yet as both start from the pure flux of naturalism, so they both pass through a denial of the distinction of good and evil based on the old ideals, and end in an egotism which brings aristocrat and democrat together in a strange and unwilling brotherhood" (187). This perception of likeness in apparently contrasting writers is typical of More and constitutes one of his primary strengths. It is the kind of insight characteristic of his criticism by means of the history of ideas.

Because a consequence of the union of naturalism and romanticism is the coexistence of extremes, he believes it is not mere chance that Tolstoy, "with his exaltation of Rousseauism and of absolute non-resistance and universal brotherhood," should be a contemporary of a philosopher like Nietzsche, "who made Napoleon his ideal and preached war and the Superman as the healthy condition of society" (186). "There is a fateful analogy between the irresponsibility of unreasoning Force and unreasoning love; and the gods of Nietzsche and of Tolstoy are but the two faces of one god" (*SE,* XI, 139-40). The essay on Tolstoy (*SE,* I, 193-224) is not concerned with his novels, but rather with his criticism, particularly with *What Is Art?* Just as More uses Nietzsche as a center of focus to trace the struggle between self-interest and sympathy, he uses Tolstoy for a discussion of the "ancient feud between philosophy and art." The feud he is concerned with is the age-old issue of the relation between beauty and truth. The major part of the essay is devoted to historical continuity, to tracing the feud from the time of Socrates to More's own day, showing how it has taken numerous forms in the conflict between imagination and reason, art and religion, fancy and insight, pleasure and virtue, and most recently, literature and science. He focuses finally on Tolstoy because he sees him as a true spokesman of certain tendencies of the age.

For a long time, religion was the battlefield for the conflict, but for the present, he says, the religious aspect of the ancient feud has been much obscured, and the most notable conflict today is between the imagination and the analytical spirit of science. But within the realm of art itself a split has developed, one side of which is still intimately connected with the religious instinct, now in a new form. Throughout the Middle Ages the dominant theme of Christianity was the anxiety for personal salvation. The humanism of the Renaissance and skepticism of the eighteenth century changed this, and at the opening of the nineteenth century many things conspired together to shift the emphasis of Christianity to the divine right of the individual and the brotherhood of man. "Deprive this belief of spirituality, and add to it a sort of moral impressionism which abjures the judgment and appeals only to the emotions, and you have the humanitarian religion of the age" (208). The division in the realm of art, therefore, is between those who emphasize humanitarianism (the early Wordsworth was the father of these) and those who emphasize art for art's sake. The career of Tolstoy, according to More, throws an instructive light on the former.

He acknowledges that Tolstoy's definition of art is very clear and consistent, the main thrust of it being that art "is not the expression of man's emotion by external signs; it is not the production of pleasing objects; and above all, it is not pleasure; but it is a means of union among men, joining them together in the same feelings, and indispensable for the life and progress toward well-being of individuals and of humanity" (Tolstoy's words). More cannot see that Tolstoy, since he distinctly denies the office of the intellect in art, has passed beyond mere impressionism, even though impressionism seemed to be one of his most hated foes. The end of art for Tolstoy, he claims, is simply to transmit feeling from man to man. "The strength of the impression conveyed is the final criterion of excellence. . . . The artist is amenable to no laws, and his work is not subject to interpretation or to criticism. . . . The whim of the individual is the supreme arbiter of taste. Sympathy, and not judgment, is the goal of culture" (211). As a revolt against the exclusiveness of art for art's sake this acceptance of humanitarianism is a real advance, More concedes, but in the final analysis he thinks Tolstoy has only substituted for the notion of art for art's sake the notion of uniting man for the mere sake of union. Here is another of those paradoxes, or coexistences of extremes, which are produced by the union of naturalism and romanticism.

The main charge that he levels against Tolstoy's brand of humanitarian religion is that it is "marred by a stain that marks it peculiarly as a falling away from the real doctrine of Christ on which he builds as a foundation" (215). This stain is the fact that while Tolstoy accepts without reservation the plain precepts of the Christian gospel and demands adherence to the strict letter of the law, he overlooks the spirit of Christ. He misses "the heart of true religion and of Christ" because he fails to understand that "the joy of the spirit is the measure of its force. . . . There is no joy in Tolstoy, and lacking joy he lacks the deepest instincts of religion" (216). As More interprets the fragmentary record of Christ's life, "it was more filled with the joy of spiritual insight than with the bitterness of earthly despair" (218). There is too much of the despair in Tolstoy. "It is because there is no note of spiritual joy in Tolstoy when he speaks from his own heart and lays aside the borrowed jargon of Christianity, it is because there is in him no charity or tenderness, but only the bleakness of disillusion, that he must be counted in the end an enemy to faith and not an upbuilder of faith" (219-20).

After using Tolstoy to demonstrate what he considers to be the present and most notable phase of the ancient feud, he says that "from the horns of this dilemma—the mockery of art for art's sake on one side, and on the other the dubious and negative virtue of the humanitarians—I find no way of escape, unless the world discovers again some positive ideal which beauty can serve" (22). Then he concludes the essay with a parable regarding the division and conflict in human nature. The parable describes a mountain with a "valley of eternal shadows" at its base and "the splendour of the pure empyrean" at its top. With this parable he means to indicate "dimly and figuratively the shadow of a solution" to the dilemma. This was an early essay (1900), however, and the solution he hints at here through the use of parable was later given more explicit expression. That solution is the positive philosophy which is always implied in the negative judgments he makes regarding any particular author or work.

Currents of Literary Criticism

Although More did not attempt in one place to give a systematic interpretation of the development of criticism as a genre during this century, there emerges from his essays on nineteenth-century critics a certain pattern that is relevant to this study of historical-philosophical continuity. Again, the absence of an essay on Coleridge is regrettable. Lamb and Hazlitt must stand alone as representatives of the Romantic Age. The other representative figures to be considered are Arnold, Pater, and Wilde.

More was fond of the writings of Lamb and Hazlitt, particularly the former; but generally speaking, he appreciated them outside of his judicial scheme. In the case of Lamb, for example, he thought it was the man Charles Lamb that made the writings precious. "Other writers—great poets and philosophers and novelists—we may admire more for their accomplishment, but none of these has so endeared himself to us personally as 'Elia,' none of them is cherished in our imagination with so sweet a savour" (*SE,* II, 87). After recreating an evening in Lamb's lodgings—the engaging talk, the play of personality—he suggests that we need the impression of such scenes on our minds in order to appreciate Lamb. "For we do not go to his Essays and Letters primarily for transcendence of intellect or creative genius, but for this spirit of illusory friendliness that runs through them all, lending to our mortal cloak of frailties and humilities a beauty that is almost a beatitude" (*SE,* IV, 178). He does not claim that intellect is lacking in Lamb, but it is "intellect turned from the deeper questions and made to play over the surface of things with a coruscating light that prevents the eye from penetrating into their depths" (*SE,* II, 93-94). Lamb's critical disquisitions, "fine and penetrating as they are in many respects," have a certain "unsubstantiality." "There is no sense of tracking the human spirit down all its wandering way of self-revelation, nor is there any effort to measure and balance the full meaning of the individual writer" (*SE,* IV, 160). (These, of course, are the principal critical endeavors More engaged in.) Lamb himself once confessed to Southey that he "never judged system-wise of things, but fastened on particulars." This tendency, says More, brought about "a misleading incompleteness" in his criticism. "No one could gather the just proportions of the Elizabethan era from his sporadic remarks, nor, to take a single case, could one gain any notion of Andrew Marvell's work as a whole from Lamb's occasional and irrational eulogies" (160). Therefore, despite his fondness for the charm of Lamb's writings, he cannot help but call attention to this "evasion of truth" that runs through all Lamb's essays, separating them from "the great tradition" (165).[24]

All of these judgments regarding Lamb ought to be weighed against More's own methods and goals as a critic—

his habit of tracking the human spirit, of striving to portray the proportions of each era, of relating the individual work to the whole, the individual writer to the age. The essay also demonstrates a fact obscured to a large extent by the effort to discern a consistent history of ideas reflected in his judgments. That fact is his breadth of appreciation, his sensitive emotional response to men and letters. His judgment is bold and uncompromising, but not narrow and intolerant. He can appreciate and love even those authors or works that fall short of his exacting standards. There is a fundamental humility in his judicial approach that his enemies failed to recognize.

In contrast to Lamb, Hazlitt, "though warped at times by prejudice, had the true critical passion . . . to get at the heart of things and strip the good from the bad" (162). This enabled him to detest a man's principles and yet love his work. Lamb, says More, could never do this. Hazlitt is similar to Lamb, however, in that he is not concerned with looking before and after, with the "linking of literary movements with the great currents of human activity." "He is not concerned with the searching out of larger cause and effect, but is intensely occupied with the individual man, and studies to deduce the peculiar style of each writer from his character and temperament" (SE, II, 73). Although More does not explicitly say so, these qualities probably, in his mind, separate Hazlitt, as they do Lamb, from "the great tradition."

According to More, the distinctive characteristic of Hazlitt's writing is passion. There is nothing quite like it elsewhere among English authors—in fact, genuine passion "is a rare, almost the rarest, trait in literature." And it is this passion which accounts both for Hazlitt's strengths and weaknesses.

It gives the tone to his critical writing; it explains the keenness and the limitations of his psychological insight; it causes the innumerable contradictions that occur in his views; it gives rapidity to his style; it imparts a peculiar zest to his very manner of quoting; it lends exhilarating interest to his pages, yet in the long run, if we read him too continuously, it wearies us a little, for not many of us are keyed up to his high pitch. We go to him for superb rhetoric, for emotions in literary experience that stir the languid blood, but we hardly look to him for judgment. (75)

Thus the virtue of his work "lies not in his analytic criticism . . . but in the fusion of passion and insight" (79-80).

These conclusions regarding Hazlitt illustrate a point which has not been given much emphasis heretofore in this study. More has often been judged as a cold and passionless personality. The error of this judgment becomes apparent to anyone who reads his letters or considers carefully the course of his life. As his treatment of Hazlitt indicates, he recognized the necessity and value of genuine passion—that it has its rightful place in life and art. In his conception of dualism, the higher will or inner check is never intended to achieve total victory over passion and vanquish it from the field of battle. He recognized that a vehicle is not propelled by its brake. Without passion there is no struggle for balance and control, and without the struggle there is no real meaning in human life.

Whereas the critical methods of Lamb and Hazlitt can be viewed as isolated products of the nineteenth century, the critical method of Matthew Arnold cannot. Indeed, More focuses on Arnold in "Criticism" (SE, VII, 213-44) in order to illustrate what he considers to be the spirit of a great tradition in criticism. The exemplars of that tradition, not complete individually—men like Cicero, Erasmus, Boileau, Shaftesbury, Sainte-Beuve, and Arnold—render literature "more consciously a criticism of life." Broadly regarded, they are "discriminators between the false and the true, the deformed and the normal, preachers of harmony and proportion and order, prophets of the religion of taste" (218). They use the past for models and standards by which they balance and weigh and measure and are ever "checking the enthusiasm of the living by the authority of the dead" (219); "they are by intellect hesitaters, but at heart very much in earnest" (218).

Because of the nature of the critical spirit, those who possess it stand with the great conservative forces of human nature, "having their fame certified by the things that endure amid all the betrayals of time and fashion" (200). But despite this, More claims, the critical spirit ultimately exerts greater influence and produces greater efficiency than does the more assertive force of the humanitarian reformers. The critical essays of Arnold, for example, will "be found in the end a broader and more lasting, as they are a saner, influence than the exaggerated aestheticism of Ruskin or the shrill prophesying of Carlyle or the scientific dogmatism of Huxley" (222).

The critical spirit is closely involved with the historical sense, which is mentioned in chapters 1 and 2.[25] This is the sense which recognizes that "the past of mankind, by the larger race-memory and particularly by that form of it which we call literature, abides as a living reality in our present" (238). In this theory of memory the critical spirit has an important office. It combines with the historical sense—indeed is probably an intrinsic part of that sense—to produce "the faculty of selection as well as of retention, the weighing of cause and effect, the constant and active assumption of the past in the present, by which the events of life are no longer regarded as isolated and fortuitous moments, but are merged into a unity of experience" (241-42). The concern for the principle of continuity in relation to judicial criticism is obvious here.

Clearly, More admired Arnold as an exemplar of the critical spirit, but he also felt that the critical spirit is something deeper than Arnold perceived, or, at least, clearly expressed. "The error of criticism in his hands, as in the hands of his predecessors, was that in the exercise of judgment it used the past too much as a dead storehouse of precepts for schoolmastering the present; it was not sufficiently aware of the relation of this faculty of judgment to the indwelling and everacting memory of things" (243). In addition to this, Arnold was lacking in another direction. Although he had considerable efficiency in the critical spirit and did not lack moral earnestness, he for the most part lacked a philosophy that could bind together his moral and aesthetic sense, "a positive principle besides the negative force of ridicule and irony; and, missing this, [he] left criticism more easily subject to a one-sided and dangerous development" (234).

These weaknesses in Arnold, though they did not seriously flaw his own criticism, had a detrimental influence on criticism that followed. More knew that the future reveals secret things, and there is no surer way to detect the weak side of a leader than by examining the career of his disciples or successors in the light of historical continuity. In this regard, Pater was one step away from Arnold in "a one-sided and dangerous development" and Oscar Wilde was the next.

In "Walter Pater" (SE, VIII, 83-115) More describes the evolution of his attitude toward Pater, which went from total admiration to repulsion to qualified admiration. His admiration was qualified, as we might expect, by his distrust of Pater's brand of hedonism, which he thought was a misguided outgrowth of Arnold's definition of criticism as the disinterested endeavor "to know the best that is known and thought in the world, irrespectively of practice, politics, and everything of the kind." He viewed Pater's hedonism as something fixed and known in the complex and illusive nineteenth century. All of Pater's work is of a piece, he says, because it is "the perfectly logical outgrowth of a single attitude towards the world" (100). That attitude is perhaps most clearly expressed in the concluding chapter of Pater's *Renaissance:* that life is but the uncertain interval before death, a brief illusion of stability in the eternal flux, and that "our one chance lies in expanding that interval, in getting as many pulsations as possible into the given time" (Pater's words). This attitude becomes a deliberate philosophy for Pater, and More responds to it in a typical way: "This exaltation of beauty above truth and emotional grace above duty, and fine perception above action, this insinuating hedonism which would so bravely embrace the joy of the moment, forgets to stay itself on any fixed principle outside of itself, and, forgetting this, it somehow misses the enduring joy of the world and empties life of true values" (114).

Pater's weakness as a critic, according to More, is that he made *a priori* judgments—he misconstrued the facts to fit a preconceived theory of hedonism. He distorted the past in his major works, and therefore in *Plato and Platonism, Marius the Epicurean,* and *The Renaissance* he misinterpreted Platonism, Christianity, and the Renaissance respectively.

In Platonism and Christianity and, to a certain extent, in the Renaissance, the beauty and joy of the flux of nature were held subordinate to an ideal above nature, the everlasting Spirit that moves and is not moved. Because Pater had lost from his soul this vision of the infinite, and sought to deify in its place the intense realization of the flux itself as the end of life, for that reason he failed to comprehend the inner meaning of these great epochs, and became instead one of the leaders of romantic aestheticism. (115)

His interpretation of Plato "falsified Plato's theory and use of facts by raising beauty, or aesthetic pleasure, above truth as the goal to be kept in sight" (112). His treatment of Christianity "placed emotional satisfaction before religious duty" (113). And his treatment of the Renaissance made "beauty and pleasure the purpose of life instead of holding them the reward or efflorescence of right living" (114).

The simple truth is that Pater was in no proper sense of the word a critic. He did not on the one hand from his own fixed point of view judge the great movements of history and the great artists in their reality; nor on the other hand did he show any dexterity in changing his own point of view and entering sympathetically into other moods than his own. To him history was only an extension of his own Ego, and he saw himself whithersoever he turned his eyes. (99)

The upshot of More's judgments here is that Pater did not have a proper understanding of the historical sense. In connection with Arnold, More had said, "The aim of culture is not to merge the present in a sterile dream of the past, but to hold the past as a living force in the present" (*SE,* VII, 237). Pater overlooked the moral charge, the call to action and duty, which the past infuses into the present.

Pater's Epicureanism is the first step away from Arnold's limitations regarding the historical sense, and the next remove in this direction is the criticism of Oscar Wilde. Wilde is concerned with the past, as More illustrates by a long passage from *The Critic as Artist,* but he seeks to lose the present in the past in order to throw off "the self-imposed and trammelling burden of moral responsibility" (Wilde's phrase). Both Pater and Wilde learned from Arnold, but they emphasized a part of Arnold's critical philosophy that was incomplete, and lacking Arnold's moral sensibility, they slighted the aspects of disciplined action and moral responsibility. And in omitting these aspects, "Pater and, to a greater extent, Oscar Wilde fell into extravagance far more deleterious to culture than was any omission or incompleteness on the part of Matthew Arnold" (237).

The Decadent Illusion

The aestheticism in the criticism of Pater and Wilde became the dominant theme in what More refers to as "the spasmodic irruption of decadent wit into English art and literature in the closing years of the nineteenth century." The focal essay in his interpretation of the 1890s is "Decadent Wit" (*SE,* X, 279-304), in which part of his purpose is to show that the decadent movement, however abruptly its peculiar manifestation may seem to have begun and ended, was not without "deep roots in the past and strong influence on the present" (279). He characterizes the dominant philosophy of the movement in this way: "Personality was to assert itself in the direction of unlimited and unquestioned expansiveness, in the claim of the individual to be purely and intensely himself, in the free pursuit of those emotions and sensations which are the root of division among mankind, while denying those rights of man, in the classical sense, which mean the subordination of the individualizing desires to the commonalty of the law of reason" (283). In this longing after the fullness of experience without consideration of the lessons of experience, More saw the heart of the decadent movement; and he saw the movement as "no vagary of a few isolated youths, but [as] the product of the most characteristic evolution of the age" (283). As Horace Gregory points out, "In both word and spirit, More had seen 'decadence' at work in a literature that started bravely enough with the Lake Poets, and declined through the course of a century to the less happy moments of Mrs. Browning, Swinburne, and William Morris."[26] But beyond the immediate native influence of Pater and Rossetti and other "virtuosos of the vibrating nerve," More traces the origins of the decadent movement to the fountainhead of German romanticism of the later decades of the eighteenth century. And he sees a more immediate foreign source in French and Russian and Scandinavian writers, specifically Dostoevsky. In Dostoevsky, he says, "Filth, disease, morbid dreams, bestiality, insanity, sodden crime, these are the natural pathway to the emancipation of the spirit; these in some mysterious way are spirituality" (300). The decadent movement was characterized by this same tendency to see physical and moral degeneration as the pathway to a redeeming spirituality. In this limited and rather quaint perception of Dostoevsky—which does not necessarily invalidate his point about the decadent movement— we can see one of More's significant limitations. As perceptive as he was in getting at the ethical core of literature, he was blind to the merits (and these merits were often moral) of most modern writers. Certain subjects and kinds of treatment repelled him enough to distract him from seeing the author's essential concerns and intentions. This limitation is treated further in chapter 7.

His evaluation of the 1890s has as its nucleus the concept

of the "decadent illusion" or, in its wider application, the "romantic illusion." As noted in chapter 2 the notion of a true and a false illusion appears at a number of points in More's writings.[27] But the distinction between the two becomes most clear in connection with the writers of the decadent movement. According to More, these writers, perhaps taking a lesson from Dostoevsky, associated art and spirituality with license and disease—this is the illusion. The decadent, unable to admit that he is simply futile or vile, poses as a martyr of the higher life. "With the composure of a saint he will tell you that physical disease is a cause of the soul's health, that nastiness of the mind itself is the price of mental expansion, that, in a word, any morbid symptom is the indication of spirituality" (292-94).

The most extensive treatment of the trend just described is found in his essay on "Arthur Symons: The Two Illusions" (*SE*, I, 122-46), where the decadent illusion is contrasted with the true illusion, which he feels is a vital part of great art. There is a true illusion "without which poetry cannot exist, without which it sinks to the level of unimaginative prose or passes into the thin aridity of metaphysics" (122). And he goes to Milton, Shakespeare, and Pope to show how this illusion works. Essentially it consists in the poet's power to lend reality to his imagined world of ideas, people, and events. But side by side with this illusion in the greater poets runs a note of disillusion: they occasionally lift the veil of illusion they are weaving and allow a view beyond. "The true illusion does not confuse the things of the spirit with the things of the world" (127). The true illusion, in other words, is when the artist creates an experience, illusory in the sense that it does not take place in the actual world of time and space, that lifts the reader's thoughts and imagination to a clearer understanding of human life. Therefore, the true illusion is followed by "a true awakening," or the awareness that the spirit's way must lead for a while through "this meadow-land of calamity, and its office is by a deliberate effort of the will to throw the glamour of light and joy and freedom on the objects by the roadside, so that the spirit may journey swiftly and pleasantly to its own upland home" (127-28).

In contrast to the true illusion is the false or decadent illusion, in which the artist casts over the physical realities of existence an illusory charm that invites the belief that the world of spirit is contained within the physical world itself. This illusion fails to satisfy the thirsting soul, and he who follows it is led deeper and deeper into the physical lust of life in pursuit of the spirit which is just not there. Such an illusion is followed by "a false awakening" in which the whole notion of spiritual values is rejected. More describes this false illusion as an inner blindness and confusion.

It is false because there enters into it no faith in the joy of things unseen, no knowledge even that such things exist; it is false because for the voice of the spirit it hears only the clamorous outcry of a man's lower personality springing from the desires of the body and the perceptions of the body, and is in the end one with what is desired and perceived. At the first this false illusion is sweet, but soon it is troubled with the bitterness of satiety; and the awakening from it leaves only the emptiness of endless regret and self-torment. (128)

After contrasting the two illusions, he proceeds with his thesis regarding Arthur Symons, which is that Symons's poetry—"the first full and sincere expression of decadence in English"—clearly displays the gradual progress of the poet's mood from the true illusion to the false illusion. Quoting generously from the poems, he attempts to trace in detail that progression, which, he says, reaches its culmination in the "false awakening" expressed in these lines:

> Who said the world is but a mood
> In the eternal thought of God?
> I know it, real though it seem,
> The phantom of a haschisch dream
> In that insomnia which is God.

168

This kind of disillusionment, More believed, must ultimately befall all those who pursue the decadent illusion. The illusion of earthly beauty is at first vivid and sweet, but as it begins to fade, there is an attempt to preserve it by heightening the colors and sharpening the emotions; but such exaggeration in order to please a jaded appetite is self-defeating and can never satisfy, but rather will leave one, ultimately, cynically disillusioned with the entire quest for beauty.

Near the end of "Decadent Wit" he puts into a few words his major complaint against the decadent movement of the 1890s. The writers of this period may fade in significance, "but other men, and this is the whole charge against decadent wit, will be forgetting that art, so long as it is human, must concern itself with the portrayal of character—triumphant or defeated, still character—just as surely as religion is concerned with the creation of character" (*SE, X,* 303-40). And he concludes with this statement by Whichcote, a seventeenth-century divine, "For we all say, that which doth not proceed from the judgment of the mind, and the choice of the will, is not an *human act,* though the act of a man."

Conclusion

In his treatment of nineteenth-century authors, the principle of philosophical-historical continuity in More's criticism is clearly revealed. On the one hand, his first principles function in every case to determine the direction of his interpretation and the nature of his conclusions. In one way or another each writer is weighed in the balance of dualism. He praises Byron for his *Don Juan,* because, beneath the sardonic laughter of its hero, there is revealed the abyss of sadness which is part of the wages of sin. He speaks respectfully of Carlyle because he has not only the sense of the phantasmagoric aspect of the world but also the conviction of the existence of the immutable element of moral law and the inexorable retribution awaiting its transgressors. He credits Tennyson with having risen here and there in the *Idylls* to a clear intuition of the conflict between the spirit and the flesh. He admires Newman as one who was keenly aware of the world of the spirit and its relation to the material world, but regrets that such a religious soul succumbed to the dogmatism or legalism of the Roman Catholic Church. In his eyes, Huxley represents science overreaching its proper sphere and threatening to explain all human experience by a rationalistic monism that denies the supernatural elements in man's nature. His favorite novelist of the period is Trollope, who he believes attained a satisfactory balance of the ethical and aesthetic in his fiction. Tolstoy and Nietzsche are, for him, examples of the strange bedfellows resulting from the blending of science and romanticism, the twin offspring of monistic naturalism. He finds the major shortcoming of the decadent movement late in the century in its false illusion, which leads men away from a true perception of the higher will and the realm of spirit transcending the realm of flesh.

In addition to this continuity of first principles, More's criticism of the literature of this age also reveals a historical continuity. Indeed, the historical forces spawned by the seventeenth century (naturalism and rationalism) and nurtured in the eighteenth are coming to full bloom in the nineteenth. From his point of view, the nineteenth century, inheriting from the preceding age a loss of faith in the religious basis of the traditional disciplines, had failed to work out the problem of finding a principle of inner urges and outward impressions. As Louis J. A. Mercier explains, More sees the men of the nineteenth century "abdicating the captaincy of their souls."

Emerson, for instance, he accuses of having closed his eyes to the complex reality of human life through the rejection of the long tradition of the existence of evil. Shelley, who had all the qualities of a great poet, has evoked but a world of fantasy, showing that he had lost contact with reality. Wordsworth wandered off into pantheistic reveries. Tennyson, who tried to make a synthesis of the ideas of his time, too often did so only through the acceptance of the compromises so characteristic of the Victorian Age. Walt Whitman with limitless unselective sympathy sang the whole welter of changing phenomena passing before his eyes, without troubling to analyze their quality or even to reject the most bizarre or eccentric urges or impressions. To William Morris, the world became a rapid succession of intangible appearances, colorful and melodious, but again too elusive for analysis, while Swinburne felt the same intangibility of phenomena so keenly that his verse seems to melt away with the dissolving seafoam and evanescent cloud. Likewise Browning's optimistic assurance that the current of life will produce of itself valuable combinations is but another fatal abdication of man's checking power over phenomena.[28]

More sees the "quarrelsome twins" of naturalism—science and romanticism—as the primary forces during the century. Their fortunes fluctuate (an uneasy peace being established about mid-century by the "Victorian compromise"), and these fluctuations determine the lines of evolution for the thought of the age. In many ways, the nineteenth century is the culmination of More's spiritual, intellectual historiography. But there are still several stages that are not completed until the first few decades of the twentieth century. These are considered later; but before they are, the next chapter, as a kind of digression, deals with More's criticism of American literature, which has a certain continuity of its own.

CHAPTER SIX

American Literature

More and the New England Tradition

Paul Elmer More's essays on American literature fit without difficulty into the continuity traced up to this point, but because they also reveal a pattern of historical development distinctively American, they warrant consideration in a separate chapter. From his point of view, the spiritual and intellectual currents that have shaped thought in America parallel rather closely those that have shaped thought in England, but there are some differences which provide America with a tradition of its own.

There is a paradoxical element in his attitude toward American literature. On the one hand, as Francis X. Duggan has noted, his interest in American literature was strong and sustained. At the beginning of his literary career in 1894 he was seriously studying Emerson and had read a good deal of Poe; in 1900 he arranged to write a biography of Franklin and hoped to write others of Washington, Hawthorne, Poe, Edwards, and Cotton Mather; and the *Shelburne Essays* are sprinkled throughout with essays on American writers. The persistence of his interest is revealed by the prominence of American names in the first volume (which is emphasized by the epigraph he quotes from Lowell—"Before we have an American literature, we must have an American criticism") and by the fact that the last volume is devoted largely to New England authors.[1] On the other hand, he tends in certain of his statements to minimize the importance of American literature. To a correspondent he wrote that he found most works on American literature distorted by the author's attempt "to make interesting . . . a subject which we must sorrowfully admit is for the greater part of trivial magnitude. Eight or ten names, none of which reaches the very first rank, do not make a literature."[2] And outside of those few, he says elsewhere, "American literature is indeed a wilderness of mediocrity."[3] He names Edwards, Emerson, Hawthorne, Poe, Whitman, and Parkman as his "choice" among American writers,[4] but in a list of authors who had appeared important to him earlier, a list including such names as Homer, Sophocles, Virgil, Sainte-Beuve, Milton, and Arnold, not a single American name appears.[5] It is the same with those few writers who spoke in a language he completely understood— Samuel Johnson, Newman, Henry More, Vaughan, and Trollope.[6] Apparently with his classical background and taste, he could not admit to American literature being truly great; but this did not diminish his persistent interest in it and appreciation of it.

Whatever his real feelings were about the greatness or value of American literature, it is certain that his interest was centered on the literature of New England. Almost without exception his essays on American literature are written about New England authors or authors who were strongly influenced by the New England tradition. American literature, he believed, began with the Puritans, reached its peak in the time of Emerson and Hawthorne, and then declined at the end of the nineteenth century. The work of Emerson's generation in New England he viewed as "the highest and most homogeneous culture this country has yet produced" (*SE,* V, 156), "a thing marvellously precious and worth cherishing,"[7] "something unique in the history of letters,"[8] "one of the very precious things in the history of the world" (*SE,* XI, 105). The trouble with his own contemporaries was that they had turned away from the New England spirit (*NSE,* I, 54-55). Duggan attributes More's preoccupation with the literature of this region to two reasons: "One of these is the strong attraction he had always felt toward New England and his Puritan ancestors. Another and more important one is that he found in the literature of New England a reflection of certain fundamental philosophical and religious attitudes of his own."[9] These reasons seem accurate, particularly the latter which is amply demonstrated by the very continuity this study is concerned with.

More's essays on American writers were written over a wide span of years and for different occasions, and doubtless he made no attempt to develop a closely linked history of American letters; however, in his concentration on the literature of New England, he clearly has outlined a consistent and fruitful American tradition. This tradition has its roots in the Puritan culture, a unique culture because of its peculiar European background modified by environment and by the necessity of carving a home out of a primitive and mysterious wilderness. "The wonder might seem to be that any literature at all ever sprang from the half-civilization that came to New England, or that any sense of art found root among a people who contemned the imagination as evil and restricted the outpouring of emotion to the needs of a fervid but barren worship" (SE, II, 175). The literature did spring up, however, and was stamped by a moral quality that he often refers to as "character." It is this character which has sustained American writing even through periods which in regard to artistic quality were quite sterile, and it is this same moral quality which accounted for the flowering of New England during the middle of the nineteenth century. But just as the brilliant flowering of American literature depended on its early New England origin, so also did its quick decay. He refers to the colonizers of New England as representing a "half-civilization" because the Puritans were the spokesmen of merely a branch of English civilization; they were divorced from the secular traditions, and therefore lacked the depth of culture needed to sustain a flourishing literature. In other words, they brought with them only one faction of the endless feud between philosophy and art considered already in connection with Tolstoy. And even today, he says, "the poverty of our art and literature" is partly due to that fact (*SE,* I, 203).

More's treatment of American literature is in no way complete. Among many authors not represented in his essays are Irving, Cooper, Lowell, Melville, Twain, Dickinson, Henry James, Howells, Robinson, and Frost. In addition to such important omissions he seldom gives fully rounded estimates of the writers he does consider. In his typical fashion, he focuses on a particular characteristic of a writer. He once praised William C. Brownell for building upon a writer's distinctive traits an appreciation of his work. "The method," says More, is "at once intellectual and psychological," for an author's distinctive trait "furnishes the key to unlock the mysteries of his art."[10] Duggan points out that this is the same method More used himself, emphasizing "Hawthorne's brooding isolation, Thoreau's aloofness and moral fiber, Emerson's optimistic faith, Longfellow's melancholy and nostalgia, Whittier's homeliness, [Henry] Adams's compound of curiosity and doubt, [Charles E.] Norton's conscience and his loss of faith: these are the traits More finds to unlock the secrets of the writings."[11] Stuart G. Brown has suggested that he did this deliberately in order to isolate those aspects of American writers which have lasting value and can be used as the basis for a fruitful American tradition.[12] Whether this is exactly true or not, there can be little doubt that, with American literature in general, one of his primary concerns was with the history of ideas.

The Spirit of Early New England

The beginnings of the New England tradition are laid out clearly in "The Spirit and Poetry of Early New England" (*SE,* XI, 3-32). This is one of those essays like "Victorian Literature" or "Decadent Wit" that synthesize major tendencies of thought and philosophy during a particular period and constitute a nucleus for other essays on individual writers. Since this is an important essay, it is useful to give a full summary of it before going on to consider its particular aspects.

The New England colonizers, says More, did not bring with them the full circumference of the diversities of the English people, and therefore their poetry should not be criticized as belonging to the main current of English literature; it is just a slender branch. This branch was further isolated from secular tradition by the very conditions of existence in New England—the struggle against a heathen wilderness. In one respect, however, the Puritans reasserted a main line of tradition in English literature which had been diverted in the Renaissance, namely character. Puritan poetry, though narrow, crude, and possessing a "nasal" quality, was not without energy and a straightforwardness of the imagination.

Women played a considerable part in creating the peculiar tone of the New World literature. Anne Bradstreet's poetry reveals the peace and self-control of the old New England family that we are likely to forget. "In a way all of New England may be said to have been snow-bound, in creed as well as in climate, but in the shelter of the hearth there was warmth for the body and there was comfort for the soul." On the other hand, Anne Hutchinson, as a spokesman against the intellectual and traditional basis of theology, "was sent into exile for teaching exactly what two centuries afterwards was to be the doctrine of Emerson's essays and Whittier's most exquisite work."

The poetry of early New England was limited both in quantity and quality, but "at least out of the limitations fixed by the origin of New England grew the peculiar attitude of the nature writers toward nature, the charm of their portrayal of the less passionate affections of the home and the family, the absence of erotic appeal, the depth and sincerity, but the perilous independence also, of their religious intuition, the invincible rightness of their character." Therefore, part of More's thesis is that some knowledge of this New

England spirit is a profitable, if not a necessary, preparation for approaching "that fine and ephemeral thing," the flowering of New England in the nineteenth century. His emphasis is on historical continuity.

The condition of seventeenth-century England—the fact that it was a time and place of violent factions—is treated in chapter 4. But after the harsh divisions of that age, England itself, according to More, returned to a kind of uneasy balance. In New England, however, it was different, because the land had been settled by only one of the national factions. "They did not bring with them the full temper of the English people or even that part of its character which has given us Chaucer and Shakespeare and Dryden and Swift and Johnson and Byron and Tennyson" (*SE*, XI, 6). Add to this the fact that conditions of existence in New England "exaggerated the seclusion of the half-civilization which the people brought over with them in their exile," and it becomes apparent why the Puritan culture of New England was unique. But it was not uniquely bad. For although the seclusion destroyed some of the secular traditions so important to the imaginative and aesthetic qualities of literature, it also produced a strong sense of conscience and tenacity of character.

And in one respect the Puritans brought no diminution to the field of art and literature, but effected rather a return to the main line of tradition from which England for a while had been partially diverted by the seductions of the Renaissance. I mean that sense of something central and formative in man, of character as distinguished from the mere portrayal of unrelated passions, which was so lamentably lacking in most of the dramatists, and which since the advent of Puritanism has been the chief honour of British letters. . . . It is highly important to remember this positive side of Puritanism when reckoning up the devastating effects of its rigid and combative morality on the imagination. (7-8)

This sense of character and of the spiritually heroic developed in early New England had a lasting influence on American literature.

Another characteristic of the early New England spirit leaving a lasting effect on American letters was the Puritan conviction of the demonic nature of the forest. The forest was associated with darkness, and the "savages" who dwelt therein were associated with the Prince of Darkness. This somewhat religious conviction was later transformed "into a kind of haunting mood of the imagination," and became the source of Hawthorne's dark psychology and no small part of that awe which Thoreau felt in the presence of the mountains and lonely forests (10).

It is obvious that in considering the spirit and poetry of early New England, he gives much more attention to the spirit than to the poetry. This may partly be because, as he says, "in truth poets in those days were something like the historian's snakes in Ireland: there weren't any." (He was writing before the discovery of Edward Taylor's poetry and perhaps would have revised his opinion if he had been aware of that poet's work.) But it is also due to his persistent tendency to see literature in a historical perspective, his passion for discovering continuity. In discussing early New England poetry, he treats the stammering Puritan muse almost tenderly, and supplies a considerable amount of appreciative response and aesthetic judgment, but his central purpose, as usual, is to search out the sources of Puritan culture and trace its influence on future thought and literature.

As a representative of the Puritan mind, Jonathan Edwards was of special interest to More because he dealt with just the kind of basic religious and philosophical questions that were always at the back of his mind: the nature of man, free will and determinism, the "religious affections," the "fruits of charity," and the problem of evil. He thought that Edwards, whom he called "an earlier and perhaps greater Emerson," had one of the clearest and most profound conceptions of dualism ever known. [13] In "Jonathan Edwards" (SE, XI, 33-65) he refers to him as "the greatest philosopher and theologian yet produced in this country," and says that he

179

could have been our greatest writer if he had not become so entangled in the exclusively logical consequences of his Puritan theology (53). The trouble is that Edwards recognized the dualism in human experience and personified the two principles as God and the devil, but then he confused the personifications with the principles they represented and studied them with terrifying boldness and logic. He is thus one of the most instructive illustrations in history of the consequences of mingling an unflinching mythology with a rigid philosophy. For once we grant the legitimacy of accepting a rigid personification of an absolute dualism, "what is there left but the tremendous picture of God dangling the poor souls of men gleefully over the mouth of an everlasting hell?"[14]

He was particularly interested in Edwards's treatise on the will, and focuses on it in his essay on Edwards. He explicates it carefully, but he makes no attempt to refute its argument; he is not opposed to Edwards's logic, but rather to his assumption that evil can be rationalized. He admits that Edwards riddled once and for all the arguments for free will commonly employed by the Arminians, but this seems to leave the human reason with only two alternatives: submission to Edward's theological determinism or to fatalistic atheisim. He viewed Edwards's theology as part of the great deistic debate which sprang from the everlasting question of the origin of evil. It was a three-cornered contest in which Calvinists, infidels, and Arminians participated. The Calvinists and infidels agreed on the matter of determinism, except that the Calvinists attributed this determinism to an omnipotent God. The deists constituted the first line of defense for the infidels because they professed belief in God and theorized on the nature of evil, but in reality viewed the world as "a perfectly working machine in which there was no room for a personal governor or for real sin" (56). The Arminians, including the bulk of orthodox churchmen, formed the third party, arguing for free will and moral responsibility. Against the common arguments for freedom of the will Edwards is victorious, but More suggests that perhaps there is a way out of the dilemma posed by that victory. That way is through "a morally satisfying form of dualism within the soul itself" (65).[15] Thus, he greatly admires Edwards's intellect, but in the final analysis considers his logical system subject to the same limitations as other "metaphysical systems."

In a similar way, he praises Edwards as a great spokesman for the religious emotions, but then characteristically qualifies that praise. Speaking of Edwards's treatises defending the Great Awakening, he says that the reader of them is often struck "by a curious, and by no means accidental, resemblance between the position of Edwards and the position of the apologists of the romantic movement in literature. There is the same directness of appeal to the emotions; the same laudation of expansiveness, at the cost, if need be, of judgment or measure or any other restraint" (48). More thought that, despite his emotionalism, Edwards lived under the control of an iron will and could not comprehend how the overstimulation of emotion in a weaker disposition would work moral havoc. Moreover, Edwards's sense of control and order were not based on a clear perception of the religious imagination. "It comes in the end to this, that, notwithstanding his verbal reservation, Edwards had no critical canon to distinguish between the order and harmony governed by a power higher than the tumultuous sway of the emotions and the order and harmony that are merely stagnation" (49).

For More, Edwards represents one side of the American character originating in the spirit of early New England; Benjamin Franklin represents the other. The lonely, introverted, God-intoxicated, almost mystical soul of Edwards is contrasted with Franklin's worldliness, shrewdness, common sense, versatility, self-reliance, wit, and antitraditionalism, Franklin being the more characteristic American intelligence. In "Benjamin Franklin" (SE, IV, 129-55) More describes Franklin's mind as "perhaps the most clarifying and renovating intellect of that keenly alert age, and to know his writings is to be familiar with half the activities of the eighteenth century" (130).[16] Then he follows this up with a lengthy discussion of Franklin's various achievements. But after enumerating those many accomplishments, he suggests that there was a certain deficiency in Franklin's character: "There was, after all, a stretch of humanity beyond Franklin's victorious good sense." We feel it chiefly in his religious convictions, and it is pressed upon us when we contrast him with Edwards:

The world in which Franklin moved lay beneath a clear, white light, without shadow of concealment, with nothing to cloud the sincerity and keenness of his vision; but far beyond, in the dim penumbra, loomed that other world of his contemporary—a region into whose treacherous obscurities those must venture who seek the comforts and sweet ecstacies of faith, and who find these at times, and at times, also, drink in only strange exhalations of deceit and vapours of spiritual pride. (149-50)

In other words, there was in Franklin none of the emotional nature and little of the spirituality that go to make the complete Christian. His strength lay in his temperance, prudence, justice, and courage—"eminently the pagan virtues." Franklin's character was not whole and complete because it did not go beyond the realm of practical, natural experience. Franklin failed to find the proper blend of reason and emotion, of the natural and the spiritual. His program for improving mankind was geared to elevate the natural man rather than the spiritual man. More thought this failing in Franklin arose from the fact that with the versatility and efficiency of his intellect he lacked the deeper qualities of the imagination: "As a writer he has all the clearness, force, and flexibility that come from attention to what is near at hand; he lacks also that depth of background which we call imagination, and which is largely the indwelling of the past in the present" (154). The standards of More's particular brand of humanism are clearly implied in this criticism. Manifestly, Franklin is being measured against that complex of religious sense, historical sense, and higher imagination that is always at the heart of More's criticism. He makes exactly the same point about Franklin's lack of background in the past in another essay and suggests how other American writers got around the difficulty: "Hawthorne by creating a mythical and purely moral past, Emerson by rising above the questions of time altogether into an atmosphere of thin spirituality, Poe by drifting out of the material and into a mere dreamland."[17]

The Flowering of New England

More treats the transition between the spirit of early New England and the flowering of American letters in the mid-nineteenth century most explicitly in "The Origins of Hawthorne and Poe" (*SE,* I, 51-70). Here he considers in some detail one particular thread of continuity linking Puritan New England with Hawthorne and Poe. That thread has to do with what Melville called "the power of blackness." He begins by distinguishing the work of Hawthorne and Poe from the work of the English writers who explored "that strange region of emotion which we name the weird." The Gothic writers such as Walpole and Radcliffe were only dilettantes, he claims, and merely dabbled in medieval superstition and gloom. But in the case of the two Americans, the preoccupation with the "weird" was not superficial; it came from the innermost core of the national consciousness. "Their work is the last efflorescence of a tradition handed down to them unbroken from the earliest Colonial days, and that tradition was the voice of a stern and indomitable moral character. The unearthly visions of Poe and Hawthorne are in no wise the result of literary whim or of unbridled individualism, but are deep-rooted in American history" (53).

He explains that in early days the superstitions of England were concerned chiefly with the fairy folk of the woods and field, "a quaint people commonly and kindly disposed, if mischievous." But with the advent of Puritanism there came a change. In the place of fairies and elves, "the imagination now evoked the terrific spectre of the Devil and attributed to his personal agency all the mishaps of life." In the New World, which was mysterious and frightening anyway, demonology was exaggerated. The people no longer beheld the pleasant vales and green hills of merry old England, which the long habitation of men had rendered almost human, but a primitive and forbidding wilderness. "There is at best something weird and uncanny about the great woods into whose depth the eye cannot penetrate and from whose interwoven shadows, especially when night has fallen and the ear has become painfully alert, come forth at intervals sounds that seem to indicate the activity of some nameless secret within the darkness" (56). The New England farmer coming home in the evening along the border of the gloomy forest experienced this sense, and it was no pleasant *Waldeinsamkeit* such as romantic poets indulge in; it was awe and ghostly terror. And this feeling was exaggerated by the actual savages who inhabited the woods.

Thus the element of dark pensiveness and gloom was a religious sentiment in early New England. More traces it through Wigglesworth's "Day of Doom," and Edwards's "Sinners in the Hands of an Angry God" through the writings of Freneau, Charles Brockden Brown, Irving, and Bryant, showing how the old supernaturalism of religion was gradually transformed to the shadowy symbolism of literature as exemplified in Hawthorne and Poe. He considers this an important tradition in American literature, reaching its peak with Poe and Hawthorne.

Necessarily this age-long contemplation of things unearthly, this divorcing of the imagination from the fair and blithe harmonies of life to fasten upon the sombre effects of guilt and reprobation, this constant meditation on earth and decay—necessarily all these exerted a powerful influence on literature when the renaissance[18] appeared in New England and as a sort of reflection in the rest of the country. So, I think, it happened that out of that famous group of men who really created American literature the only two to attain perfection of form in the higher field of the imagination were writers whose minds were absorbed by the weirder phenomena of life. (69)

In "A Note on Poe's Method" (*NSE,* I, 77-87), he defines one of the distinguishing marks of Poe's work as his rigorous intellectual analysis. Poe not only practiced logical concentration, but raised it to a principle of art. More feels that "The Philosophy of Composition" is essentially an accurate explanation of how "The Raven" was written. "The point is that this *conscious* logical analysis was present with him throughout the whole work of composition to an abnormal degree, now preceding, now accompanying, now following the more inscrutable suggestions of the creative faculty" (83). This rationalistic analysis was Poe's original note.

Another distinctive aspect of Poe's work, in More's opinion, is that as beautiful as much of it is, it leaves untouched the richest source of human feeling. This resulted from Poe's too rigorous exclusion of what he calls "the heresy of The Didactic." He put truth and beauty in opposition and dealt with beauty to the exclusion of truth. "It is natural, but it is none the less unfortunate, that such a man should have developed an aesthetic theory which rejected from the province of poetry any claim of truth beyond that of fidelity to a chosen sensation, and which emphasized so strongly the element of melancholy inherent in the perception of physical beauty" (86). Because of the incompleteness of Poe's perspective, More would not compare him with "those normal poets who deal with the larger and more universal aspects of nature and create loveliness out of the more wholesome emotions of our common humanity." Because of his limitations, Poe's was a narrow achievement; "Yet it is to the honour of Poe that in all his works you will come upon no single spot where the abnormal sinks to the unclean, or where there is an effort to intensify the effect of what is morbid emotionally by an appeal to what is morbid morally. The soul of the man was never tainted" (86). Poe, in other words, avoided the false or decadent illusion. The same cannot be said, More points out, for his continental disciples. Poe differs from the French symbolist poets who later admired him because he exercised the kind of restraint which indicates that regardless of how delicate his psychological balance was, he possessed an active inner check at least in aesthetics.

More's opinions on Hawthorne run through several essays. In "The Solitude of Nathaniel Hawthorne" (*SE,* I, 22-50), he indicates that isolation (which More generally calls "solitude") is the one dominant motive running through all of Hawthorne's tales, and it is so persistent in its repetition that "to one who reads Hawthorne carefully his works seem to fall together like the movements of a great symphony built upon one imposing theme." More shows this theme in Hawthorne's first novel, *Fanshawe,* his last fragment, *The Dolliver Romance,* and in the work coming between these, giving special attention to *The Scarlet Letter* and *The House of the Seven Gables.* He then points out some interesting relationships between Hawthorne and his works, particularly in regard to the concept of isolation, and concludes with comments on the universality of this concept. "Other authors may be greater in so far as they touch our passions more profoundly, but to the solitude of Nathaniel Hawthorne we owe the most perfect utterance of a feeling that must seem to us now as old and as deep as life itself."

In "Hawthorne: Looking Before and After" (*SE,* II, 173-87), he claims, in accord with his concern with historical continuity, that Hawthorne lived during the only period in the history of this country which could have fostered worthily his peculiar genius; "he came just when the moral ideas of New England were passing from the conscience to the imagination and just before the slow, withering process of decay set in." More uses three quotations from Cotton Mather that display the temper of the Puritan conscience, and then shows how the ideas in these quotations appear in "Ethan Brand" as ideas that are no longer matters of conscience, but converted by the imagination into art. Mather represents the seeds of the flowering of New England, Hawthorne the blossom, and Mary Wilkins Freeman the withering of the blossom. "The Tragedy of New England came," he says, "when Hawthorne wrought the self-denial of the ancient religion into a symbol of man's universal isolation, when out of the deliberate contemning of common affections he created the search for the Unpardonable Sin. In the pages of Mrs. Freeman we hear only an echo, we revive a fading memory, of that sombre tragedy" (184-85).

He viewed Hawthorne as a fine artist and a serious moralist; indeed, he seems to see the genius of Hawthorne in his peculiar blending of moral with aesthetic judgment at its best, and he found no taint of morbidness or unwholesomeness in him. "If there is to be found in his tales a fair share of disagreeable themes, yet he never confounds things of good and evil report, nor things fair and foul; the moral sense is intact. Above all there is no undue appeal to the sensations or emotions" (*SE,* I, 43). He considers Hawthorne by right of inheritance a Puritan; all the intensity of the Puritan temperament remained in him, and all the overwhelming sense of the heinousness of human depravity. But these, cut off from the old faith, took on a form of their own. Religious dogma, in short, became the symbolism of art, and the change, More thought, was for the better. Thus, though the impression received from Hawthorne's fiction does not approach the terror of Edwards's "Sinners in the Hands of an Angry God," Hawthorne is finally the more appealing writer, for he gives us allegorically an everlasting truth, one known alike by Christian, Greek, and Hindu: we are born alone and die alone, and alone reap the fruits of our actions, all earthly ties being meaningless and transient. Thus we may "count it among the honour of our literature that it was left for a denizen of this far Western land, living in the midst of a late-born and confused civilisation, to give artistic form to a thought that, in fluctuating form has troubled the minds of philosophers from the beginning" (49-50). Hawthorne is "the one artist who worked in materials thoroughly American and who is worthy to take a place among the great craftsmen of the world" (*SE*, II, 173).

The terms "dualism" and "inner check," which are so frequently implied in More's essays, come explicitly into play in his essay on Longfellow. Longfellow has been greatly loved by the public, but critics have spoken of him with reservation and sometimes even contempt. In More's opinion, the critics are mainly right. One of the weaknesses in Longfellow, he explains, is that he uses images and sentiments that have been used more effectively and beautifully by greater poets. This gives his poetry an aura of the commonplace. But the real weakness in Longfellow does not arise from plagiarism or lack of originality, but rather from the fact that his imagination moved on a lower plane.

This distinction between the higher and lower planes of the imagination goes so near to the very roots of taste and criticism, it is a matter so elusive withal, that I would run the risk of an insistence which may seem like the proverbial breaking of a butterfly upon a wheel. The question turns upon that dualism, or duplicity, in human nature, often misunderstood and to-day more often ignored, the perception of which does yet in some way mark the degree of a poet's or a philosopher's initiation into the mysteries of experience. (*SE*, VI, 135-36)

The greater or lesser depth or consciousness of the dualism of human nature on the part of the artist therefore determines the plane of imagination on which he moves. Longfellow lacked the deep sense of that dualism felt and expressed by great poets.

Closely connected with Longfellow's inadequate comprehension of dualism was his lack of restraint. "One feels this lack of the inward check in much of Longfellow; the lines flow from him too smoothly and fluently; they have not been held back long enough to be steeped in the deeper and more obstinate emotions of the breast" (145). When the proper resistance came to him, it was commonly produced by difficulties of form rather than by his own artistic inhibition. "Thus of all his poems, the dramas in blank verse are about the flattest, and in general his power increases with the intricacy of the rhymes imposed" (145). The sonnets, especially those associated with Dante, More believed constitute Longfellow's greatest poetry.

Whittier, whom More read "with ever fresh delight" and praised as the warm poet of hearth and home, also suffers from a lack of resistance, a faulty inner check. He did not receive the proper criticism that would have instructed him in how to check his moral and political fervor; indeed, one of the dominant influences on him, the Quaker's inner light or transcendentalism, seemed only to confirm him in his habit of "uncritical prolixity." The other dominant influence, abolitionism, gave his poems the sound of cant. He could never subordinate his moralism to his craft. The great English romantics were at times formless and unrestrained but were redeemed by the magnitude of their achievement. Whittier has no such apology; lacking refinement and taste, he is merely commonplace. Nevertheless, he has a unique importance in the New England tradition, for "more completely than any other poet he developed the peculiarly English *ideal of the home* . . . and added to it those *homely comforts of the spirit*. . . . With Longfellow he was destined to throw the glamour of the imagination over 'our common world of joy and woe' " (*SE*, III, 36). The home may be a lowly theme for poetry, says More, but it is a spurious culture whose appreciation of Milton and Shelley dulls the ear to paler beauty, and Whittier is in fact often a relief from the more pretentious accomplishments of the masters. At his best, he is "a genius of pure and quiet charm" (48).

Although More's defense of Whittier and Longfellow is partly the result of his preference for inner serenity and unvexed faith and for morality over technical virtuosity, his preference rests ultimately on dualist standards, as do his reservations about them as well. Thus, Whittier's devotion to the home, like his religious fervor, is an outward manifestation of his desire for a release from the flux.

Like Longfellow and Whittier, Whitman, whom More admired as one of the "most original and characteristic" of American poets, suffers from a lack of self-restraint. His revolt from convention was too complete. As we might expect, Whitman's sensual detail was unattractive to More, but he objected to it on the grounds of taste rather than moral principle. Whitman's inner check failed to keep such detail within the bounds of good taste. Despite this objection, it is very clear that he perceived the quality of greatness again and again in Whitman. He believed this poet occasionally possessed a verbal felicity that Emerson had not attained. And he even found something richer in him than the sustained urbanity of Emerson offered. But of course he did not find his lawless brotherhood appealing. He was just not attracted to a gregariousness that practically surrendered all standards for the sake of an affectionate and undiscriminating embrace. But while Whitman's undisciplined democracy left him cold, he could still appreciate the poet's vitality. He was responsive to the sudden vistas of beauty that frequently open up in Whitman's verse, and he did not miss the sudden flashes of genuine understanding. In regard to form, he thought that when Whitman breaks from the poetic convention of exact rhythm, he cuts himself off from a desirable kind of restraint which grows out of the demands of human nature.

It was inevitable that More should find an affinity for the writings of Emerson and Thoreau. Both were concerned with conduct, both were New Englanders, both were concerned with the worth of the individual, and both were alive to the realm of spirit transcending the physical world. Of the two, his personal preference appears to go to Thoreau. Not that he valued Thoreau's writings more than Emerson's; it seems that his own personal experience caused him to be more deeply moved by Thoreau. Stuart G. Brown sees two qualities in Thoreau which appealed particularly to him: "a healthy individualism, a manly strength and willingness to grapple with the elements of experience and make something of them; and a kind of humility which recognized a transcendent and other-worldly power behind the screen of natural phenomena."[19] More fits Thoreau into the New England tradition in this way:

Much of this contemplative spirit of Thoreau is due to the soul of the man himself, to that personal force which no analysis of character can explain. But, besides this, it has always seemed to me that, more than in any other descriptive writer of the land, his mind is the natural outgrowth, and his essays the natural expression, of a feeling deep-rooted in the historical beginnings of New England; and this foundation in the past gives a strength and convincing force to his words that lesser writers utterly lack. (SE, I, 13)

This passage is characteristic of More in several ways. First it illustrates his concern with the historical evolution of ideas, values, and tendencies. Second, it suggests that a writer's work is enhanced by his being part of a tradition, by his having "a foundation in the past," and thus reflects More's notion of the historical sense. And finally, the reference to the mystery of individual genius—"the soul of the man himself," "that personal force which no analysis of character can explain"—reflects one of the basic premises of More's humanism: the inexplicable uniqueness of the individual human soul and its potential for achievement through free-willed responsibility. As demonstrated again and again, these are the elements that give his criticism direction and unity and cohesion, a wholeness greater than any of its parts.

In his essay on "Thoreau's Journal" (SE, VI, 106-21), More is primarily interested in attacking German romanticism and in showing Thoreau's divergence from it. He uses the case of Thoreau to show wherein the transcendentalism of

Concord was an echo of the German school, and wherein it differed. Naturally, More is unsympathetic toward German romanticism; it ran contrary to some of his most fundamental philosophical principles. It was too much simply a flux, sweeping along unrestrained. Predictably, he concludes that Thoreau differs from the German romantic school mainly because he possesses "character." "It comes at the last chiefly to this: the freedom of the romantic school was to the end that the whole emotional nature might develop; in Thoreau it was for the practice of a higher self-restraint. The romantics sought for the common bond of human nature in the *Gemüth;* Thoreau believed it lay in character" (127). He traces the sources of Thoreau's attitudes, and in the light of the course of spiritual history in this and preceding chapters, it is no surprise to find him listing prominently among those sources the inheritance of Puritan religion and "the spirit of fine expectancy derived from the poets of the seventeenth century, who were Thoreau's chief mental nourishment" (127).

Another characteristic of Thoreau that More finds congenial is his opposition to humanitarian movements. In "A Hermit's Notes on Thoreau" (*SE,* I, 1-21), he says: "Philanthropy and humanitarian sympathies were to him a desolation and a woe. . . . Similarly his reliance on the human will was too sturdy to be much perturbed by the inequalities and sufferings of mankind, and his faith in the individual was too unshaken to be led into humanitarian interest in the masses" (15-16). More is sympathetic with Thoreau's broader outlook on human experience that caused him to be uninterested in revolutions and reforms of the moment. He quotes with approval Thoreau's statement, "God does not sympathize with the popular movements."

This distaste for humanitarianism crops up in several of the essays on American literature. He regrets, for example, that Freneau and Whittier were so involved in causes and popular movements. In his discussion of *The House of the Seven Gables* he describes Holgrave as "the type of a whole race of men who were to take revenge on the despotism of the spirit by casting it out altogether for the idealized demands of the hunger of humanity" (*SE,* II, 185-86). This statement, by the way, indicates the main reason why he was antagonistic toward humanitarianism: he saw it as a form of naturalism or the rejection of the spiritual elements in man, along with disproportionate reliance on merely outward or institutional reform.

Regarding Emerson, More's attitude is rather ambivalent. It is the kind of ambivalence already noted in his essays on other major writers: he has great admiration for their artistic achievement and genius, but because of his concern with human values and the way they are shaped by historical tendency, he expresses reservations about the implications and possible consequences of these writers' philosophical premises. In the case of Emerson, he was attracted by certain deep and abiding insights deriving from Plato. And as Lynn H. Hough puts it, "his heart beat a little faster whenever he thought of the sage of Concord."[20] But he also recognized that Emerson sowed many seeds from which rather unwholesome weeds grew. He was never an uncritical Emersonian. In fact, his purpose in writing "The Influence of Emerson" (*SE,* I, 71-84) was to show that Emerson has occasionally been valued and copied and admired for the wrong things, and, like Poe and Whitman, he was unfortunate in his disciples. More considers him to be the New England conscience deprived of its belief in a concrete and personal God and relying on the gleams and suggestions of eternal beauty and holiness. There is something inspiring about this, but it is not without danger. This kind of reliance tends to produce in Emerson a certain indifference to moral and personal responsibility, and his philosophy based on it lends itself to being misunderstood and perverted. For example, More thought much of Christian Science was "a diluted and stale" product of Emersonianism. He thought that Emerson's optimistic philosophy, when expressed with the noble accent and from the deep insight of an

Emerson, was a radiant possession; but it is folly and inner deception when repeated parrot-like by people with no mental training and no depth of spiritual experience. He ends the essay with the phrase *Corruptio optimi pessima* (the corruption of the best is the worst) to describe what Emersonianism runs to when divested of the common sense and strong character that were the ballast to the master's shining optimism.

More noticed very early a "double consciousness" in Emerson,[21] but he came to see his transcendental philosophy as "a kind of vanishing dualism." His dualism was only apparent, because upon close scrutiny it becomes resolved in the transcendental unity. More distrusted this kind of synthesis or reconciliation of the One and the Many. He thought that religion and philosophy rest not only on a statement of the dualism of good and evil, the One and the Many, knowledge and ignorance, etcetera, but on a realization of the full meaning and gravity, practical and intellectual, of this dualism.

Now Emerson certainly recognizes the double nature of experience, but it is a fair question whether he realizes its full meaning and fateful seriousness. He accepts it a trifle too jauntily; is sometimes too ready to wave aside its consequences, as if a statement of the fact were an escape from its terrible perplexities. To be reconciled so cheerfully to this dark dilemma is not a reconciliation of the dilemma itself, but argues rather some deep-lying limitation of spiritual experience. (*SE,* XI, 89)

More's attitude toward the quality of Emerson's dualistic vision is encapsulated in this comparison of the Concord sage with Socrates, who is More's ideal dualist: "Emerson, like Socrates, had found no difficulty in combining scepticism with an intuition of pure spirituality, though, unlike Socrates, to maintain his inner vision intact he shut his eyes resolutely on the darker aspects of nature" (135).

As with Thoreau, More finds character to be the dominant note of Emerson's work, and this character grows out of the

Puritan heritage. The formative element of his ancestral inheritance combines in Emerson with romanticism to produce Emersonianism, which More defines as "romanticism rooted in Puritan divinity" (83). German romanticism found fertile ground in America but there remains this vital distinction: "the spontaneity and individualism of the romantic movement on the Continent went with a dissolution of character against which the Puritan mind, so long as it held true to its origin, was impregnably fortified" (83). Romantic spontaneity might work on Emerson to cause him to repudiate theological dogma and deny a personal Jehovah, but with all the divinity of Massachusetts in his veins, he could never be moved to confuse spiritual aspiration with the sicklier lusts of the flesh; and despite some centrifugal wandering, he never overstepped the bounds of character.

More points out that Emerson's work fluctuates between romantic expansiveness and character. When it grows out of his confidence in individual inspiration, "it tends to looseness and formless spontaneity of style. When, on the contrary, he turns to the note of character, his language becomes instantly terse and restrained, and falls naturally into symmetrical form" (85). More praises the kind of self-restraint he sees in a poem like "Days," centering on a free-willed choice between the low and the high. He says that if such restraint had come oftener and had been under Emerson's control, he would have been "one of the very great poets of the world." But beside these poems displaying "masterly form and restraint" are others, "and these the more numerous, in which he surrenders himself to the shifting breath of inspiration like a rudderless boat, to such a degree, indeed, that over much of his work his own word 'whim' might be set as a superscription" (86-87).[22]

More saw "Charles Eliot Norton" (*SE*, XI, 95-114) as a kind of counterbalance to Emerson. Norton stood for the traditional New England conscience and sense of evil that he thought Emerson slighted. He was a cultured man "to whom the lessons of the past had become a personal experience;" to the multiform flowering of the time he brought a note of sound cosmopolitanism. He also acted as a restraining influence. To the community at large, he functioned "undeniably as critic and check," and this was often resented. "Yet is not character always in some way negative?" asks More. "Is it not of the very essence to act as a check upon the impulsive temperament, and even upon the ranging enthusiasms of the soul?" (111). Norton's negation was a useful contribution, for "especially in the hour of expansive liberty that came to New England when it had broken from the bondage of religion, it was desirable that the principle of restraint, broadened indeed by contact with the world, but not weakened or clouded, should have its voice and embodiment" (111-12).

More calls Emerson "the most outstanding figure of American letters." But his preeminence is not due only to his personal endowment of genius, but also to the fact that, "as the most complete exponent of a transient experiment in civilization, he stands for something that the world is not likely to let die" (69). In other words, he is one of the most outstanding figures of a group that produced that mid-nineteenth-century high point of our literary culture. Of Emerson's generation he says,

When we consider the work of that generation it seems as if we saw the energy of a strong people, nourished through long discipline and austere abstentions, now suddenly freed from repression and displaying itself in manifold, and all too brief, expansion. Each man had his particular share in that activity: to one it was the exercise of wit, to another the sentiment of home and hearth, to another the comfort of religion, to another the re-creation of aboriginal life, to another the critical judgment, to another the symbolism of a brooding imagination, to another the freedom of nature, to another the justification of the untrammelled spirit. (109-10).

After the fullness and quality of this renaissance came a decline.

The Dispossessed Conscience

More's essays "Charles Eliot Norton" (*SE,* XI, 95-114) and "Henry Adams" (*SE,* XI, 114-40) are so closely connected in their central ideas as to constitute almost a single essay on the final decay of New England conscience and faith. Norton and Adams are both descended from the New England settlers who left their homes in the Old World in order to find religious and political liberty and who in pursuit of that aim had gradually overthrown the tradition and authority of their ancestors. But the liberty of denying may become a habit, says More, and the history of New England is the history of a growing denial of the Puritan affirmations. Throughout the development of New England thought there had been the gradual elimination of the content of faith—a passage from Calvinism to Unitarianism to free thinking—until there was nothing left but a great denial. Yet, throughout this development the full moral impulse of the Puritan conscience remained; and this is the key for interpreting the generation of Henry Adams: that generation represents the Puritan conscience dispossessed, in a void, seeking a new place of rest.

The essay on Adams is devoted primarily to *The Education of Henry Adams.* More says that "Adams' scholarship, his imagination, his verbal dexterity, his candour, his cynical vivacity, his range of reflection," must give him a high place in the American literature of his time. But the tragedy of Adams's education is that of a man "who could not rest easy in negation, yet could find no positive faith to take its place" (140). In trying to understand Adams, one must remember that with his intellectual negation there remained almost in full force the moral impulse of the New England tradition. To see into the inner life of Henry Adams, one must, if possible, get "into the state of a man whose conscience was moving, so to speak, *in vacuo,* like a dispossessed ghost seeking a substantial habitation" (124). And in this Adams is

197

representative of his age. Because Adams is unable to find a substantial habitation for his conscience, he ends his career in "sentimental nihilism" (140).

One of the main ideas in "Charles Eliot Norton" is that this man, even with his sturdy conscience and common sense, was not consistent. While he little regretted the passing of the old religious belief, since he thought that agnosticism would force upon man a new sense of responsibility, he was alarmed to find America entering a new barbarian age. Here is the inconsistency. Welcoming a creed that destroys the very principle of authority, he still bemoans the irresponsibility of a world that acts in accordance with that creed. "It is the inconsistency of a conscience that has outlived faith and not found philosophy, the will of New England working out in its own peculiar manner the problem of the nineteenth century" (126-27).

Another outgrowth of conscience that has outlived faith, according to More, was the surge of humanitarianism coming around the turn of the century. As previously noted, he considered humanitarianism to be at the heart of much modern religion, and also that, from his point of view, humanitarianism was primarily materialistic. He suggests that with the loss of the content of faith during the nineteenth century, "the hunger of humanity begins to assert itself unhampered by any vision beyond its own importunate needs," and he wonders if the new ideal of humanitarianism will create "in turn another half-civilization, blindly materialistic as its predecessor [the half-civilization of early New England] was harshly spiritual" (*SE*, II, 187).

Another movement or philosophy of late nineteenth- and early twentieth-century America that More concerned himself with was pragmatism. He pointed to pragmatism as a culmination of the philosophizing of the nineteenth century. Its general tendency is plain: "it is at once romantic and scientific, an adventurous revolt against the dogmatic intellectualism in which science has involved itself and at the same time thoroughly evolutionary, even Darwinian, in theory" (*SE*, VII, 252). While greatly admiring William James, he considers his attempt to escape from skepticism by accepting for truth what persists longest in the experiences of life as the most dangerous of sophisms; for to do so is to accept the flux of passing experience within us as the totality of consciousness. He agreed heartily with James's refutation of rationalistic monism, but saw the alternative which he presents as rationalistic also. More defines pragmatism as a philosophy which tries "to defend rationally a system which is professedly an attack on rationalism" (197). It is simply the metaphysic of the Many as opposed to the metaphysic of the One, or idealism. According to More, James was an ardent foe of all forms of absolutism or monism, but he went to an equally undesirable extreme of absolutism of the Many, or pluralism. Therefore he failed "to bring spiritual relief from the prison house of metaphysics" (*HP*, 158n). "What, at bottom, is the Pluralism of Mr. James, but the same ancient presumption of the reason which he has himself so shrewdly denounced. His feeling for flux and change and multiplicity as an undeniable part of our conscious experience is a reality, a great and desirable reality, set over against the monist's exclusive sense of unity," but it is not the whole of reality. In other words, James has refuted one theory which attempts to account for things in terms of one side of the dualism in human consciousness, but in so doing, he has relied too much on the other side of that dualism. Therefore, More cannot accept James's Pluralism as a true substitute for dualism—it is simply the rejection of the One for the Many.

Thus, pragmatism, in More's view, was a movement in the direction of disintegration. As it was not science, so it was not religion. And when the last balance is made up, he suspected that James would be found among "the disintegrating and deteriorating forces of the age" (*SE*, XI, 159). More's own position consisted in a rejection of both James's pragmatism and F. H. Bradley's idealism.

Forces beat upon us from every side and are as really existent to us as ourselves: their influence upon ourselves we know, but their own secret name and nature we have not yet heard—not from Mr. James, or Mr. Bradley, or another. Until that prophet has appeared, I do not see what better thing we can do than to hold our judgment in a state of complete skepticism, or suspension, in regard to the correspondence of our inner experience with the world at large, neither affirming nor denying; while we accept honestly the dualism of consciousness as the irrational fact. (*SE,* VII, 211)

This skepticism combined with his religious faith make up More's distinctive style of humanism.

The historical pattern of More's criticism of American literature can now be summarized. According to his scheme, American literature had its beginnings in the cultural privations and religious excesses of Puritan society. These led the Puritans to a morbid sense of isolation and sin and to a rigorous emphasis on character, and these products of the early New England spirit constitute the native springs of the literature which came after. Yet this heredity of Puritan ideas is partly balanced by the American environment, notably in the role of the forest (and its "savage" denizens) as reinforcing Puritan notions of inscrutable evil. The course of American letters is a history of the fortunes of these products in their various permutations. Here they are emphasized and there neglected by various writers, until they gradually decline in the late nineteenth century, mingle with foreign influences, and almost totally disappear in the twentieth century. The spirit of early New England comes to find contrasting expression in Edwards and Franklin, and then passes through a transitional stage in the late eighteenth century when it appears in modified form in Freneau and Charles Brockden Brown and later in Irving and Bryant. The isolation and gloom become apparent in Hawthorne and Poe, the sense of sin in Hawthorne, and the morality and character with varying emphasis in Hawthorne, Emerson, Thoreau, Longfellow, and Whittier. Later, Hawthorne's kind of morality withers in its seclusion and dies, as evidenced in the stricken souls of Mary Wilkins Freeman's characters. Emerson's strong inheritance of character becomes overshadowed by his expansiveness and optimism and his influence descends to Mary Baker Eddy on one side and to Whitman and William James on the other, and to the broad humanitarianism of the late nineteenth and early twentieth centuries. The homely tradition of Longfellow and Whittier finds its last expression in such a little known figure as Donald G. Mitchell. Charles Eliot Norton inherits the high sense of character, his common sense and concern with evil are a healthy contrast to Emerson, but his sturdy conscience is without the anchor of a substantial faith. And in Henry Adams the New England conscience comes to its final decline in sentimental nihilism. By the time Poe's amoral virtuosity has come down to the twentieth century by way of French symbolism, this influence, along with the two other major importations of French naturalism and evolutionary science, come to dominate the early part of the twentieth century.

CHAPTER SEVEN

The Twentieth Century

More and the Modern Spirit

In an article written in 1920, Stuart Sherman compliments More on the abundance of fine portraits he has given us of writers who are dead, but complains that he has neglected his contemporaries. Such neglect, Sherman thought, was a retrogression from the purpose indicated by Lowell's epigraph to the first volume of the *Shelburne Essays*—"Before we have an American literature, we must have an American criticism." More, says Sherman, "has done too little to meet his poor living fellow-countrymen half way; and give and receive the recognitions which are among the functions and the rewards of letters."[1] This comment, coming when it did, is an accurate one. There are really no essays among the eleven volumes of *Shelburne Essays* which give critical attention to the literature of the twentieth century. A possible exception is the essay on Yeats in volume I, but even here it is the early Yeats that More is considering and not the later poems which mark Yeats as a modernist. Sherman's comment would have to be qualified, however, in the light of the *New Shelburne Essays,* a series of three volumes begun in 1928. In the late 1920s, when he was in his sixties, More did turn his attention to his living fellow countrymen—indeed, to the conditions of contemporary literature in general. His essays in this area are not numerous, but he has expressed himself amply enough that we can be quite clear about his attitudes regarding the major tendencies of modern literature.

Generally speaking, those attitudes are negative. He seems to write on contemporary literature only to denounce it. And when his critical principles and his system of values are considered, it should not be surprising that he found so little to interest him in contemporary literature. The dominant tendencies of the modern spirit—naturalism, determinism, rejection of tradition, search for pure art, etcetera—were just those tendencies that he repeatedly derogates as he traces their evolution since the Renaissance. In his essay "The Idea of the Modern," Irving Howe has attempted to define the distinguishing characteristics of literary modernism. He presents nine formal and literary attributes of modernism.

1. Avant-garde as a special caste has arisen.
2. The problem of belief has become exacerbated, sometimes to the point of dismissal.
3. A central direction in modernist literature is toward the self-sufficiency of the work.
4. The idea of esthetic order is abandoned or radically modified.
5. Nature ceases to be a central subject and setting of literature.
6. Perversity—which is to say: surprise, excitement, shock, terror, affront—becomes a dominant motif.
7. Primitivism becomes a major terminus of modernist writing.
8. In the novel there appears a whole new sense of character, structure, and the role of the protagonist or hero.
9. Nihilism becomes the central preoccupation, the inner demon, at the heart of modern literature.

Of these attributes there is probably not one with which More would have been in total sympathy; most of them he would have found fundamentally destructive of true literary art. For example, Howe points out that for the modern writer, "the usual morality seems counterfeit; taste, a genteel indulgence; tradition, a wearisome fetter." It becomes a condition of being a writer to rebel, and a modernist culture soon learns to respect, even to cherish, signs of its division. It sees doubt as a form of health. It hunts for ethical norms through underground journeys, experiments with sensation, and a mocking suspension of accredited values. Upon the passport of the Wisdom of the Ages, it stamps in bold red letters: *Not Transferable*. It cultivates, in Thomas Mann's phrase, "a sympathy for the abyss." It strips man of his systems of belief and his ideal claims, and then proposes the one uniquely modern style of salvation: a salvation by, of, and for the self.[2]

More viewed doubt (i.e., a true skepticism) as a form of health, but he would never have condoned searching for ethical norms "through underground journeys" or "experiments in sensation," and would have been appalled at the notion that the "Wisdom of the Ages" is "not transferable." Furthermore, salvation "by, of, and for the self" he would criticize as an illusion of romantic egotism. It finally comes down to the fact that he was simply not temperamentally suited to tolerate, let alone appreciate, modern literature as "modern" is used in Howe's sense.[3]

In his long career in literary criticism, More never accepted as his province the responsibility for criticizing the creative artists of his own day. When, late in the 1920s, he published some essays on his contemporaries, he did it at the instigation of others or out of a sense of obligation to assert his values in the face of the challenge presented to them by modern tendencies. He apparently felt that society and literature were better served by a critic who sought to preserve the best of the past and to vitalize it in the present by persuasion, example, and imaginative appeal. In reply to an inquiry made by one of his favorite students, he wrote:

As for your question why I had deserted authors of our own day for those of yesterday,—I haven't. I never set out to write serious criticism of contemporary literature. I have of course reviewed hundreds of new books, but only as a journalist. I have pretty thoroughly confined my essays to writers who were worthy of serious consideration. . . . And besides, criticism of the essay sort

205

is a different thing from reviewing, and has a purpose of its own. Why should not a man write about Shakespeare or Milton or Wordsworth, if he chooses? Is there any crime in that? I never set out to be a nurse to the sucking poets of the day.[4]

If he appears a little touchy in this defense, it may be because he remembers his own statement in "Walter Pater:" "The hardest test of the critic, in the exercise of his special function, is his tact and sureness in valuing the productions of his own day" (*SE*, VIII, 84). He may at this time (1924) have begun to feel a little self-conscious about the fact that he had virtually ignored "the productions of his own day."

In 1926 the *Revue de Paris* asked him to contribute an article on present tendencies in American literature. He was not inclined to accept the invitation because he doubted his competence to deal with the subject,[5] but his wife and Irving Babbitt "overpersuaded" him.[6] In preparing the article, which in the English version is "Modern Currents in American Literature" (*NSE*, I, 53-72), the truth of his own dictum regarding "the hardest test of the critic" being the evaluation of contemporary writing must have been brought forcibly home to him. He describes to his sister the difficulties he experienced:

I feel very much as the traitor must have felt in the old days when his hands were hitched to one horse and his feet to another, and then they pulled. . . . To read Gregory Nyssen and write about the Logos in the morning, and then to pass the evening trying to make out what Sherwood Anderson and Dreiser and Cabell stand for, is a soul-and-body-wracking distraction. And I get no forarder [*sic*]. These Americans perplex and trouble me. It would be so easy to condemn them *en bloc* as unclean and unartistic; and it would be equally easy to praise them lustily for their frankness and Americanism and other qualities which most critics find in them so abundantly—but to strike the balance! and to see what it is all derived from and pointed towards![7]

The last part of this statement indicates that, for him, a good deal of the challenge in criticizing contemporary literature lay in the question of continuity—"to see what it is all derived from and pointed towards." This, of course, was the primary concern in all of his criticism. But finding continuity becomes a particularly difficult undertaking in regard to contemporary literature, simply because it is always difficult to see in clear and wise perspective what is nearest at hand.

In the *Shelburne Essays,* More had characterized the modern philosophy of life as the product of a blending of inner romanticism and outer naturalistic science (*SE,* VIII, 234-35); in the first volume of *New Shelburne Essays,* he develops this notion in greater detail. The history of European culture since the Renaissance, he says in the preface, turns on the varying fortunes of two hostile views—humanism and naturalism. The primary difference between these views, of course, is that humanism recognizes a dualism of the natural and the supernatural in man and asserts that the distinctive mark of man is a consciously directive will. In recent times the philosophy of naturalism has come pretty well to dominate our thought, and from this fountainhead has flowed two currents of influence.

On the one hand we have the illicit usurpation of science which came to a climax in the mid-nineteenth century, and which taught us to believe that the world runs forever in a set groove under some complex of mechanical laws, and that man like the animals is no more than a cog in the huge fatalistic machine. The modern form of this hypothesis is what our psychologists call behaviorism; its outcome in literature is the sort of realism that still actually dominates our fiction. On the other hand, we are haunted by a suspicion that this world of ours, so far from exhibiting the tight regularity of a machine, is an infinite flux of accidents without calculable pain or meaning. From this creed derives the literature that undertakes to represent man as the merely passive channel for an ever-flowing stream of sensations. (xi)

It may appear, he continues, that these two views are mutually exclusive. Indeed, they are in a sense contradictory, but it should be observed that they have a common origin in the denial of that element in man that is outside of nature and is

207

the seat of consciously directive purpose. Thus the two views are alike in being "anti-humanistic" and in depriving life of "any serious interest or deep emotions for representation." Both views, as previously discussed, are traceable to the immersion of man in the stream of nature, which originated with Bacon. In the Aristotelian scheme, man was both in nature and above it; with Bacon, there arose a tendency to see man only as a creature of nature governed by natural forces and to ignore the self-determining higher will of his humanity. More had examined the two views rather thoroughly in the *Shelburne Essays*. In the *New Shelburne Essays*, the second view, having to do with the infinite flux of accidents, receives special attention.

No one is likely to defend More very strongly as a critic of modern literature, at least not in his appraisals of individual American writers. But he is consistent, and certainly he is accurate in delineating major currents and tendencies. Moreover, unless his humanistic philosophy is simply dismissed out of hand as false and outdated, then his denunciations of the modern spirit, which are well-grounded in a spiritual-intellectual historiography, still warrant consideration as meaningful judgments. Taken in the context of his world view, those judgments may fall short of the mark here and overshoot it there, but in general they are well worth considering insofar as the essays relate to "main currents" and the continuity of general attitudes.

The Demon of the Absolute

The title of the first volume of *New Shelburne Essays, The Demon of the Absolute*, reflects a continuity with the former series. Absolutism, in its various forms, was the demon of the *Shelburne Essays*, too, even if no title called attention to it. In the title essay of this volume, More defines the Demon of the Absolute as rationalistic monism or "reason run amuck." This Demon can be seen at work in a number of areas: in politics when men contend for some final unchecked authority in the

State; in religion when faith is presented as involving the alternative between an absolute omnipotent God or no God at all, or between an infallible church or undisciplined individualism. "But nowhere has it produced more stupid contrariety than among the critics of art and literature" (2).

The malignity of the Demon in the field of criticism is readily seen, he says, in the controversy over standards. The question leads to a polarity until we find "the genius who champions a complete irresponsibility of temperament" ranged against "a monster of pedantry" (5). Luther once likened human nature to a drunkard on horseback: prop him up on one side, and over he topples on the other. It is the same, says More, with taste and morals. "As soon as we are convinced that no absolute standard exists, forthwith we flop to the other extreme, and swear that there are absolutely no standards at all; so hard is it to keep the middle path of common sense" (7). It is the middle path that he advocates. There is no absolute law of taste, but certain standards do exist which approximate universality. In fact, the law of taste is "the least changeable fact of human nature," and there is a central tradition of taste that remains the same (13-14). Tradition does not create standards but may serve as evidence that certain works of art embody qualities "which it is very much our concern to appreciate, and which we have every reason to use as a criterion" (19).

The result of the Demon's involvement in the question of taste and standards is that many modern critics and artists have rejected the notion that they are responsible to comply with standards based on any kind of tradition or universals. "It is a nice question to ask," says More, "whether belief in the absolute irresponsibility of the artistic temperament has engendered the modern ideal of absolute art, or the contrary" (29). He is satisfied to leave the solution of such a problem to the Demon himself, who alone knows his own mind. Meanwhile, he sets out to attack what he calls "the fetish of pure art." Modern writers, he says, are uneasy about the slavish submission of their elders to the Idol set on a pedestal by Bacon. "Some of the more courageous rebels have even sought a way of escape by claiming for the imagination a complete independence of the laws of life, by what has been dubbed, without intentional irony, the dehumanization of art. But that is only to fall from one absolute into another, to exchange servitude for vacuity" (xii). The principal targets of his attack are Benedetto Croce and José Ortega y Gasset, both influential aestheticians of the time. In the writings of both these men he hears the voice of the Demon appealing to the lust for an irresponsible absolute. "The simple truth is," he concludes, "that the effort to create pure art is nothing more than idolatry to a fetish of abstract reason" (36). In other words, such an artistic effort is a form of rationalistic monism.

More's views on the connection between art and life are treated at some length in chapter 2. It is sufficient here to point out that his refutation of Croce and Ortega y Gasset rests on this attitude: he grants at once that there is a difference between art and life, but insists on the falseness and futility of the logical deduction that art can therefore dispense with "the stuff of humanity and nature." And this part of his argument is worth quoting again:

Always the great creators have taken the substance of life, and, not by denying it or attempting to evade its laws but by looking more intently below its surface, have found meanings and values that transmute it into something at once the same and different. The passions that distract the individual man with the despair of isolated impotence they have invested with a universal significance fraught with the destinies of humanity; the scenery of the material world they have infused with suggestions of an indwelling otherworld. And so by a species of symbolism, or whatever you choose to call it, they have lifted mortal life and its theatre to a higher reality which only to the contented or dust-choked dwellers in things as they are may appear as unreal. (36-37)

Against the concept of so-called pure literature, or dehumanized literature, as it is reflected in the aesthetic theorizing of

Croce and Ortega y Gasset, More poses two major objections: first, it leads to incomprehensibility; second, because it cuts itself off from the universal appeals that we find in the great art of the past, nothing great can come of it.

He summarizes what he believes is the result of the modern search for absolute or pure art and how it relates to the dominant trend of realism in this way:

As, successively, one after another of the higher elements of our composite nature has been suppressed, a lower instinct has taken its place. The submergence of the humanistic conception of man as a responsible creature of free will has been accompanied by an emergence of the romantic glorification of uncontrollable temperament; this has been supplanted by a realistic theory of subjection to the bestial passions, and this, at the last, by an attempt to represent life as an unmitigated flux, which in practice, however it be in literature, means confinement in a madhouse. (40)

This process of evolution has been carried on in the name of absolute art; but, says More, the actual goal attained is an absolute of quite another order—a form of rationalistic monism. The main goal of the process was liberation, but according to More, no true liberation has been achieved, but rather a progressive descent in slavery.

The last section of *The Demon of the Absolute,* dealing with "The Phantom of Pure Science," is primarily a critique of Alfred North Whitehead's philosophy and is intended to demonstrate more havoc wrought by the Demon, this time in the field of science. Although More's views on science are discussed prior to this, the conclusion to his critique of Whitehead's philosophy, which basically he considered to be scientific absolutism masquerading as religion, is worth noting here in order to describe his interpretation of the modern spirit and its continuity with the past. This is Whitehead's analysis of the present condition of the popular mind: "A scientific realism, based on mechanism, is conjoined with an unwavering belief in the world of men and of the higher animals as being composed of self-determining organisms.

211

This radical inconsistency at the basis of modern thought accounts for much that is half-hearted and wavering in our civilization." To this More replies:

My reading of history is different. I should assert that our vacil-lating half-heartedness is the inevitable outcome of the endeavour, persistent since the naturalistic invasion of the Renaissance, to flee from the paradox of life to some philosophy which will merge, no matter how, the mechanical and the human together. I should assert that the only escape from our muddle is to over-throw this idol of Unity, this Demon of the Absolute, this abor-tion sprung from the union of science and metaphysics, and to submit ourselves humbly to the stubborn and irreducible fact that a stone and the human soul cannot be brought under the same definition. (51)

Thus, at bottom, More's answer to the threat posed by the Demon is to hold tightly to the two laws, discrete, not reconciled—the law for man, and law for thing.

Modern Currents in American Literature

The tone of "Modern Currents in American Literature" (NSE, I, 53-76) is decidedly less temperate than the tone in most of the *Shelburne Essays*. There are several possible expla-nations for this. It may be that in his maturity More was more confident of his judgments and therefore less patient with tendencies he regarded as deleterious. His reading of history, traced throughout this volume and as contained in *The Greek Tradition*, perhaps promoted a rigidity in his basic assumptions regarding human nature and experience. Perhaps he saw reflected in current American literature the consum-mation of the forces destructive to humanism that were in-cipient in the Renaissance. But whatever the reason, he does not mince words in his criticism of his fellow countrymen. This is unfortunate, from one standpoint, because some of his denunciatory phrases (e.g., his description of Dos Passos's *Manhattan Transfer* as "an explosion in a cesspool") have called attention to themselves to such an extent that some of his more subtle and discerning judgments have been over-looked. But on the whole, it may be said that his method of treatment of these writers makes less for tact than for cutting discriminations between their qualities and their defects.

He begins by defining the scope of his treatment of the subject. His theme, which is the modern movement as a conscious school, leaves no place, he says, for considering such accomplished novelists and poets as Edith Wharton, Edwin Arlington Robinson, and Robert Frost.[8] He is dealing with the philosophy of modernism rather than a comprehensive interpretation of the art of those writers who happen to live in a time we call modern. The modern movement in America derives, he points out, from a similar movement in England, which, in turn, took its cue from France or perhaps Russia. But in one article of their creed the Americans stand by themselves: "without exception they are animated by a whole-hearted contempt for New England Puritanism and all that it means" (54). In the light of the New England tradition described in the preceding chapter, this point is very significant. More admired that tradition and felt the moderns made a mistake in rejecting it. He emphasizes this break with New England by pointing out that the leading modern realists—Dreiser, Anderson, Lewis—were from the Midwest. Also, he notes that so far as the moderns acknowledge any ancestors in this land, it is to Whitman and Poe and, among the more recent writers, Stephen Crane they pay homage. The repudiation of New England's primacy entails several animosities that unite the otherwise centrifugal modernists into a brotherhood: "Hatred of Puritanism, rejections of 'moralism' and 'religionism,' emancipation of art from the responsibilities of life" (57).

He divides the moderns into two groups, "two different and often antagonistic schools, the aesthetic and the realistic." Of the aesthetic school, Amy Lowell was perhaps the leading spirit. In her "more regular verse" the "vein of genuine talent cannot be questioned, and some of her pieces have a beauty of hard incisive imagery of no common order." But she sometimes appears "a genius hag-ridden by theory" (58). As another example of this school, he cites James Branch Cabell, whom he finds an interesting if enigmatical figure. Cabell's chief limitation, in his view, is that he confuses the true and false illusions, and fails "to discriminate between ideas and ideals, that is between an intuition into the eternal truth of things behind the curtain of appearances and an attempt to wrap the hateful facts of reality in veils of deliberate illusion" (61). He finds Cabell's *Beyond Life* the most interesting of his books, but although the theory of art it contains "arrests one's attention," he is critical of it because it ultimately makes "a divorce between the true in life and the beautiful in art which must spell death to any serious emotion in literature" (62).

In discussing the realistic school, he credits Edgar Lee Master with discovering the characteristic theme of contemporary American realism—the sordidness of the Midwestern town. He notes that *Spoon River Anthology* is in its way a notable achievement, but the "unfailing dullness" of its author's subsequent work indicates that the *Anthology* is only "a malodorous flash in the pan" (69). If popularity were the test, Sinclair Lewis's *Main Street* would be a most significant work. But More suspects that *Main Street* owed its vogue "in part to its title, which is a veritable stroke of genius, and in part to its flattery of those who like to believe that, whatever their sins, they are better folk than the dull hypocrites who grovel and boast in so typical a community as Gopher Prairie. . . . Otherwise it is hard to account for the success of so monotonous a tale written in so drab and drizzling a style" (69). Sherwood Anderson, although he occasionally reveals a genuinely poetic talent, lacks restraint; he is unable "to check the flood of animal suggestions from his subconscious self." At its worst, his work is "a painful illustration of what 'the stream of consciousness' means when it is allowed to grow putrid" (71-72).

Of all the writers discussed in the essay, Dreiser receives

214

the fullest treatment. More considers him the most powerful and typical of the modern realists. Of greater significance than any of Dreiser's novels is his autobiography. This emphasis is important to note because the same is true of More's interest in other moderns—Anderson and Cabell, for example. Because modern fiction seemed to him based on a false philosophy, he was not fond of such fiction; but he was interested in the autobiographical writings of these novelists because there he could get at the sources of attitudes and philosophies, and this he was fond of doing. Drawing his information from Dreiser's *A Book About Myself,* he summarizes Dreiser's early life to show the influences that produce the typical realist. When he moves from this to a discussion of *An American Tragedy,* he says that the real tragedy of that work is that Dreiser knew only the "shabby underside" of life, and that he knew more of "the police courts and the dregs of science" than of the larger tradition of literature, and that religion had only appeared to him in the garb of "the travesty of superstition and faded fanaticism" (68-69). If Dreiser had known more of great literature, he might have produced the great American novel.

Near the end of the essay, More makes a comparison between Cabell and Dreiser that quite accurately summarizes his judgment of the two schools of American moderns. Cabell, he says, tries to substitute an aesthetic philosophy of beauty for the moral law of character, but seems to end up with the thesis "that the pursuit of perfect beauty leads in the end to inevitable disillusion and disappointment." On the other hand, Dreiser, "so far as his creative instinct does not break through his parochial theory of art, simply reproduces the surface of life as he has seen it, with no attempt to reorganize it artistically or to interpret its larger significance" (72).

The Lust of Irresponsibility

In the preface to volume IX of the *Shelburne Essays,* More characterizes the predominant philosophy of his day as "a faith in drifting." In volume III of the *New Shelburne Essays,* which is titled *On Being Human,* he develops this notion of drifting in detail as it relates to modern literature. He asserts in "A Revival of Humanism" that in the end the distinguishing mark and largely the cause of the pessimism of modern literature is a false philosophy that "looks upon human nature with the inflamed vision of a monocular Cyclops, seeing man only as the slave of his temperament, or as a mechanism propelled by complexes and reactions, or as a vortex of sensations, with no will to govern himself, no centre of stability within the flux, no direction of purpose to rise above the influences that carry him hither and thither" (6). In another essay in this volume, "The Modernism of French Poetry," he appears to suggest that this philosophy has its basis in a single psychological principle that may be expressed in a single phrase: "the lust of irresponsibility." He holds the lust of irresponsibility, "which may of course easily pass into the lust of dominion," to be one of the primary and universal instincts in human nature, "though in most men it is more or less concealed by imbecility of will, or is held in check by the traditional conventions of society" (111).

Consequently, the cause of the general decay in contemporary literature, according to More, is the widespread acceptance of the theory (which has a kind of psychological basis) that there are no moral laws governing life, or none at least that apply to art—a point he had developed in *The Demon of the Absolute.* Insofar as both aestheticism and realism deny the relevance of moral purpose in art, while both lust after irresponsibility, they are both, in his eyes, naturalistic:

The writer, whether realist or symbolist, will belong to the broader school of naturalism, in so far as he eliminates that faculty of responsible selection in the field of consciousness which, for the humanist, belongs to man only along with the "nature" common to man and the rest of the animal kingdom. And further it should be noted that both branches of the naturalistic school

216

are alike in this, that they rob human activity of any purpose or ultimate meaning. (55)

The only difference is that the realist shows the ugly and the bestial as the ultimate truth of things, while the modern symbolist shows the illusion and futility of life through art that is fantastically unreal. Thus More's criticism of naturalism applies to both schools equally. In *On Being Human,* however, several of the essays treat aestheticism separately and at length.

The essays "Proust: The Two Ways" (*NSE,* III, 43-68) and "James Joyce" (*NSE,* III, 69-96) serve to demonstrate his criticism of modern aestheticism. The school of pure art that he attacks in these essays is one whose outlines are clearer today than they were in More's own time. In the novel, this school is usually traced beginning with Flaubert and running through the most characteristic work of James, Joyce, Proust, Virginia Woolf, Camus, and other twentieth-century writers. The ideal of this literary school is the novel which shows rather than tells, the novel of "pure presentation" that is devoid of authorial commentary and whose primary value is aesthetic—moral and social value being minimized or excluded. The resultant art, as More describes it in connection with Proust, attempts to extract the reality of life from all associations with practical utility and conventions and reveals it as a kind of pure vision.

More detested the notion that art constitutes a reality and a system of values completely separate from life. And his main purpose in the essay on Proust, though this essay treats several aspects of the Frenchman's work and is not devoid of appreciative response, is to discredit that notion. "The simple truth, which ought to be known to any adult mind," says More, "is that pure art, art completely severed from actuality, just does not exist. Art may interpret, and so in a fashion re-create; it cannot create *ex nihilo.* This chatter about receiving the ineffable joys of Paradise from a reality unattached to

217

anything real is the watery moonshine of an outworn romanticism" (58). There is something paradoxical about Proust's position, says More. On the one hand, Proust claims, and his disciples claim for him, that his art is in no sense "a prolongation of life"—that is, it is apart from life. But on the other hand, his art is rooted in one of the most concrete of animal passions. In fact, More concludes, Proust's art "is a criticism of life as didactic as any Matthew Arnold would demand, though a criticism pointing in a very different direction" (59). The answer to the paradox lies in the fact that the modern symbolist and realist in fiction "are merely accidental diversions on the main road of naturalism" (60).

More summarizes Edmund Wilson's treatment of Proust in *Axel's Castle,* explaining that the trouble with Proust, according to Wilson, is not that he lacked moral insight, but that he represents the farthest outpost of the symbolistic movement as a reaction against nineteenth-century naturalism, and nothing further can be expected of this literature that has attempted to build up a "world of the private imagination in isolation from the life of society" (Wilson's words); art for art's sake has brought us to the great vacuum. The remedy for this, in Wilson's opinion, is for literature to return to the "life of society." And what the life of society means to Wilson, More points out, referring to a particular article in *The New Republic,* is colored by Marxian communism. More disagrees with this remedy. He says it plunges us more deeply into the vicious circle to substitute the communistic naturalism of Marx for the individualistic naturalism of Proust. The proper remedy, according to More, is "that men must be brought once more to feel their responsibility to a law within nature but not of nature in the naturalistic sense of the word" (68). It is because Wilson and others like him can see no reality in this something not of nature, and will grant no authority to its commands, that, seeking reality, they fly distractedly from admiration of Proust to admiration of Marx.

In "James Joyce," More acknowledges that "by nature Joyce was a moralist endowed with that penetration into the secret issues of life which can scarcely exist without a keen sense of religious values; and he was, indeed is, an artist gifted with genius, nothing less, for the subtleties of style" (70). But More is puzzled by how a man who could write the last scene of "The Dead" in *Dubliners* could also have written *Ulysses* and *Finnegan's Wake* (which More refers to as *Work in Progress*). The essay attempts to answer this question. And the answer More arrives at is basically that Joyce was gradually moving from *Dubliners* to the *Portrait* to *Ulysses* toward "a theory of irresponsible art"—he was seeking a pure art, art for art's sake; "the changing factor is the self-liberation of the artist from the spiritual values and dogmatic authority of tradition, and the consequent forging of 'conscience' out of the uncontrolled spontaneity of his individual consciousness" (79).

Such a pursuit of art as an abstraction divorced from the responsibilities of life, as far as More is concerned, leads to nothing, "and idealistic beauty loosed from belief in the higher reality of spiritual ideas is no more than a mist fluttering in the infinite inane." What generally happens to the artist who sets out on such a pursuit is that

in his reactionary search for reality he is precipitated down and down into the depths of his own being, into that vast dark region of the soul below the ordered and rationalized life. Being unable to sink lower he will feel that at last his feet are set on a foundation of facts which he calls the nature of man. His art will be to reproduce in flowing language the vapours that float up unsolicited through the conscious mind from the abyss of the unconscious. Rational selection and spiritual authority have been repudiated, and the only law governing the flux is the so-called association of ideas, the fact that one image by some chance similarity evokes another, and one sensation fades into another. (80)

This metaphorical description of the stream of consciousness technique clearly indicates why More distrusted it. From his point of view, nothing really worthwhile can be produced by a method that repudiates rational selection (involving free will) and spiritual authority. Joyce's development, consequently, is another manifestation of the lust of irresponsibility. And the nature of Joyce's later work is to be explained by the fact that "the romantic notion of art for art's sake, set loose from any responsibility to the authority of spiritual law and traditional inhibitions, merges into a naturalism which rejects from reality all but the physical and in the end all but the ugly" (87).

The failure of both Proust and Joyce, from More's standpoint, is that, despite their great skill and genius, their works lead to nothing ultimately worthwhile; on the contrary, they illustrate the futility of an art divorced from moral values and the consequences of the instinct toward irresponsibility allowed to go unchecked.

More's concept of responsibility relates to his concept of humanitarianism. He considered the brotherhood of man to be the real religious dogma of his times. And while he had nothing against loving his brother (the love of humanity is actually the cornerstone of his humanism), he did object to an abstract kind of brotherly love that ignores the free-willed responsibility of the individual soul. He deplored the attitudes in some modern books that make of humanitarianism a cloak for what is lax and materialistic in the age. He meant by this the false emphasis on man's responsibility for the material welfare of man in general to the neglect or exclusion of the individual soul's responsibility to itself. The humanitarianism he so frequently attacked was actually a false humanitarianism (emphasizing outward or institutional reform) growing out of the lust of irresponsibility as related to the individual's need for inward control. A man who in his own life fails in a very concrete way to meet his moral and spiritual responsibilities can still ease his conscience by engaging in an abstract social sympathy that in terms of genuine effort and sacrifice costs very little. Man's most significant responsibilities, from the humanistic standpoint, are thus abnegated under the license of a so-called humanitarian love. Any genuine humanitarianism, like any genuine art, from More's point of view, would have to be based on a recognition of man's dual nature and on a sense of his responsibility to the supermundane powers.

It is manifestly clear that More's antagonism toward modernist literature grew directly out of his opposition to the philosophical concepts on which he thought that literature is based. He felt that, more than in any previous age, the philosophy of naturalism dominated the main patterns of thought during his time, and the literature reflected this. He firmly believed that no lasting and worthwhile literature is possible unless the writer recognizes the dual nature of man and is guided by that recognition in expressing his view of human experience. In short, his appraisal of much modern literature is based on his view that in basic assumptions such literature represents a culmination of assumptions continued from and proved inadequate in earlier literature.

The only hopeful sign he could see was in the revival of humanism. He called attention to "the little group of critics of life and letters scattered over the land, who have set their faces against the all-invading currents of irresponsible half-thinking, and, with full knowledge of what has been thought and done in the past, are trying to lay the foundations of a new humanism for the present" (NSE, I, 73). He included in that group such men as Irving Babbitt, F. J. Mather, P. H. Frye, S. B. Gass, Robert Shafer, and W. C. Brownell. All of these humanists he thought were openly or virtually in protest against the monism of the modern spirit and its fruits.

It is appropriate to end this chapter by repeating More's exposition on the positive ideals of humanism.

Against those who teach that man is totally submerged in natural law, the humanist lays emphasis on that in man which distinguishes him generically from other animals and so in one part of his composite being lifts him out of the more narrowly defined kingdom of nature; and the humanist assumes for himself this title as opposed to the naturalist because this super-added element, or faculty, however named, is what marks off a man as man. In a word, the humanist is simply one who takes his stand *on being human*. Against those who still hold that man is only a fragmentary cog in the vast machine which we call the universe, moved by the force of some relentless, unvarying, unconscious law, the humanist asserts that we are individual personalities, endowed with the potentiality of free will and answerable for our choice of good or evil. Against those who reduce man to a chaos of sensations and instincts and desires checking and counterchecking one another in endlessly shifting patterns, the humanist points to a separate faculty of inhibition, the inner check or the *frein vital*, whereby these expansive impulses may be kept within bounds and ordered to a design not of their making. Against those who proclaim that a man can only drift, like a rudderless ship, with the weltering currents of change, the humanist maintains that he is capable of self-direction, and that character, as different from native temperament, is a growth dependent on clarity and strength of purpose. Against those who, to appease the stings of conscience, assure us that we are what we are by no fault of our own, that, as we have no responsibility for our character, so the lesson of wisdom is to shuffle off any sense of regret or remorse or fear; and against those who go further in flattery and, through each and every appearance of delinquency, assert the instinctive total goodness of unredeemed nature—against these the humanist contends that as free agents we are accountable for defalcations and aberrations and that self-complacency is the deadliest foe to human excellence. On the other hand, the humanist will not stand with those who jeer at human nature, as if men were in no better state than rats in a trap, rushing distractedly hither and thither, hurling themselves upon their bars in a pitiable frenzy of impotence. (*NSE,* III, 7-8)

CHAPTER EIGHT

Conclusion

Summary of Historical Continuity

In the foregoing chapters I have attempted to synthesize and examine, century by century, the continuous historiography that is always implicit, sometimes explicit, throughout Paul Elmer More's literary criticism. It becomes necessary now to formulate a summary of this spiritual-intellectual history. In its general outline it runs as follows.[1]

The world view inherited by Western thought from the classical civilizations had at its heart a dualistic concept of the world: the one and the many. The "one" is the absolute principle of self-concentration that makes for unity and is called by More "the infinite." The "many" is the exact opposite—the limitless expanse of impulse and desire, which he usually refers to as "the flux." According to Aristotle, the goal of reason is to keep the limitless expanse of impulsive flux in proper relationship (i.e., the golden mean) to the unity of the infinite. This represents classical dualism.

Up until the Reformation this classical principle of restraint was embodied in the doctrines of the Christian religion, though somewhat obscured. On the one hand was man with his instincts, desires, and intellectual faculties, and on the other hand was an opposite, supernatural force within man but emanating from God. The task for man was, through faith and reason, to make the impulsive elements of his nature subject to the higher elements of control and restraint.

The peculiar form of religious enthusiasm developed in the Middle Ages wrought out an idealism of its own. The soul of the individual man seemed to the Christian of that day to be the center of the world, about which the divine drama of salvation revolved; and on the position taken by the individual in this drama depended his eternal life. A man's personality became of vast importance in the universal scheme of things, and a new justifiable egotism of intense activity was born, allied to introspection. There was necessarily an element of anguish in this thought of personal importance, but on the whole, while faith lasted, it was overbalanced by feelings of joy and peace; for, after all, salvation was within reach. The idealism of such a period found its aim in the perfection of man's soul, and the development of one's fullest humanity in contrast to animality in the life of its individual members was the one theme of surpassing interest.

But unfortunately, during the religious controversies of the Reformation and Post-Reformation, supernatural restraint was commonly vested in an infallible church or infallible Bible, so that the individual soul was relieved to some extent from the responsibility of grappling with the dualism and, of its own strength, exerting proper restraint. There was still, however, a genuine dualism—the limitless flux potentially held in restraint by the infinite "one."

The new humanism which came in with the Renaissance modified, but did not entirely displace this idea; the faith of the earlier ages remained essentially intact for some time. But increasingly during the seventeenth and eighteenth centuries, under the impact of rationalism and the Baconian view of science, the supernatural book and church were discredited, and men became more and more reliant on human reason rather than divine revelation. Almost as a reaction to the supernaturalism of earlier ages, the philosophy of naturalism (i.e., the denial of a discrete supernatural nature in man) began to emerge. This tendency is revealed in a comparison between the seventeenth and eighteenth centuries. To the great writers of the seventeenth century human nature was a thing to distrust as containing tendencies of ruinous evil. But along with this fear of undisciplined nature went a kind of religious sense, a belief in the efficacy and virtue of certain supernatural emotions, in an infinite appetite that revealed itself in enthusiasm. The following age, especially as represented by the prevalent Deism, brought a reversal of this attitude. Human nature (used almost without deviation as a synonym of reason) was considered good, and strong emotion or enthusiasm was condemned as contrary to nature and was therefore considered perilous. In that distrust of free emotion lay the strength of the time, the power that made its belief in nature ancillary to its belief in order and subordination; but here, too, lay the cause of its limitations, for this dread of enthusiasm cut off the great inspirations of the preceding age as well as the disturbing passions. The irresistible tendency of religion is to project the dualism of consciousness into the supersensible realm and to create a mythology (using the term in no derogatory sense). When reason came into its own in the eighteenth century, heaven and hell were swept away for devotees of rationalism; the religious sense, which had become atrophied through dependence on a mythology authoritatively provided for it by the infallible church or infallible Bible, seemed to fail altogether. And that situation, with various eddies of revolt, has prevailed since the deistic movement of the eighteenth century—a blustering denial of man's uneasiness and an organized effort to drown that feeling in social sympathy.

By the closing years of the eighteenth century the long illusion of man's personal value in the universe had been rudely shattered; his anchor of faith had been rent away. Then came the readjustment that is still in progress, and is still the cause of so much unrest and tribulation. In place of the individual arose a new ideal of humanity as a whole—a pretty theory for philosophers, but in no wise comforting for the homeless soul of man, trained by centuries of introspection to deem himself the chosen vessel of grace. This readjustment precipitated a season of revolt. The individual, still bearing his burden of self-importance, and seeing no restrictive laws to bind him, gave himself to all the wild vagaries of the revolutionary period. Unfortunately, the romantic movement, with its return to seventeenth-century enthusiasm, retained the eighteenth-century acceptance of nature, but now without restriction, thus leaving to itself no inner check. The individual found a new solace in reverie, which seemed to make him one with the wide and beneficent realm of nature. Indeed, romanticism was a form of naturalism since it did not recognize that man's higher being is separate from the world of nature, that is, supernatural. In this absorption into nature the romantic poet was too apt to forget that, after all, the highest and noblest theme must forever be the struggle of the human soul. He was liable to several errors: he was too ready to substitute vague reverie for honest thought, too ready to give himself up to the unrestrained flux of instincts and passions, too ready to place his faith in the limitless expansiveness of man's emotional nature as ultimately and inevitably leading to progress.

While this was going on in the history of man's internal development, natural science was making a similar progression in man's external relationships. The doctrine of an expanding, constantly changing, self-creating universe corresponds with the flux of the inner world. And from the union of this inner romanticism and outer naturalistic science during the nineteenth century arose the problem of the modern philosophy of life, which may be called indifferently scientific or romantic. As this philosophy is concerned with conduct and the inner life rather than with material phenomena, it may be regarded as the offspring of romanticism; as it enjoys its great authority from a supposed connection with the actual discoveries of physical law, and has obtained its precise character from the evolutionary hypothesis, it may with equal propriety be regarded as the bastard offspring of science. The keynote of this new philosophy in any of its various forms is a kind of laissez faire, a belief that, as the physical world has unrolled itself by its own expansive force, so human society progresses by some universal instinct, needing no rational and selective guidance, no imposition of moral restraint, no conscious insight.

The central thrust of More's historiography is reflected in this critique of the concept of progress.

It is just the craving for flattery, the itch of an uneasy vanity, a longing to escape from the ancient indictment of the human heart as desperately wicked and deceitful above all things, that has been the driving force behind the whole movement of human thought from the Renaissance to the present day. Bacon felt this when he announced that the "happiness of mankind" was to be attained by discrediting the restrictive wisdom of the past, and by setting out on a course of physical discovery which should look to "the endowment of human life with new inventions and riches." Mankind had suffered, he thought, not from any innate overreaching after power, but from its mere lack of knowledge. Give man power over nature and the heart will take care of itself. The deists felt the same pull when they taught that "social evils were due neither to innate and incorrigible disabilities of the human being nor to the nature of things, but simply to ignorance and prejudice." Let men once be told that the universe is totally reasonable in design and of course they will be reasonable in their conduct. . . . Rousseau made it the principle of education when he showed how a child, if left to develop its own nature without restraint or discipline, would grow up into a perfect man. And at last the philosophers of evolution gave it the sanction of science when they declared that, as one species is transmuted into a higher species by the mechanical law of fitness, so the generations of mankind grow from better to better by the mere gravity of an innate propensity, without taking thought and without painful self-direction. The idea of Progress as it was finally formulated in the nineteenth century might be described as organized vanity decking itself out in the flummery of science.[2]

Thus, starting from the critical observation that, judged by its fruits, the philosophy of naturalism as it had developed since the Renaissance had led men astray, because it had led to types of monistic pantheism and materialism, or to a pluralism which remained monistic since it did not distinguish man from the rest of nature, More worked to restore the element of classical dualism which had become obscured since the Renaissance.

This interpretation of history in its general ideas is of course not unique with More. But he is original in giving it a clear, basic philosophical foundation that he traces in literature. He is also original in the way he discovers the relation of particular writers and works to each other and to broad historical tendencies. Often these relationships are obscure and paradoxical and he displays great learning and remarkable intellectual power in ferreting them out.

Why was he so obsessed with the genealogy of ideas? The answer lies in what Whitney Oates refers to as More's "Quest of the Spirit."[3] The more one studies his writings, particularly the *Shelburne Essays,* the deeper becomes the sense that More is not only conducting a vast adventure among the masterpieces of literature, he is all the while seeking to find his own way. As Lynn H. Hough says, "He is re-creating the past for the sake of making his own mind."[4] More himself says in one of those passages in *Pages from an Oxford Diary* where he is reflecting back on the direction and meaning of his career that he had always been led on by the hope that in some piece of literature, some autobiography, or some more artificial revelation of the human heart he should "surprise the secret of existence" (*POD,* V).

More's study of human thought and experience as set forth in the varied and searching studies of the *Shelburne Essays* moved him toward certain notable conclusions. Lynn H. Hough summarizes them in this way:

Great principles emerged to which one must be loyal at whatever cost. Great systems of thought, which at last emasculated the very life they were trying to interpret, began to be seen in their true quality. Not even reason itself must be allowed to commit suicide. And the use of reason to rob life of its truest meaning

228

must be repudiated. It will be repudiated if it is seen for what it is. More saw these things at every turn in the literature and the philosophy of the world.[5]

It is important to see that More's quest meant listening to as many human voices as possible. They must all be heard. They must all be analyzed and appraised. And in this process he discovered that certain permanent distinctions remain despite the many rationalistic efforts (naturalistic at one extreme and mystical at the other) to reduce life to a unity.

Summary of Philosophical Continuity

It would be unnecessarily repetitious here to restate once again More's concept of dualism, which informs all of his literary criticism and tends to make of it a continuous whole. Chapter 2 defines that dualism, and repeatedly in the following chapters it is illustrated in all of its various and specific manifestations. What here must be synthesized and defined, however, is the unique complex of historical sense, religious sense, and higher imagination that is the product of that dualism and that constitutes the fundamental continuity of More's critical thought.

When More uses the terms historical sense, religious sense or religious imagination, and imagination or higher imagination, he is referring to slightly different manifestations of the same human faculty. He once said he was born a Platonist, and certainly his conception of the faculty of the imagination is Platonic. In "Definitions of Dualism" (SE, VIII, 247-302) he distinguishes between the "subjective" and "objective" imagination, a distinction that calls to mind Coleridge's notion of a primary and secondary imagination. The objective imagination is the faculty by which we organize our perceptions of nature and external experience. "The subjective imagination is the use of the faculty by which we project our complex inner experience into nature as existences apart from the soul" (260-61). The subjective imagination is therefore the faculty of creation, and art becomes the attempt, by means of the subjective imagination, to establish the experience of the individual in tradition. "In so far as it deals with beauty, it is an attempt to adapt the beauty of nature as seen through the objective imagination to the demands of the subjective imagination. It differs from the pathetic fallacy by implying a distinct and more or less revocable addition to nature rather than a fusion of nature and the soul" (263). What it comes down to in the end is that imagination, in the highest sense, is for More the primary quality of man's higher nature, which enables him to comprehend the realm of eternal Ideas (in the Platonic sense) and connect or relate the mutable material world with that higher, immutable world.

It is this faculty that enables man "to hold the past as a living force in the present" (*SE, VII, 237*). It is the power of "grasping in a single vision, so to speak, the long course of human history and of distinguishing what is essential therein [the eternal Ideas] from what is ephemeral" (*SE, IX, 36*). The imagination is therefore "an accomplice of time as well as of the law of subordination; indeed, its deepest and noblest function lies in its power of carrying what was once seen and known as a living portion and factor of the present, and there is no surer test of the quality of a man's mind than the degree in which he feels the long-remembered past as one of the vital and immediate laws of his being" (19). Once, as he looked back on his lifetime of scholarship, More wondered about the attraction his books had held for him all the time. He concluded:

Not every man's thoughts and visions and desires, as by them he would remould the gross material of experience, are capable of passing into enduring literature, but rather those which conform with actual truths, visualizing a beauty finer than that comprehended by the seeing eye, grasping a law of justice more infallible than the tangled events of this earth ever obey, conveying a significance beyond any evaluation of the senses. By such distinctions I lay hold of a strange philosophy which tells me that the soul's assurance of truth is not a dream . . . but an intuition more or less perfectly grasped of veritable realities. These books on which I depend for most of my noetic life are effective just as they are a history of what has been known of these realities by other souls in the past and set down for the recreation of any who can spell out the record [the higher imagination being the faculty by which these realities are known and communicated]. So do they charm into peace because they lure us to the belief that some time, if not here and now, our soul may be lifted to that world of immutable Ideas which lie in all their splendour before the eye of Plato's God. (*CF, 214-15*)

Spelled out rather clearly in this passage is the ultimate criterion of his judicial criticism, and how the imagination functions in that process is clearly implied.

Thus the historical sense, the religious sense, the artistic sense, and even the political sense have their ultimate basis in the imagination. The nature of the historical sense is clear from the foregoing paragraph. The religious sense parallels and is linked with it: "In that power of the past to impose itself on the heart as a thing no longer subject to decay lies the natural bond between tradition, or memory in its transcendent sense, and faith which is the faculty of beholding the eternal beneath the transient" (*SE*, VII, 133). And the religious sense is in turn linked with the artistic sense, because the true artist is one

who, by the subtle, insinuating power of the imagination, by just appreciation of the higher emotions as well as the lower . . . gives us always to feel that the true universal in human nature, the faculty by which man resembles man as a being different from the beast, is that part of him that is "noble in reason," the master and not the slave of passion. True art is thus humanistic rather than naturalistic; and its gift of high and permanent pleasure is the response of our own breast to the artist's delicately revealed sense of that divine control, moving like the spirit of God upon the face of the water. (*NSE, I, 24*)

In the area of politics the imagination again functions in a similar way. Institutions are "those symbols and efficacies of the imagination, which swallow up the individual man in involuntary actions and then render back to him his life enriched by manifold associations, and whose traditional forms are the hands of the past laid caressingly on the present" (*SE,* IX, 176). "The State to the imagination is a vital reality, to the unimaginative sense it is a mere name for a collection of men living together in the same territory" (177). He compares this somewhat Burkean conservative acceptance of the imaginative entity of a nation with the Rousseauistic theory of the *volonté générale* (which he sees at the heart of liberalism) and to socialism, concluding that "the one may be called the true illusion of the imagination which conforms a man in the upward motions of his nature, the other as part of the false illusion which promises liberty but in the end leaves the soul a prey to its own downward gravitation" (179). Thus in any field of human endeavor the higher way is revealed by those who think that an entity grasped by the imagination is just as real to their spiritual life—more real in fact—as an object visible before them is to their sensuous life.

It is this complex of the imagination, derived from a dualistic interpretation of Plato, that constitutes the fundamental continuity of More's literary criticism—indeed of his thought in general. It is the controlling premise which determines the interests, the methods, and the judgments of his criticism. This conception of the imagination evolved and expanded to some extent during the course of his career, but in its essential form was present in all of his writing and gives to his large and varied body of criticism a peculiar unity and wholeness. He himself was well aware of this; he knew that his work must stand or fall taken as a whole. This is why he insisted, despite the pressing advice of close friends, on placing all of his criticism under one general title.

More's Achievement

In his essay on Coleridge, John Stuart Mill says, "A true thinker can only be justly estimated when his thoughts have worked their way into minds formed in a different school;

have been wrought and moulded into consistency with all other true and relevant thoughts; when the noisy conflict of half-truths, angrily denying one another, has subsided, and ideas which seemed mutually incompatible, have been found only to require mutual limitations."[6] We are in a much better position to estimate More's thought than were people of the last several decades. From our vantage point, it is clear that the young liberal critics carried the day against More and the New Humanists in America's "battle of the books." The moral approach to literary criticism was pushed into the background by the social-oriented criticism of the thirties and was displaced much further by the rise of the New Criticism. These approaches have now had ample time to demonstrate their scope and limitations. The New Criticism has had a profound effect upon the literary criticism of our century. Much of that effect has been salutary: more attention is now properly given to works of literature themselves; that attention is more penetrating and systematic; and criticism is recognized as high creative endeavor. But formalistic analysis fails to confront some important aspects of the literary experience and often succumbs to the temptation of overly ingenious but sterile interpretation of structure and imagery. And it has contributed to the development of recent radical approaches such as "deconstruction," which undermine the traditional assumptions about relationships between author and reader, literature and life, and reduce literature to arbitrary sequences of linguistic signs whose meanings are disconnected from the author's intention or the world outside the text. But despite these developments in radical aesthetics, a renewed interest in literature as a criticism of life is apparent among many teachers and critics, an interest resulting to a large extent from a reaction to the excesses of formalistic approaches and recent antimimetic theories. The current conservative trend in American politics, mirrored to a degree by cultural and academic trends, makes this an apt time for a reassessment of More's work. The "noisy conflict of half-truths, angrily denying one another," as Mill puts it, has subsided; moreover, we have witnessed the evolving losses and gains resulting from those literary battles early in our century.

The young liberal critics of the twenties clearly carried the day. But paradoxically this fact, rather than discrediting More's ideas, in one important respect bears them out. If his interpretation of historical tendency is correct, particularly his interpretation of the modern tendency, then it was inevitable that his work should have been pushed into the background, since it is an expression of ideas and attitudes antipathetic to the mainstream of contemporary liberal thought. This is not to say that More is entirely unknown or without admirers today. As Austin Warren points out, "It is a 'VULGAR ERROR' that, with the deaths of Babbitt and his ally, P. E. More, in the 1930s, the 'New Humanism' movement became extinct." It simply "went underground."[7] Nearly every English faculty includes a member who, while realizing More is not fashionable, finds that he speaks to that member's most genuine interests and concerns in literature.

Daniel Aaron suggests that More's being bracketed with Babbitt has been unfortunate in two ways: it obscures the real differences between the two, and it links More closely with the New Humanism controversy, resulting in his philosophical and political views receiving more attention than his literary criticism.[8] The truth of the latter part of this statement will diminish as that controversy of the late 1920s recedes into the past. More's literary essays will be evaluated on their own merits.

Any evaluation of More should take into consideration the context of his career. In some important respects he was a pioneer in American criticism. As Lynn H. Hough points out, "More was perhaps the first great American critic to meet English critics, not only on their own ground and quite level eyes, but also without the slightest sense of self-consciousness."[9] During his early work particularly he stood

234

alone without the guidance and stimulation of other major critics. "There was almost a critical vacuum in this country and England," he wrote to a friend, "and I see now that my writing suffers from absence of the right kind of friction and emulation. Yet it was something of an achievement—I say it unblushingly—just to keep going in such a desert."[10]

The context of his career partly explains why he placed little emphasis on aesthetic and literary theory. He was nurtured in a tradition in which literary criticism found its first implements in moral doctrine and social values and was considered primarily a phase of philosophic study that must be schooled by ideas and traditions instead of sensibility and the craft of language. Austin Warren says he was sensitive to poetry but lacked "instruments of analysis;" his metaphorical descriptions of style—the *je ne sais quoi* approach—was a "period defect" and not an indication that he intended to exclude considerations of style and form.[11]

More is not an important critic in the sense that he changed our conception of what literature is. In fact, contemporary antimimetic theorists who view literature as a linguistic process quite separate from actual life will view him as quaint and obsolete. But the fact remains that such theories, though fashionable in some academic circles, are not very comprehensible or engaging to the general reader—or scholar; and this holds true within English faculties as well as outside of them. Paul Elmer More read literature of the past to determine what it meant for him and his age, what difference it makes in human life; and in so doing he helped us better understand what it means to us. Regardless of how sophisticated literary theory becomes, the interest in literature on the part of the great mass of serious readers will be directed toward what it teaches about life. More is short on aesthetic theory, but he says many penetrating and useful things about what and how literature teaches about life.

He began his career as a generalist in an age of specialization. He was the last, or near last, of a certain type of scholar-critic. He was erudite, remarkably well read, knowledgeable in a number of languages, a philosopher and theologian as well as literary man. He was willing to tackle the large questions with a boldness that appalls contemporary critics intimidated by the complexity and overabundance of knowledge and information accumulated in our age. He was a master of the genealogy of ideas. He followed them from country to country and from century to century like a tenacious detective. He had a special feeling for the New England in which so much of our own intellectual and aesthetic life had centered. He was at home with the great masterpieces of English literature. The many-sided and evasive mind of the East had revealed many things to him as he studied Sanskrit. His knowledge of Greek philosophy and Christian history and doctrine are impressively reflected in his six-volume work on *The Greek Tradition*. He had a close understanding of German thought, and French critics like Sainte-Beuve were at his fingertips. He saw everything in terms of everything else and was constantly discovering more or less hidden and unsuspected relationships. In his preface to the eighth volume of *Shelburne Essays,* he describes his own criticism as "not so much directed to the individual thing as to its relation with other things, and to its place as cause or effect in a whole group of tendencies." A generalist of his caliber may not come along again. Where would such a person be trained? Our schools no longer have programs to stimulate such wide scholarship. The classics, which were More's foundation, have nearly disappeared from our curricula. Our schools may produce brilliant scholars, but with few exceptions they are specialists.

Although More has been irresponsibly dismissed in some quarters as a mere worshipper of the past and almost blind to the present, actually he tempered his judicial criticism by his very considerable concern for historical continuity. He viewed a given piece of literature as a link in the chain of historical tendency. And the criteria on which he based his judicial criticism were a kind of synthesis of what had actually been proved to be associated with the unchanging elements in literature and life and which had advanced the happiness of mankind. In other words, he used a semi-inductive and historical method in arriving at his judicial criteria, and his Platonic concern with a flexible adjustment of the changeless One and the changing Many helped to give his better critical essays an air of perpetual modernness. One ought to bear constantly in mind his dictum that "The aim of culture is not to merge the present in a sterile dream of the past, but to hold the past as a living force in the present" (*SE,* VII, 237). One is reminded, of course, of T. S. Eliot's "Tradition and the Individual Talent" (which owes a significant debt to More[12]), but it should be remembered that in More's case, his traditionalism did not cause him to surrender to any codified institutionalism such as Roman Catholicism or Anglicanism or monarchy. He maintained a skepticism regarding any kind of infallibility and of the "Demon of the Absolute." Only by keeping steadily in mind his concern with historical continuity can one comprehend the special nuance of what he meant by tradition and by judicial criticism.

There is a prophetic quality in his interpretation of intellectual history, and part of estimating the value of his work is determining how true a prophet he was. In general, experience has proved him right in his conjectures regarding the consequences of certain major tendencies. He strongly indicated, for example, that the nineteenth century erred in supposing that science would be an unqualified good and would guarantee happiness and especially world peace. We have lived to see that technological progress is not identical with nor does it always promote the progress of human happiness and peace. We have watched the prestige of rationalism decline in many quarters in direct proportion to the mounting achievements of science, an event caused partially by several terrible wars. We have seen that nearly a half century of the kind of materialistic humanitarianism that More condemned has not brought happiness and contentment to society. Great material prosperity seems to have produced great discontent, and this not simply due to the unequal distribution of wealth. Some of the greatest discontent is to be found among the most wealthy, and particularly among their children. There are many opinions regarding the nature and causes of the problems of contemporary culture, none of them conclusive. An opinion based on More's work is certainly worthy of unprejudiced consideration. The breadth and depth of his learning certainly warrants respect, and his sincerity and total commitment to the highest human values cannot be doubted—or faulted.

No critic is ever right in the sense that he says all there is to say about a work of literature, or in the sense that what he does say cannot be shown by someone else to be incomplete or inaccurate in some way. We should judge a critic's virtue not by his freedom from error but by the nature of the mistakes he does make, for he will make them if he is worth reading. And he is worth reading if he has in mind something besides his perceptions about the work itself, if he has in mind the demands he makes upon life. Those critics are most to be trusted who allow these demands, in all their particularity, to be detected by their readers. There is never any doubt about what More demands of life—energy, discipline, balance, and scope in the individual and in society. At the behest of his dualistic vision, he no doubt overvalued certain qualities of literature and undervalued others. But his mistakes are in the open, and so are the lively principles by which he made them. To enjoy More as a critic it is not necessary to agree with his particular literary judgments, not with any of them. It is only necessary to be aware of the generosity and commitment of his enterprise.

List of Abbreviations

CF   *The Catholic Faith.* Complementary Vol. of *The Greek Tradition.* Princeton: Princeton University Press, 1931.

CIE   *A Century of Indian Epigrams.* Boston and New York: Houghton Mifflin, 1898.

CNT   *The Christ of the New Testament.* Vol. 3 of *The Greek Tradition.* Princeton: Princeton University Press, 1924.

CW   *Christ the Word.* Vol. 4 of *The Greek Tradition.* Princeton: Princeton University Press, 1927.

HP   *Hellenistic Philosophies.* Vol. 2 of *The Greek Tradition.* Princeton: Princeton University Press, 1923.

JL   *The Jessica Letters.* New York and London: G. P. Putnam's Sons, 1904.

NSE, I   *The Demon of the Absolute.* Vol. 1 of *New Shelburne Essays.* Princeton: Princeton University Press, 1928.

NSE, II   *The Sceptical Approach to Religion.* Vol. 2 of *New Shelburne Essays.* Princeton: Princeton University Press, 1934.

NSE, III   *On Being Human.* Vol. 3 of *New Shelburne Essays.* Princeton: Princeton University Press, 1936.

P   *Platonism.* Princeton: Princeton University Press, 1917.

POD   *Pages from an Oxford Diary.* Princeton: Princeton University Press, 1937.

RP   *The Religion of Plato.* Vol. 1 of *The Greek Tradition.* Princeton: Princeton University Press, 1921.

SE, I   *Shelburne Essays*. No. 1. Boston and New York: Houghton Mifflin, 1904.

SE, II   *Shelburne Essays*. No. 2. Boston and New York: Houghton Mifflin, 1905.

SE, III   *Shelburne Essays*. No. 3. Boston and New York: Houghton Mifflin, 1905.

SE, IV   *Shelburne Essays*. No. 4. Boston and New York: Houghton Mifflin, 1906.

SE, V   *Shelburne Essays*. No. 5. New York and London: G. P. Putnam's Sons, 1908.

SE, VI   *Shelburne Essays*. No. 6. Boston and New York: Houghton Mifflin, 1909.

SE, VII   *Shelburne Essays*. No. 7. Boston and New York: Houghton Mifflin, 1910.

SE, VIII   *The Drift of Romanticism. Shelburne Essays*. No. 8. Boston and New York: Houghton Mifflin, 1913.

SE, IX   *Aristocracy and Justice. Shelburne Essays*. No. 9. Boston and New York: Houghton Mifflin, 1915.

SE, X   *With the Wits. Shelburne Essays*. No. 10. Boston and New York: Houghton Mifflin, 1919.

SE, XI   *A New England Group and Others. Shelburne Essays*. No. 11. Boston and New York: Houghton Mifflin, 1921.

Notes

Chapter One

1. Robert E. Spiller et al., *Literary History of the United States,* 3d ed. (New York: Macmillan, 1963), 1151.

2. Austin Warren, "Paul Elmer More: A Critic in Search of Wisdom," *Southern Review* 5 (1969): 1103.

3. Russell Kirk, Foreword to *The Essential Paul Elmer More: A Selection of His Writings,* ed. Byron C. Lambert (New Rochelle, N.Y.: Arlington House, 1972), 9.

4. T. S. Eliot, "Paul Elmer More," *Princeton Alumni Weekly,* 5 Feb. 1937, 374.

5. H. L. Mencken, *Prejudices,* 3d ser. (New York: Knopf, 1922), 178.

6. Austin Warren, "The 'New Humanism' Twenty Years After," *Modern Age* 3 (1958): 81.

7. Most of the essays first appeared in *The Atlantic Monthly, The Independent* (of which More was literary editor, 1901-03), *The Evening Post* of New York (on which he held a similar position, 1908-09), and *The Nation* (of which he was assistant editor, 1906-09; editor in chief, 1909-14; and advisory editor, 1914-17).

8. Francis X. Duggan, *Paul Elmer More* (New York: Twayne, 1966), 43.

9. Louis J. A. Mercier, *The Challenge of Humanism* (New York: Oxford University Press, 1933), 205.

10. Walter Lippman, "Humanism as Dogma," *Saturday Review of Literature,* 15 Mar. 1930, 817.

11. More to William Roscoe Thayer, 11 Oct. 1911. Quoted in Duggan, *Paul Elmer More,* 40.

12. See the preface to the first volume, *The Religion of Plato* (Princeton: Princeton University, 1921), vi-vii.

13. Paul E. More, *The Drift of Romanticism,* vol. 8 of *Shelburne Essays* (Boston: Houghton Mifflin, 1913), vii-viii. All other references to More's works will be abbreviated (see list of abbreviations on pp. 239–40) and included within parentheses in the text.

14. "The Charge Against the Critics," *The Independent,* 6 Feb. 1902, 353.

15. More to William Roscoe Thayer, 2 Oct. 1911. Quoted in Arthur H. Dakin, *Paul Elmer More* (Princeton: Princeton University, 1960), 120. This same point is discussed in Duggan, *Paul Elmer More,* 40.

16. Harry H. Clark, "A Study of Paul Elmer More," *The American Review* 5 (1935): 492.

17. Barrows Dunham, "Paul Elmer More," *Massachusetts Review* 7 (1966): 160.

18. Eliot, 373.

19. The central pattern of organization and treatment in both Dakin's *Paul Elmer More* and Robert M. Davies, *The Humanism of Paul Elmer More* (New York: Bookman, 1958) is the chronological tracing of the development of More's thought.

20. Folke Leander, "More, Puritan a Rebours," *American Scholar* 7 (1937): 442-43.

21. Paul E. More, *Selected Shelburne Essays* (New York: Oxford, 1935), xxii.

22. Lynn H. Hough, "Paul Elmer More and our American Civilization," *Christian Century,* 30 Oct. 1924, 1407.

23. Horace Gregory, "On Paul Elmer More and his Shelburne Essays," *Accent* 4 (1944): 144.

24. H. J. Harding, "American Thinker," *Contemporary Review* 185 (1954): 36.

25. Clark, 495.

26. Stuart P. Sherman, *Americans* (New York: Charles Scribner's Sons, 1922), 331.

27. Warren, "Paul Elmer More," 1092.

28. "The Teaching of the Classics," *The Independent,* 6 Aug. 1908. Reprinted in Byron C. Lambert, ed., *The Essential Paul Elmer More:*

A Selection of His Writings (New Rochelle, N.Y.: Arlington House, 1972), 262-67.

29. Louis Kronenberger, "On Critics, Pedants and Philistines," in *Highlights of Modern Literature,* ed. Francis Brown (New York: New American Library, 1954), 90.

30. Gorham B. Munson, *Destinations: A Canvass of American Literature Since 1900* (New York: J. H. Sears, 1928), 21.

Chapter Two

1. Matthew Arnold, "Wordsworth," in *Criticism: The Major Texts,* ed. W. J. Bate (New York: Harcourt, Brace & World, 1952), 478.

2. More to William Mode Spackman, 16 Feb. 1929. Quoted in Arthur H. Dakin, *Paul Elmer More* (Princeton: Princeton University, 1960), 258n.

3. Paul E. More, "Marginalia," *The American Review* 8 (1936): 17-18.

4. Ibid., 22-23.

5. More to Robert Shafer, 22 Oct. 1931. Quoted in Francis X. Duggan, *Paul Elmer More* (New York: Twayne, 1966), 20. Cf. SE, VI, 65-66. Dakin thinks that More's discovery of Baur might have occurred later than 1891—Dakin, *Paul Elmer More,* 44.

6. For an extensive consideration for More's Platonism see Robert M. Davies, *The Humanism of Paul Elmer More* (New York: Bookman, 1958), 98-126. In his summary, Davies says the principal contributions of Plato to More's thought are to be found in five areas: "(1) The doctrine of Ideas—of undiminished significance to More throughout his entire life. (2) The psychology of the ruling principle with its manifestations in 'the inner check.' (In a way More's concept of sin as a slackening of will is an outgrowth of the belief of the inner check.) (3) The concept of the dark Necessity (with its correlative of a limited god). (4) The concept of the aristocratic state in the Platonic sense, in contrast to the democratic state, as set forth in *The Republic.* (5) The revolt against metaphysics, or the improper use of reason in the field of intuition."

7. Davies, 114.

8. More to Robert Shafer, 13 Sept. 1931. Quoted in Dakin, *Paul Elmer More,* 311-12.

9. Robert Davies quite rightly distinguished theistic humanism from religious humanism because the latter term has been used in a loose sense to describe a group of twentieth-century humanists who see religion as a devotion to man's ideals and aspirations apart from superhuman revelation. The theistic humanist, on the other hand, sees man's higher nature as definitely related to the superhuman, to God. See Davies, 20-21.

10. Davies, 131.

11. More, "Marginalia," 17.

12. Ibid., 18.

13. M. D. C. Tait, "The Humanism of Paul Elmer More," *University of Toronto Quarterly* 16 (1947): 111.

14. Cf. T. S. Eliot's statement in "Tradition and the Individual Talent" regarding "the historical sense" which involves a perception "not only of the pastness of the past, but of its presence; the historical sense compels a man to write not merely with his own generation in his bones, but with a feeling that the whole of the literature of Europe from Homer and within it the whole of the literature of his own country has a simultaneous existence and composes a simultaneous order." T. S. Eliot, *Selected Essays,* (New York: Harcourt, Brace, 1932), 4. It is possible that Eliot was indebted to More in this regard. Eliot's essay appeared in 1917, More's in 1915. Eliot reviewed volume IX of the *Shelburne Essays* in *The New Statesman* 7 (24 June 1916): 284. It is interesting also that the term "historical sense" was used by More (see SE, IV, 68) before Eliot used it. See Stephen L. Tanner, "T. S. Eliot and Paul Elmer More on Tradition," *English Language Notes* 8 (1971): 211-15.

15. More to Stuart P. Sherman, 20 Jan. 1922. Quoted in Dakin, *Paul Elmer More,* 194n.

16. Humanitarianism is a central theme in *The Jessica Letters,* and although this is a novel, it is obvious that Philip Towers, one of the main characters, is a direct spokesman for More himself. In fact, the fictionalized framework probably allows him to be even more direct and candid on this subject than he otherwise would be.

17. More to Richard W. Boynton, 18 June 1918. Quoted in Dakin, *Paul Elmer More,* 117n.

18. Henry D. Thoreau, *The Variorum Walden,* ed. Walter Harding (New York: Washington Square Press, 1967), 55.

19. J. Duncan Spaeth, "Conversations with Paul Elmer More," *Sewanee Review* 51 (1943): 541.

20. This is More's character speaking in a novel, and the tone of this passage is not the tone More would use in one of his essays, but there can be no doubt that the ideas reflect essentially his own feelings regarding humanitarians.

21. More, "Wealth and Culture," *The Independent,* 1 May 1902, 1061.

Chapter Three

1. More to Alice More, 14 Mar. 1925. Quoted in Arthur H. Dakin, *Paul Elmer More* (Princeton: Princeton University, 1960), 229.

2. More to Alice More, 16 Apr. 1925. Quoted in Dakin, *Paul Elmer More,* 229-30.

3. Barrows Dunham, "Paul Elmer More," *Massachusetts Review* 7 (1966): 160.

4. J. Duncan Spaeth, "Conversations with Paul Elmer More," *Sewanee Review* 51 (1943): 541-42.

5. More to Prosser Hall Frye, 24 Sept. 1928. Quoted in Francis X. Duggan, *Paul Elmer More* (New York: Twayne, 1966), 51.

6. Dunham, 164.

7. Two incidental sidelights might be mentioned here regarding More's attitude toward Shakespeare. Both point out typical elements in More's pattern of thought. (1) More says in *Aristocracy and Justice* (SE, IX) that "If anywhere Shakespeare seems to speak from his heart and to utter his own philosophy it is in Ulysses' speech on degree in *Troilus and Cressida*" (p. 57). More's point of view here clearly indicates his aristocratic tendencies and high regard for order. (2) When More visited England in 1924, he wept at Shakespeare's tomb; not so much over Shakespeare, apparently, as over the fact that the church there in Stratford seemed to him to be "the heart of England." He goes on to say that "the true life of the country is symbolized in the churches" (More to Irving Babbitt, 5 Sept. 1924. Quoted in Dakin, *Paul Elmer More,* 223). The implication here is that More's love of the warmth of religious tradition overshadowed, or perhaps to be more accurate, defined his appreciation for Shakespeare's contribution to art.

8. This was written in 1905. T. S. Eliot is often credited with rediscovering Donne and the metaphysical poets. It is interesting

that in this early essay More's comments on Donne indicate that he was fully aware of Donne's genius. See particularly pp. 74-75.

9. More to Stuart P. Sherman, 1 Mar. 1915. Quoted in Dakin, *Paul Elmer More*, 154.

Chapter Four

1. Stuart P. Sherman, "An Imaginary Conversation with Mr. P. E. More," in *Americans* (New York: Charles Scribner's Sons, 1922), 326-27.

2. More to Percy H. Houston, 3 Dec. 1923. Quoted in Arthur H. Dakin, *Paul Elmer More* (Princeton: Princeton University, 1960), 200n.

3. More to Alice More, 12 Nov. 1921. Quoted in Dakin, *Paul Elmer More*, 200.

4. More to Stuart P. Sherman, 27 May 1909. Quoted in Dakin, *Paul Elmer More*, 123.

5. Ibid., 123-24.

Chapter Five

1. J. Duncan Spaeth, "Conversations with Paul Elmer More," *Sewanee Review* 51 (1943): 435.

2. More to Robert Shafer, 22 Oct. 1931. Quoted in Arthur H. Dakin, *Paul Elmer More* (Princeton: Princeton University, 1960), 312.

3. More to Robert Shafer, 13 Sept. 1931. Quoted in Dakin, *Paul Elmer More*, 311.

4. Paul E. More, ed., *The Complete Poetical Works of Lord Byron* (Boston: Houghton Mifflin, 1905).

5. Paul E. More, "The Wholesome Revival of Byron," *The Atlantic Monthly* 82 (December 1898): 801.

6. Ibid., 806.

7. Ibid., 807.

8. "The Desired Poet," *The Evening Post,* 16 July 1904. Quoted in Dakin, *A Paul Elmer More Miscellany* (Portland, Maine: Anthoensen Press, 1950), 79.

9. This desire for rest and peace mentioned here is the subject of "The Quest of a Century" (SE, III, 244-65) in which More discusses the gap between rest and motion and its relation to faith.

"It was the peculiar quest of the nineteenth century," he says, "to discover fixed laws and an unshaken abiding place for the mind in the very kingdom of unrest; we have sought to chain the waves of the sea with the winds" (264).

10. Some characteristics of Tennyson made him the spokesman for his age, particularly his tendency to compromise, but More recognized that he had other characteristics which were not Victorian—"a sense of estrangement from time and personality which took possession of him at intervals from youth to age." For More's treatment of them see particularly SE, VII, 87-94. For example, he describes in this way the scene in "The Holy Grail" in which the grail appears: "The vision, in other words, is nothing else but a sudden and blinding sense of that dualism of the world and of the human soul beneath which the solid-seeming earth reels and dissolves away, overwhelming with terror and uncomprehended impulse all but those purely spiritual to whom the earth is already an unreal thing" (90). "With Tennyson, unfortunately, the task is always to separate the poet of insight from the poet of compromise" (94).

11. For definitions of these terms and a summary of the distinctions between them, see the section on "Science" in chapter 2.

12. More to Alice More, 8 Nov. 1918. Quoted in Dakin, *Paul Elmer More*, 183-84.

13. More might be considered to have been a member of the Protestant Episcopal Church, though he was never confirmed as an actual member. Dakin describes how More, though unconfirmed, when near death received the Holy Communion from an Episcopal bishop and priest (this is allowed by the Episcopal Church). The two clergymen wanted him to have every benefit the Church could give and hoped that he would ask of his own accord to be confirmed. The bishop finally broached the subject himself, and More said he would think it over. "For a few days he was greatly disturbed, torn between his respect for tradition, of which the Church seemed to him to be one of the nobler strands, and between his individualistic and Protestant tendencies, his suspicion of deathbed conversions, and his desire to remain true to his own best light." In the end he decided against confirmation (Dakin, *Paul Elmer More*, 384).

14. Paul E. More and Frank L. Cross, eds. and comps., *Anglicanism: The Thought and Practice of the Church of England, Illustrated from*

the Religious Literature of the Seventeenth Century (London and Milwaukee: Morehouse, 1935). For More's views on the Church see the introductory essay to this volume, "The Spirit of Anglicanism." And for a summary of how Newman fitted into the spirit, according to More, see particularly pp. xxx-xxxi.

15. George R. Elliott criticized "A Revival of Humanism" (NSE, III, 1-24) as heading for Rome. "In the first place," More answered, "humanly speaking, there is no danger of my going over to Rome. It behooves me to be modest on this head. A man who has changed as he never expected he would change ought not to be too certain of his future. Nevertheless I do feel secure in saying that my conversion to Rome seems to me impossible" (More to George R. Elliott, 12 Apr. 1930. Quoted in Dakin, *Paul Elmer More*, 284).

16. Paul E. More, "Marginalia," *The American Review* 8 (1936): 20.

17. G. K. Chesterton, *Charles Dickens: A Critical Study* (New York: Dodd, Mead & Co., 1906).

18. In the essay on Trollope, More refers to this concept as "the canon of poetic justice." See the discussion of Trollope which follows.

19. The artistic significance of authorial comment has been more widely recognized and more seriously considered since Wayne Booth's study of it in *The Rhetoric of Fiction* (Chicago: University of Chicago Press, 1961).

20. See the section "Art and Life" in chapter 2.

21. More to Prosser Hall Frye, 3 Oct. 1929. Quoted in Dakin, *Paul Elmer More*, 275.

22. For example: "Both the sense of disillusion, which was really inherent in him from his youth, and the passion for truth hindered him in his 'creative' work, while they increased his powers as a critic;" "his life was a long endeavor to supplant the romantic elements of his taste by the classical;" "what attracted him chiefly was that middle ground where life and literature meet, where life becomes self-conscious through expression, and literature retains the reality of association with fact" (SE, III, 69, 73, 78). Each of these statements could be applied to More himself.

23. See the section dealing with this topic in chapter 4.

24. More will be said of this tradition below in connection with Matthew Arnold.

25. See pp. 7, 68-70.

26. Horace Gregory, "On Paul Elmer More and his Shelburne Essays," *Accent* 4 (1944): 145.

27. See pp. 48-49.

28. Louis J. A. Mercier, "Challenge of Paul Elmer More," *Harvard Graduate Magazine* 34 (June 1926): 559.

Chapter Six

1. Francis X. Duggan, "Paul Elmer More and the New England Tradition," *American Literature* 34 (1963): 542-43.

2. More to William Roscoe Thayer, probably early Dec. 1900. Quoted in Arthur H. Dakin, *Paul Elmer More* (Princeton: Princeton University, 1960), 102.

3. "American Literature," *The Independent,* 16 July 1903, 1887. Identified as More's work in Dakin, *Paul Elmer More,* 388.

4. More to Nicholas Murry Butler, 31 Oct. 1932. Quoted in Dakin, *Paul Elmer More,* 85n.

5. More to Prosser Hall Frye, undated (probably August 1910). Quoted in Dakin, *Paul Elmer More,* 111-12.

6. More to Alice More, 12 Nov. 1921. Quoted in Dakin, *Paul Elmer More,* 200.

7. Paul E. More, "A Critic Among the Prophets," *The Nation,* 5 Sept. 1912, 207.

8. Paul E. More, "The Flowering of New England," *The Villager,* 3 (16 Aug. 1919), 79.

9. Duggan, "Paul Elmer More and the New England Tradition," 544.

10. Paul E. More, "Admirable Criticism," *The Independent,* 14 Nov. 1901, 2710.

11. Duggan, "Paul Elmer More and the New England Tradition," 558.

12. Stuart G. Brown, "Toward an American Tradition," *Sewanee Review* 47 (1939): 496.

13. More to Irving Babbitt, 3 May 1913. Quoted in Dakin, *Paul Elmer More,* 153-54.

14. Ibid.

15. More does not elaborate on that inner dualism here. A more extensive answer to Edwards's argument can be found in More's *Platonism,* (P, 127ff).

16. In 1900 More did a short biography of Franklin for Houghton Mifflin Riverside biographical series. It is not a critical biography, and the main critical insights it does contain are, for the most part, repeated in this *Shelburne Essay* on Franklin.

17. Paul E. More, "Franklin a Man of His Day," *The Evening Post* (New York), 17 Jan. 1906. Quoted and identified as More's in Dakin, *A Paul Elmer More Miscellany* (Portland, Maine: Anthoensen Press), 23.

18. I do not know whether the phrases "American renaissance" and "the flowering of New England" were original with More, but it is interesting to note that these phrases, used by him early in the century, later became the titles of two significant books on American literature by F. O. Matthiessen and Van Wyck Brooks respectively.

19. Brown, 481.

20. Lynn H. Hough, *Great Humanists* (New York: Abingdon-Cokesbury, 1952), 180.

21. More to Alice More, 12 Mar. 1894. Quoted in Dakin, *Paul Elmer More,* 46.

22. The fact that More's essays on Edwards and Emerson were originally solicited by the editors of *The Cambridge History of American Literature* (New York: G. P. Putnam's Sons, 1917) would seem to be a testimonial to the recognition of More's concern with the continuity of literary history as contrasted with critical evaluation in a vacuum.

Chapter Seven

1. Stuart P. Sherman, "Mr. P. E. More and the Wits," *The Review* 2 (1920): 54. Revised and reprinted as "An Imaginary Conversation with Mr. P. E. More" in *Americans* (New York: Charles Scribner's Sons, 1922), 317-38.

2. Irving Howe, ed., Introduction to *Literary Modernism* (New York: Fawcett, 1967), 14.

3. Francis X. Duggan, *Paul Elmer More* (New York: Twayne, 1966), 123, has noted that perhaps the most telling example of

More's estrangement from contemporary literature is the difficulty he had with T. S. Eliot. Although he was intimately acquainted with Eliot, generally shared the poet's religious and political views, and had the benefit of long conversations and an extensive correspondence with him, More was never at ease with Eliot's poetry. The trouble, according to Duggan, seems to have been his unwillingness or inability to meet the formal demands of contemporary literature. Describing More's attitude toward Eliot's later poetry, Duggan says, "Since Eliot's personal values and his poetic themes were now traditional and orthodox, so should be the form of his poetry; in continuing in his former vein, he is giving comfort to the enemy. A poet must be granted freedom in his choice of form, More admits, but a wrong form can negate what he means to convey: 'Eliot has never as an artist come into the open. He still is a leader for radical young men who loathe and detest what he now stands for.' "

4. More to Maurice Baum, 31 Mar. 1924. Quoted in Arthur H. Dakin, *Paul Elmer More* (Princeton: Princeton University, 1960), 217.

5. More to Robert Shafer, 8 Oct. 1926. Quoted in Dakin, *Paul Elmer More,* 248.

6. More to Alice More, 4 Dec. 1926. Quoted in Dakin, *Paul Elmer More,* 249.

7. Ibid.

8. In 1921 Frost stayed overnight at More's home. Of this visit More wrote to his sister: "I have always rather admired his poetry, which is modern in some respects, but has balance and measure and deals with the real things of life. It was a pleasure to talk with him—we sat up until about one—and hear how sound his views of art and human nature are. . . . It was rather exhilarating to listen to him, and I think too he went away somewhat encouraged from his contact with a kindred soul" (More to Alice More, 10 Mar. 1921. Quoted in Dakin, *Paul Elmer More,* 193).

Chapter Eight

1. Much of the summary which follows is More's own words from a number of different sources. In the interests of readability I have omitted quotation marks and references that would distinguish between his words and my own. Such documentation in this particular case I think serves no real purpose, but may be distracting.

2. Anonymous review of J. B. Bury, *The Idea of Progress, An Inquiry into its Origin and Growth,* in *The Villager* 4 (April 9, 1921), 188.

3. Whitney J. Oates, "A Quest of the Spirit," in *The Lives of Eighteen from Princeton,* ed. Willard Thorp (Princeton: Princeton University Press, 1946).

4. Lynn H. Hough, *Great Humanists* (New York: Abingdon-Cokesbury, 1952), 185.

5. Ibid., 188.

6. John Stuart Mill, *Autobiography and Other Writings,* ed. Jack Stillinger (Boston: Houghton Mifflin, 1969), 263.

7. Austin Warren, "The 'New Humanism' Twenty Years After," *Modern Age* 3 (Winter 1958-59): 81.

8. *Paul Elmer More's Shelburne Essays on American Literature,* ed. Daniel Aaron (New York: Harcourt, Brace & World, 1963), 3.

9. Hough, *Great Humanists,* 179.

10. More to George Roy Elliott, 31 Mar. 1929. Quoted in Arthur H. Dakin, *Paul Elmer More* (Princeton: Princeton University, 1960), 273.

11. Austin Warren, "Paul Elmer More: A Critic in Search of Wisdom," *Southern Review* 5 (1969): 1103.

12. Stephen L. Tanner, "T. S. Eliot and Paul Elmer More on Tradition," *English Language Notes* 8 (1971): 211-15.

Index

Q
Queen Anne, 92, 93
Queen Elizabeth, 92

R
Radcliffe, Ann, 183
Rationalism, 41–47; and classicism, 105; and deism, 96, 97–100; and dualism, 30, 117; and humanitarianism, 107; and monism, 50, 140, 170, 208, 210–11; and the Renaissance, 84, 224; and romanticism, 115; and science, 75–76, 237; mentioned, 11, 63, 113, 119, 143
"Raven, The" (Poe), 185
Reasonableness, 46–47, 49
Religio Medici (Browne), 76
Religious imagination, 75–78, 80, 81, 83, 84, 86, 96, 97, 99, 101, 117, 125, 143, 144, 145, 181
Renaissance, The (Pater), 163, 164
Republic, The (Plato), 243n.6
Reynolds, Sir Joshua, 105, 109
Richards, I. A., 15
Robinson, Edwin Arlington, 176, 213
Romanticism, 51–57, 133; German, 11, 166, 191–92; and humanism, 121–22, 131; and Newman, 144–45; and the Oxford Movement, 144–45; and puritanism, 195; and Rousseau, 112–13; and science, 113–19, 226; and Shelley, 131; and Tolstoy, 155, 157; mentioned,

4, 6, 9, 35, 47, 63, 105, 152, 170–71, 207, 218
Rome, 61, 65, 144, 248n.15
Romeo and Juliet (Shakespeare), 71–72
Rossetti, Christina, 135
Rossetti, Dante Gabriel, 118, 166
Rousseau and Romanticism (Babbitt), 113
Rousseau, Jean-Jacques, 37, 53, 84, 87, 107–13, 132, 136, 139, 151, 154, 155, 227, 232; *Emile,* 110
Ruskin, John, 162

S
Sainte-Beuve, Charles Augustin, 8, 15, 17, 28, 152–53, 161, 174, 236
Sanskrit, 1, 14, 236
Schlegel, August Wilhelm von, 53
Schlegel, Friedrich von, 53
Schleiermacher, Friedrich Ernst Daniel, 37
Science, 48–51; and the Demon of the Absolute, 211–12; and dualism, 88–89; and naturalism, 36, 54, 170–71, 207, 224–27; and the philosophy of change, 134, 135, 138–41; rational, 113, 117, 119; rationalism, 75–76, 97; mentioned, 4, 9, 47, 63, 81, 96, 102, 152, 156, 193, 198, 199, 201, 237, 247n.11
Scientism. *See* Science
Selected Essays (Eliot), 244n.14
Shafer, Robert, 37, 125, 221